Information Systems for Strategic Decisions

T
bo
re
I

Information Systems for Strategic Decisions

K. J. Radford
Department of Administrative Studies
Atkinson College, York University
Downsview, Ontario

Reston Publishing Company, Inc., A Prentice-Hall Company
Reston, Virginia

Library of Congress Cataloging in Publication Data

Radford, K. J.
Information systems for strategic decisions.

Includes index.
1. Management information systems. 2. Decision-making. I. Title
HF5548.2.R247 658.4′032 78-2660
ISBN 0-87909-389-7

10 9 8 7 6 5 4 3 2 1

Printed in the United States of America

Intelligence is the soul of all public business

Daniel Defoe

Contents

Preface

Much of the discussion and published literature on information systems to date has been about systems concerned with the internal administration and operations of an organization. Considerably less attention has been given to the information requirements of the more strategic managerial activities of planning and policy making, in which the future directions and objectives of the organization are decided.

There have been a number of reasons for this concentration on the internal aspects of management in the design and implementation of present day information systems. The greatly increased demands for routine transactional data processing that are inherent in modern society and business have had the effect of directing information systems thinking away from strategic activities. The introduction of the computer in support of this data processing has often given emphasis to the servicing of routine transactions as opposed to the support of less completely-specified and less quantitative aspects of management. In some cases, the very availability of the computer has contributed to the growth of the internally-oriented information system at the expense of developments in other areas.

The introduction of computers into organizations has been accompanied in many instances by very great difficulties. In some cases, the magnitude of the task was underestimated by enthusiastic specialized personnel, with the result that promises of performance were not met. In other circumstances, many human factors in the operations affected were neglected, so that the resulting computer-supported systems did not meet the normal or unanticipated needs of users. In many cases, system development was pushed ahead with little attention to cost-effectiveness. Sometimes specialists opted for technically sophisticated systems, rather than for a less expensive alternative that met operational requirements with less technical risk.

Hopefully, some, if not all, of these difficulties are now behind us. Overall competence in the use of the computer in support of managerial activities has grown in recent years. Many modern information system implementations have shown evidence of a greater maturity of approach, in which the emphasis of system design is placed on the role of information in the organization rather than on transaction processing alone. The computer is now increasingly regarded as essential supporting equipment for an information system rather than the major factor on which the system design must be based.

With these trends of thought firmly entrenched, it is now widely appreciated that the purpose of an information system is to support managerial activities of all types at all levels of an organization. This makes it imperative that the information needs of the strategic aspects of management be considered along with those of the more familiar activities of internal regulation and control when the design of an organizational information system is undertaken. The purpose of this book is to provide a basis for design of this comprehensive type of information system.

The text starts with a review in Chapter 1 of the development of information systems in recent years, which leads later in the chapter to a discussion of the elements of a modern information system. Two major components are identified: first the familiar internal information system, and second, the strategic information system that serves managerial activities such as planning and policy making. The discussion leads to an initial statement of requirements upon which the design of the overall information system can be based.

One of the most important of these requirements is that the information system must serve and support the activities involved in the direction and management of the organization of which it is an integral part. The second chapter of this text is therefore devoted to a description of these managerial activities. The organization is viewed as a complex system operating within an environment. The various aspects of management are classified under the headings of strategic planning, management control, and operational control. The strategic information system component is primarily concerned with the first of these sets of activities, while the internal system serves the other two.

The prime functions of an information system are the acquisition, transmission, presentation, and retention of information useful in decision making. The types of decisions that arise in management are described briefly in Chapter 3. Since support of the decision-making procedures in an organization is a vital role of the information system, knowledge of the nature and pattern of decision making is essential in the design and implementation of that system.

The internal information system is described in detail in Chapter 4. This chapter draws material from an earlier book, *Information Systems in Management*.* The discussion builds on this material to provide a comprehensive description of the component of the overall information system that serves the processes of internal regulation and control.

Chapter 5 is concerned with the nature of the information that is used in strategic planning and management. These activities relate primarily to the setting of objectives and future directions for the organization. This chapter provides a complete discussion of the characteristics of strategic information in the context of a modern organization. Reference is made to the extensive literature on military and political intelligence and also to the growing body of evidence that faulty acquisition or use of strategic information is often the cause of disasters in both community and organizational settings.

The subject of Chapter 6 is the design and implementation of the strategic component of the overall information system. This design is brought together with that of the internal system in Chapter 7. Factors that are crucial to the success of an information system are discussed at this point. The chapter ends with a treatment of the costs and benefits of an organizational information system and of the methods by which they can be evaluated.

Acknowledgements

I am indebted to all those authors whose work I have referenced very freely. My special thanks are due to Dr. Malcolm Dando of the University of Sussex for his valuable suggestions on the structure and content of the text and to Professor Nigel Howard for his continued help and collaboration in the area of organizational decision making.

Much of the research upon which Chapters 5 and 6 were based was done most thoroughly by Beverly Fingerhut. She also read and checked the text that was prepared by Laurine Ackert, Leslie Crosby, Doreen Deacon, and Terry Spier. My thanks are extended to all these ladies, without whose efforts this book could not have been produced.

Some of the research upon which some sections of this book is based was supported by research grants to the author from the National Research Council of Canada. This support is most deeply appreciated.

K. J. RADFORD

* K. J. Radford, *Information Systems in Management* (Reston, Va.: Reston Publishing Company, 1973).

Information Systems for Strategic Decisions

1

An Introduction to Information Systems

Information is an essential commodity in all modern activities. Individuals, organizations, and communities use information in every aspect of their day-to-day affairs. Most organizations have some sort of information system to handle and process the information needed in the various aspects of their work. The system may be elaborate and highly developed or it may be informal and casual in its operation. The system may have been specifically designed and implemented for its task or it may have evolved naturally over a period of time. In recent years, the idea of introducing into an organization an information system that is specially designed to support its managerial and decision-making activities has received increasing acceptance. Some of these systems have met both their design specifications and the expectations of those involved in their creation. Other systems have been less successful. The systems that have not been successful have most commonly been those designed to meet very sophisticated specifications. In many such cases, the specifications called for systems that were more complex than could be attained using the skills and experience available at the time.

The conceptual foundation on which the design of modern information systems is based derives from many sources and disciplines. These sources include not only current organization theory and recent developments in computer technology and information science, but also the observed pattern of organizational decision making and the recorded behavior of managers in an organizational setting.

The great impact of computers on organizational activities in recent years has caused many authors to take the position that computer technology is the dominant consideration in all information systems. Others, however, take the view that the information requirements of the organization are of primary importance. Those supporting this second view see the computer more as a tool, the application of which should be governed by the perceived needs of the various parts of the organization for information. The treatment in this text will be based on this second approach. The starting point will be the work of Norbert Wiener.

In his original treatise on cybernetics, Wiener compared the acquisition and processing of information in human beings and animals with the similar activity required in the control of machines and other organized activities.[1] Wiener described information-handling in living beings in the same terms used to describe comparable organizational activities. He saw our own information system as a highly developed component of the overall human system. Further, he used the human information system as a general model for the construction of information systems in man-made organizations. He regarded the information system as an essential device, both for enriching the information resources of an organization and for bringing about a greater understanding of the environment in which the being or organization operates.

Some of the statements in Wiener's work reflect the relatively primitive state of computer science at the time that his books were written. However, his basic ideas regarding the role of information in the direction and management of an organization have not lost their force with the passage of time. He regarded communication between the component parts of an organization or community as vital to its activities, stating that "the community extends only so far as there extends an effectual transmission of information."[2] Wiener saw an information system as the means by which the necessary communication can be established and maintained. His statement that an organization

[1] Wiener, Norbert, *Cybernetics: Control and Communication in the Animal and the Machine,* MIT Press, paperback edition, 1965 (first published 1948).

[2] Ibid., p. 158.

"is held together . . . by the possession of a means for the acquisition, use, retention, and transmission of information,"[3] provides a basic outline of the tasks of a modern information system. It is noteworthy that Wiener did not state specifically what constitutes information in his statement. The exact nature of information and the distinction between data and information are points to which we will return shortly.

The parallel between the information system that exists in humans and that which must be created in organizations has many interesting aspects. For example, the human information system can be considered to have developed naturally over a long period of time and to have evolved in a manner dictated by the needs of the human being operating within his environment. By analogy, the characteristics of the organizational information system can be expected to evolve with time and to be influenced by the environment in which the organization operates.

Other aspects of the human information system provide considerable insight into the manner in which an organizational information system should be designed. For example, the human information system is closely integrated with other components of the overall system. These other components include those involved with the internal management of the human body (the regulatory system), those concerned with decision making (parts of both the brain and the nervous system), and those concerned with taking action once a decision has been made (the motor systems). The functions of the human regulatory system can be compared with those of administration and control of the internal operations of an organization. Much of the higher-level activity of the brain is concerned with selecting of objectives and future courses of action for the individual in relation to his or her environment. This activity is analogous to strategic planning in an organization.

The degree of integration in the human system and the manner in which the various systems are interconnected provide examples of efficiency of design that can guide those involved with organizational information systems. However, as with many other such analogies, the comparison between human information systems and organizational information systems loses some applicability and usefulness when pursued to too great a level of detail.

[3] Ibid., p. 161.

The Evolution of Information Systems

Norbert Wiener's explicit listing of the organizational requirements of information systems in terms of the acquisition, use, retention, and transmission of information is a comparatively recent development. Various systems for processing information were in use by organizations many years before Wiener's analysis. For example, Murdick and Ross have described such a system used in a small country store in the late nineteenth century.[4] As was typical in those days, the store was owned and operated by one man. The owner was both president and chief executive, undertaking all the functions required to operate the store including sales direction, market research, accounting, inventory control, public relations, and so on. The owner personally gathered all the information necessary to carry out his various functions, either using it as it was gathered or storing the information in his memory for later retrieval. Data that were too numerous or too detailed to be retained in his memory were recorded in a ledger or on pieces of paper that were impaled on a spike. Once a decision was made, the owner usually undertook the necessary action himself.

Within the confines of a small operation, the owner-operated information system was often very efficient. It made use of the highly-integrated information system of the owner himself. Information was expressed and stored in that system in a form that was readily understood by all the components of management. Communication between these components was excellent because all were served by the owner's own integrated information system. The amount of information involved in the relatively simple operation of the one-man store did not usually cause an overload of the communication channels that were being used.

The owner-operated information system could also be expected to be efficient if more than one person worked in the organization, provided that those involved were relatively close in their experience and knowledge. The similarity of purpose and experience of the individuals in such circumstances usually allowed a close communication between them and facilitated the interaction between their respective stores of information.

[4] Murdick, R. G. and J. E. Ross, *Information Systems for Modern Management*, Prentice-Hall, 1971, pp. 156–157.

In more recent times, an increasing proportion of our affairs have been conducted by larger organizations. Many of the smaller enterprises have been superseded by larger corporations or incorporated into them. Private business and industry have grown as the size and scope of the national economies of the leading industrial nations have expanded. This growth has been accompanied by a corresponding increase in the activities and involvement of government. Industrialization has also resulted in an increase in the size of the urban communities in which many of us live. This increase has been accompanied, in most cases, by a decrease in the size of rural communities.

The development of modern mass economies has had a number of effects on the organizations involved in both the public and private sectors. In the first place, the growth of organizations has made it much more difficult for one man to control and direct the activities of an enterprise in the manner of the owner of the country store. As the staff size of an organization increases, the amount of authority that must be delegated naturally increases also. Responsibility for routine activities and the accompanying decisions is delegated to managers at the middle and lower levels of the organization. Senior management concerns itself with the less routine activities of planning and policy making. These activities are concerned with setting the future objectives and directions of the organization.

A necessary counterpart of delegation of authority is the reporting of the results of the activities that have been assigned. Delegation of authority must, therefore, be accompanied by the establishment of a communication channel through which these results can be reported and discussed. The greater the degree of delegation, the greater is the number of communication channels needed as part of the information system. A greater degree of delegation, however, also increases the chance that some of the necessary channels may become blocked or distorted. Some organizational communication channels may carry formal, structured, and periodic reports. Other channels may exist to facilitate less structured passage of information and to foster informal discussion of the activities of the organization.

A second effect of the growth of an organization is that the breadth of experience and knowledge of individual members of the organization tends to decrease. In the early stages of expansion, the owner, president, or director of a small organization usually does the hiring himself, normally choosing persons with whom he can communicate easily and readily. As the organization grows, however, the hiring process itself is delegated. The delegation of hiring authority usually results in the hiring of individuals with a wider range of characteristics. It is quite common that individuals with different backgrounds place different interpretations upon information that has been acquired. This diversity of viewpoint often is a source of strength to an organization. It can, however, be a cause of misunderstanding, especially if those involved are engaged in some form of competition or conflict. For this reason, greater attention to communication between individual members is needed as the organization grows in size. This need is particularly acute if the expansion of the organization involves geographic dispersion of units. In a dispersed organization, both the separation of individuals and the absence of frequent personal contact increase the need for clarity and ease of understanding in organizational communications.

Another factor with which modern organizations must contend is the greatly increased complexity of the activities in which they are involved. This complexity is due in most part to the pace and pattern of modern life, and has led to an increased degree of specialization by those who work in organizations.[5] Increased specialization tends to decrease the amount of knowledge and experience common among members of an organization. In addition, specialization encourages communication between those with similar backgrounds and decreases passage of information between individuals with different interests and specializations.

The complexity of the external environment in which modern organizations operate has greatly increased the amount of information that must be processed within an organization. The nature of the modern environment has also increased the complexity of the necessary information handling. A striking example of this increased complexity is the administration of a company payroll. The owner of the country store usually paid an employee a previously agreed upon amount withdrawn directly from the cash register. The owner then charged the amount to costs. A modern payroll system has the same basic function. However, modern social conditions require that a payroll system also incorporate a large number of other features. In the first place, the gross amount paid to an employee is usually determined by a formal agreement which must be scrupulously observed. Second,

[5] Toffler, A., *Future Shock,* Random House, 1970, Chapter 8.

modern payroll systems are usually required to make deductions from the gross pay for some or all of the following: income taxes, health care programs, dental care programs, pension schemes, unemployment insurance, charitable donations, taxable allowances and benefits, union dues, parking fees, payroll savings plans, garnishments, disability insurance, and numerous other social and administrative functions. As a result, a modern payroll system is a very large and complicated operation usually requiring computer support to accomplish the necessary data processing tasks.

Organizations have met the demands of the increased complexity of their activities by diverting an increasing proportion of their effort and resources to administrative tasks and information systems.

In the late nineteenth and early twentieth centuries, the information gathering activities were devoted almost entirely to reporting the financial condition of the organization. As managerial skills developed, financial and accounting activities were expanded to include evaluations of the efficiency of subcomponents of the organization in a market-oriented economy. More sophisticated techniques based on concepts developed in economics were introduced under the general heading of management accounting. These techniques included responsibility accounting, in which managers are provided with information identifying any variations from planned performance in the areas for which they have responsibility.[6] Considerable emphasis was (and still is) given to cost analysis and profitability accounting in the application of these techniques.

The early information systems developed in organizations were oriented almost entirely toward the financial and managerial accounting functions. As unit-record equipment and, later, computers became available, these machines were used to undertake the considerably increased clerical and data processing workload that were associated with the prevalent accounting functions. It is noteworthy that the main initial effect of the introduction of the computer into organizations was an increase in the amount of routine clerical and data-manipulating capacity available to the accounting function. Design and implementation of information systems at this time was often entirely in the hands of accountants and computer specialists. Due to this circumstance, many of the first systems introduced into operation gave highest priority to financial and accounting matters. The concept of

[6] Higgins, J. A., "Responsibility Accounting," *The Arthur Anderson Chronicle,* April 1952.

an information system designed to serve a wide range of managerial functions was often given little attention. Primary emphasis at the time was given to the work involved in introducing the new computer-supported financial and accounting systems.

In many cases, the introduction of computer-based information systems gave rise to considerable controversy within the organizations concerned. Prior to the general use of computers in organizations, D. R. Daniel had described a crisis in management information.[7] He called for new organizational approaches and improved information handling to ensure that managerial effectiveness was not hampered by lack of pertinent information. Early attempts to introduce systems to meet these requirements often resulted in disappointment.[8, 9] To many, the crisis described by Daniel in 1960 was still in effect at a much later time.

Problems still to be overcome in 1973, as described in a survey paper written by J. C. Emery at that time,[10] included (a) alienation, suspicion, and hostility between information system specialists and managers; (b) a tendency for specialists to dictate system characteristics not closely related to the requirements of management; (c) failure by specialists to deliver systems with performances matching specifications; (d) indifference by information systems specialists to costs and inattention to the relation of benefits to cost; (e) inattention to human factors in the design of systems; and (f) failure to provide the flexibility in system design and operation needed to meet the changes that are inevitable in a living organization. Despite these problems, many useful and efficient information systems have been developed in recent years. In particular, information systems that were implemented with the cooperation of both specialists and managerial personnel were shown to provide significant benefits to an organization.[11]

[7] Daniel, D. R., "Management Information Crisis," *Harvard Business Review,* September-October 1961, pp. 111–121.

[8] Dearden, John, "How to Organize Information Systems," *Harvard Business Review,* March-April 1965, pp. 19–27.

[9] Dearden, John, "MIS Is a Mirage," *Harvard Business Review,* January-February 1972, pp. 90–99.

[10] Emery, J. C., "An Overview of Management Information Systems," in H. L. Morgan, ed., *Proceedings of the Wharton Conference on Research on Computers in Organizations,* published in *Data Base,* vol. 5, nos. 2, 3, and 4, Winter 1973.

[11] Hanold, Terrance, "An Executive View of MIS," *Datamation,* November 1972.

The Nature of Information

Before proceeding to a discussion of the design of an organizational information system, it is necessary to examine the meaning of the term *information*. The concept of information is one with which we are all familiar. However, the exact nature of information is not easy to describe or comprehend. Perhaps the most explicit definition in the technical literature defines information as recorded experience that is, or can be, used in decision making.[12]

In an organizational setting, recorded experience can take many forms. It may, for example, consist of sets of values of well-defined measures or parameters such as are found in the financial statements of a corporation. On the other hand, it may be much more qualitative in nature and consist of a verbal description of events and phenomena, possibly interspersed with numeric data. In most practical situations, the recorded experience available to an organization consists of a mixture of purely quantitative data and descriptive material.

The definition quoted above makes an important distinction between information on the one hand and recorded experience on the other. The distinction is that recorded experience becomes information only when it is or can be applied in a decision process. Under the terms of this definition, it is possible to be in possession of large amounts of raw data and descriptive material but yet to have little or no information. This situation can arise when the data and material at hand are not pertinent to the particular decision process under consideration or when the data and material are not interpreted with respect to that decision process. In different circumstances, however, a very small amount of raw data can provide a very great deal of information. This occurs when a particular piece of data happens to be just that which is necessary to resolve a current decision problem.

The value of the information that can be extracted from an amount of data or raw material depends therefore upon the use to which it can be put. For example, a body of data on the availability of supplies of iron ore is probably of little value to a decision maker involved in

[12] Churchman, C. W., *Prediction and Optimal Decision*, Prentice-Hall, 1961, p. 100. For other discussions of the nature of information, see: K. W. Deutsch, *The Nerves of Government*, The Free Press, 1966, p. 82; and Norbert Wiener, *The Human Use of Human Beings*, Avon Books, paperback edition, 1967, p. 26 ff.

planning programs of secondary education. The same data, however, would no doubt be vital to the president of a company that is engaged in extracting and marketing metallurgical coal.

A valuable concept concerning the amount of information that can be obtained from a particular piece of raw data or descriptive material can be derived from information theory. This concept relates the amount of information obtained to the probability that the event, state, or phenomena described will actually occur.[13] If the event concerned is expected by the individual receiving the message, his estimate of the probability of its occurrence is high. The amount of information conveyed by a message reporting such a well-anticipated occurrence is therefore low. Its addition to the amount of information held by the individual, his information set, is correspondingly low. On the other hand, if the event or state reported is unexpected, both the amount of information conveyed by the message and its addition to the information set of the recipient are correspondingly larger. This is the concept upon which reporting by exception is based.

The amount and value of information extracted from a message or report does not necessarily increase with the quantity of material contained. The process of extraction of information by an individual may, in fact, become less efficient as the quantity of material increases and the person involved becomes increasingly overloaded. In such circumstances, meanings may be obscured and vital information overlooked as the capability of the individual to process the material diminishes under overload conditions.

The material collected and processed by an information system frequently contains a substantial amount of data that is irrelevant to the activities of the organization concerned. The existence of this irrelevant material makes the interpretation of raw data and material much more difficult. Such extraneous data may cause the individuals reviewing the material to become overloaded. It may also conceal the true relevance of the material under study to the situation confronting the recipient of the material. The task of separating irrelevant content from relevant material is best achieved by a skilled interpreter. In practical circumstances, the manager who is the eventual user of the information is often the best interpreter. When there is widespread agreement between those concerned as to the meaning of a particular recorded experience, the data and material representing this experi-

[13] Pierce, J. R., *Symbols, Signals and Noise,* Harper Torchbooks, 1961, Chapter 5.

ence is generally regarded as "factual". If there is no such agreement, the information derived from any given quantity of raw material may vary widely from analyst to analyst.[14]

The commodity that is acquired, transmitted, processed, and stored by an information system is usually a mixture of (a) "factual" data; (b) material that has been subjected to interpretation in its passage through the system; and (c) other content that is openly acknowledged to be the opinions of individuals both within the organization and outside it. The output of the system is presented to managers who are faced with decision problems and who place their own individual interpretation on the material and derive information, each in his or her own way.

Despite the above distinctions, the commodity that is processed by an information system is generally referred to in the literature as "information." This convention will be preserved here. However, where it is necessary to the clarity of the discussion, a distinction will be drawn between information as recorded experience used in decision making and the raw data and material that comprises the recorded experience. At all other times, the reader is asked to draw the appropriate meaning from the context in which the terms are used.

The Components of an Information System

A modern organization can be regarded as a system that sets goals and endeavors to achieve them.[15] It has objectives and it uses resources in undertaking activities in pursuit of these objectives. A modern organization operates within an environment and can respond to events and phenomena in that environment in the course of its activities. The organization can respond also to various internal situations. It can, therefore, achieve its objectives in different ways and under different conditions. An organization can also work to increase the efficiency with which it uses its resources to achieve its objectives.

The more purposeful organizations are those that most readily change their objectives in response to changing internal and external

[14] Cherry, Colin, *On Human Communication,* The MIT Press, paperback edition, 1966, Chapter One.

[15] Ackoff, R. L., "Towards a System of Systems Concepts," *Management Science,* vol. 17, no. 11, July 1971, p. 666.

conditions. A purposeful organization selects ends as well as means. It places different values on different outcomes and continually seeks those outcomes that it regards as most desirable. The work of managing such an organization consists of two major sets of tasks. The first of these relates to the overall direction of the organization and involves the setting of future goals and objectives. This first set of tasks consists primarily of policy formulation and planning and is carried out at the senior levels of management. The second set of tasks is concerned with the internal regulation and control of the organization as it carries out those activities needed to achieve the ideals and objectives that have been selected. This latter set of tasks involves the general administration of the organization's resources and the direction of operations in a manner that ensures efficient use of these resources.

The management and operation of an organization can be compared with the running of a ship. The captain stands on the bridge and surveys the environment surrounding the ship. He then selects the course that he judges best, making any adjustments to the course that he deems necessary in view of changes in the environment. At the same time, he oversees the internal operations of the ship that are delegated to junior staff personnel. He receives reports from time to time summarizing the progress of these delegated operations. The captain uses these reports to assess the efficiency of operations and to facilitate any necessary adjustments to the allocation of resources among the various activities of the ship.

The categories of information required by managers at the various levels of an organization have been described by Daniel in the following terms:[16] (a) *environmental information*—relating to the social, political, and economic aspects of the environment in which the organization is operating; (b) *competitive information*—describing the performance, plans, and activities of other competing organizations; and (c) *internal information*—concerning the operations of one's own organization. The role of the information system is to acquire information in each of these three categories, process the information according to requirements laid down by those who use it, transmit and report the information to those who need it in the course of their day-to-day work, and store the information, when necessary, in a form appropriate for efficient later retrieval. The information system de-

[16] Daniel, D. R., "Management Information Crisis," *op. cit.*, p. 113.

signed to carry out this role in a modern organization consists of two major components: (a) the internal information system and (b) the strategic information system. Each of these components of the overall system serves one of the major sets of tasks of management mentioned above. The two components and their roles in the support of management can be described briefly, as follows:

The Internal Information System

This component serves managers engaged in the internal regulation and control of the organization, providing processing support for the multitude of transactions that must be undertaken in the day-to-day operations of the organization. This component keeps track of the expenditure of resources and provides managers with reports in which these expenditures are compared with planned and budgeted estimates. It reports also the degree to which the objectives that are to be achieved by the expenditure of resources have, in fact, been accomplished. The internal information system includes most of the activities that have come to be called "electronic data processing," or EDP, in many organizations. These activities most often involve repetitive processing of routine tasks that in an earlier age would have been undertaken by clerical staff. In a modern system, standard procedures are established for the accomplishment of these tasks. The great speed and data storage potential of the computer can be used to provide efficient and accurate processing of the necessary transactions.

Most of the managerial activities that are supported by the internal information system are concerned with the administration of resources and the conduct of operations. These activities are the responsibility of middle-level managers in a typical organization. The information provided by the internal component of the overall system allows these mid-level managers to monitor the processing of routine procedures and to modify these procedures as is found necessary in the changing conditions in which the organization operates.

Another important function of the internal information system is to provide summary information on the conduct of routine internal activities to the more senior levels of management. This information permits these managers to assess the effectiveness of the expenditure of the resources of the organization in terms of the achievement of its objectives. This information also serves as an important input for the more strategic managerial activity of choosing future objectives for the organization and selecting new paths along which the energies of the organization can be conducted.

The Strategic Information System

This component of the overall information system serves and supports the strategic activities of management that are most often described by the terms planning and policy making. The strategic component of the information system receives summary information on the state of the organization from the internal component, while searching the external environment for information likely to affect the future course or activities of the organization. The material processed by this strategic component often consists of a high proportion of non-quantitative and descriptive information as opposed to the more quantitative content of the internal component of the system.

The strategic component of the information system has received less attention to date than its internal counterpart. This has been due in part to the natural adaptability of computers to quantitative data and the important role that financial information plays in the management of most organizations. This lack of emphasis has also probably been caused by the more elusive characteristics of the information with which the strategic component of the system must deal. The nature of strategic information is such that it is inherently less amenable to processing than numeric data. Numeric data refer to well-defined quantities and are well-understood by all concerned. The highly subjective character of the strategic information often militates against the creation of a common information system for use by all concerned in the organization. Information that has a high interpretive or subjective content tends to be held much more confidentially by those who have collected it. The tendency has been, therefore, for a manager to collect and store such information for use solely within his own office. Recent developments in strategic components of information systems do not run directly contrary to this natural desire of managerial personnel. More recent systems do, however, provide facilities for more effective acquisition, transmission and storage of strategic information in support of decision processes at the highest levels of management.

The Elements of an Information System

Each component of the overall information system contains elements that carry out tasks concerned with the management of the organization's information. These tasks were specified originally by

Norbert Wiener (as already referenced) as being the acquisition, use, retention, and transmission of information. The only modifications to this early specification made necessary in light of modern experience are the replacement of the word "use" by the word "processing," and the reinterpretation of the word "transmission" to include reporting.

The task of acquiring information is undertaken in an organization by a variety of elements that can be grouped conveniently under the heading "sensors." These elements have their counterparts in the human system in the eyes, ears, and the other sense organs. Organizational information sensors may be passive in that they detect and acquire only the data and information that is normally channelled to them. On the other hand, sensors may be active, seeking out information that would not otherwise be acquired. Sensors may be so placed that they primarily collect information within an organization or they may be deployed so as to obtain mainly external data. Sensors may be semi-automatic, machine-like devices that record data according to pre-programmed instructions. On the other hand, data may be gathered by individuals who use initiative in seeking out information of particular interest as and when it is required. All members of an organization play the part of an information sensor to some extent in the course of their normal day-to-day activities.

The transmission of information in both the internal and strategic components of the system is undertaken by communication channels. These channels connect the sensors to facilities that process the material that has been acquired. Some interpretation of raw material may take place during its passage between the points connected by communication channels in an organization. Interpretation of this kind occurs in the human system when messages passed via the nervous system are subjected to a degree of selection and modification at the synapses. Communication channels also pass data and information to and from memory according to the requirements of the decision centers. Other channels pass messages from the decision centers to the parts of the organization that initiate action.

The material acquired by the sensors is processed so that it provides information to the decision centers in the manner and format most appropriate to the decision process in which it will be used. The processing activity may consist of one or more of the following activities: collation, aggregation, interpretation, and condensation. Collation seeks to place in order material collected from various sources. Aggregation consists of collection of like items and may include summarization by reporting a total effect rather than each of its component parts. Interpretation implies the addition of meaning to collected information, usually by the inclusion of subjective judgments in addition to or in place of the original material. Condensation may occur during aggregation and interpretation and is usually undertaken with the objective of economizing on the use of storage or transmission facilities.

Many of these processing activities are undertaken in conjunction with memory devices. Some memory devices are used as buffer storage to hold data and information for short periods during processing. Other memory devices serve as longer term storage for material that is judged to be of possible future interest to the organization. Rudimentary memory devices exist in all organizations in the form of filing cabinets, notebooks, and other media in which recorded information is stored. In modern information systems, many of the memory devices make use of magnetic or optical storage media. These devices are usually linked to a computer to ensure accurate recording and rapid access to the material at a later date.

The reporting function is inherent in the transmission of information by communication channels. The basic (but often overlooked) requirement of the elements of the system that are engaged in reporting to decision centers is that the information should be reported in the quantities and form that are appropriate to the use to which it is to be put. In some parts of an organizational informational system, information is reported as output from one mechanized process and is used directly as input to another such process. In these cases, care is taken to ensure that the output and input are matched so that the transfer of information is complete. In many other cases, however, reports from an information system are presented directly to a manager. In some instances in the past, lack of attention to the design of that interface has resulted in either too much or not enough information being presented to the manager. In other cases, information has been offered in a format that was not acceptable or understandable to the human recipient.

The Human Information Processing System

The degree to which the output of the information system meets a manager's needs for support in decision making depends on two factors: (a) the nature and form of the information presented and (b) the human capability for absorbing, processing, and using information. The information system designer has no control over the second of these factors. The characteristics of the human information processing system must, therefore, be taken into account when making decisions regarding the form of the output from the organizational system. Lack of attention to this requirement may result in the output of the organizational system being unacceptable or less valuable to the managers concerned.

The human information processing system consists of (a) a number of sensors that detect patterns and stimuli in the vicinity of the individual; (b) a series of channels for communication of information within the body; and (c) the brain, which contains the higher decision centers of the human system. The sensors are in essence special detectors, each of which has a role with respect to one of the five senses: sight, hearing, smell, taste, and touch. The stimuli detected by the sensors are passed toward the decision centers in the brain via the nervous system. The nervous system consists of a series of communication channels in which there are a number of junctions called synapses. Some filtering of the input from the sensors takes place in the synapses. The filtered material then passes through stages of memory that act as buffers in the communication system. Additional filtering and some interpretation of the input from the sensors takes place in these buffers. The resulting messages are then passed to the brain. Once a decision has been made, further messages are conveyed by similar communication channels to the parts of the body where action is to be initiated.

The sensors and the nervous system in the human body together constitute a most efficient means of recognition of patterns in the environment of the individual and of passing messages toward the decision centers in a format that is most appropriate for interpretation of the input.[17] The exact process by which pattern recognition is achieved is not fully understood at the present time. However, it seems clear that there are two sorts of memory involved, short-term and long-term. The input from the sensors first enters the short-term memory. In what appears to be a multi-stage process, this input is changed with

[17] Hunt, E. and W. Makous, "Some Characteristics of Human Information Processing," in Tsu-lieh Tou, ed., *Advances in Information Systems Science,* Plenum Press, 1969, pp. 283–335.

respect to both its information content and its physical nature. In the first stage, the input to the short-term memory is compared with previously-stored images of similar conditions. The updated impressions resulting from the comparison are then transferred to long-term memory, from which they can be recalled later as necessary.

This memory transferral process provides man with a very high capacity for visual pattern recognition of familiar items. For example, recognition of a friend seen on the street is accomplished in a fraction of a second. Familiar objects are detected even if they are partly masked by minor alterations or camouflage. In addition to pattern recognition, human beings are also very good at recognizing items in context, especially in terms of written or spoken material.[18]

Despite its capacity for prodigious feats of recognition of patterns and items in context, however, the human information system has many deficiencies when viewed in the light of modern organizational activities. These deficiencies appear to be due at least in part to the very characteristics of the memory process that allow us to achieve high capability in other areas. The deficiencies seem to arise from two major sources: (a) the comparative slowness of the transfer of material from short-term memory to more permanent storage and (b) the limited capacity of the short-term memory itself. There is some evidence that the size of the short-term memory is the more important of these deficiencies.[19]

If an individual is presented with very large amounts of data and material, he or she may very quickly become overloaded.[20] Overloaded individuals may delay giving attention to certain types of material in an attempt to adjust to the overload condition. They may favor familiar material under such conditions and they may establish a set of priorities for processing information of different types.[21] Some experiments have suggested that overloaded individuals use less information in decision making than those who are presented with what

[18] Ibid., p. 320.

[19] Miller, George A., "The Magical Number Seven, Plus or Minus Two: Some Limits on our Capacity for Processing Information," *The Psychological Review*, vol. 63, March 1956, pp. 81–97.

[20] Weick, Karl E., "The Twigging of Overload," in H. B. Pepinsky, ed., *People and Information*, Pergamon Press, 1970, Chapter 3, pp. 67–129.

[21] Katz, D. and R. L. Kahn, "Communication: the Flow of Information," *The Social Psychology of Organizations*, Wiley, 1966, Chapter 9.

is apparently a near-optimal amount of material.[22] Other observations suggest that individuals often process material inaccurately under conditions of overload.

The characteristics of human information processing have an important bearing on information system design and implementation.[23] The human information system provides an interesting and useful model upon which the design of the organizational system can be broadly based. The high degree of integration of the human information system with the other components of the body is a feature to be emulated in the design of the organizational system. Of particular importance, however, is the fact that the organizational information system and its human counterpart must interface at the point at which information is provided to managers. The characteristics of that interface are probably one of the most important aspects of information system design. The overriding consideration is that the output of the information system at all levels must be determined by the needs of the manager and by his ability to absorb the material presented.

Initial Specifications for an Organizational Information System

The foregoing discussion provides material upon which some broad initial specifications for an organizational information system can be based. Foremost among these specifications is the requirement that the information system must serve and support managerial activities throughout the organization. Emphasis must be placed on designing an information system to meet managerial needs. The temptation to endeavor to influence organizational activities in order to accommodate the characteristics of a particular type of information system must be avoided at all times.

The organizational activities to be supported range from routine transaction processing (such as payroll preparation, servicing of ac-

[22] Driver, M. J. and S. Streufert, "Integrative Complexity: An Approach to Individuals and Groups as Information Processing Systems," *Administrative Science Quarterly*, June 1969, pp. 272–285.

[23] Mintzberg, H., *Impediments to the Use of Management Information*, a study carried out on behalf of the National Association of Accountants, New York, N.Y., 1975.

counts payable and receivable, and inventory control) to planning and policy making. The services provided by the information system must support traditional staff functions such as accounting and personnel management as well as the operations of the organization. The information system must provide appropriate service from the topmost to the lowest levels of the organization.

A second important requirement of the information system is that it must match the pattern and structure of management at all levels of the organization that it serves. This pattern and structure may be dynamic, changing to meet variations in conditions encountered by the organization. The design of the information system must, therefore, be sufficiently flexible to meet the changing needs of management quickly and economically. The process of management is closely-related to decision making.[24] The design of the information system must therefore be based on the pattern of decision making in the organization that it serves and it must support decision processes at all levels of management.

As noted earlier, a third requirement to be met in the design of the information system is that the output of the system at every point at which it interfaces with managers must be matched with (a) the information needs of managers at the point of output and (b) the capacity of the managers involved to absorb, process, and use the information provided. It is not the overall quantity of information presented on any occasion that is important, but rather the quantity of information that can penetrate the management process and be used to advantage in decision making.[25] The bottleneck in most organizational decision making does not result from a shortage of pertinent information. The deficiencies lie in the area of determining what of the available information is significant and arranging the interface between the organizational information system and the equivalent human system of the manager. The design of the output and of the information system should emphasize the selecting of information that is significant and the conveying of information in concentrated form into the mind of the manager.

Detailed specifications for an organizational information system

[24] Simon, Herbert A., *The New Science of Management Decision,* 2nd ed., Prentice-Hall, 1977, p. 39.

[25] Wiener, Norbert, *The Human Use of Human Beings,* Avon Books, paperback edition, 1967, p. 127.

must include those relating to two major components of such a system: an internal component, serving routine decision processes and transactions in the regulation, administration, and control of the organization; a strategic component that supports strategic decision making. Both components must carry out the tasks of acquisition, processing, retention, and transmission of information needed by the organization. Each component must incorporate: (a) sensors to be employed in the acquisition of data and information; (b) communication channels to transmit the data and information to decision centers; (c) processing facilities for recording and restricting data and information into a form suitable for use in the organizational decision processes; and (d) memory devices for retention of data and information during processing and for later recall as necessary.

No matter how elaborate a formal information system is set up in an organization, it will and should be complemented by informal communication between staff members. The informal system of communication is much less structured than its formal counterpart and is therefore much more flexible in changing conditions. On the other hand, it is much less likely to cover in sufficient detail all aspects of any situation confronting an organization. The informal communication system is based to some extent on social relationships that exist in the organization, and it is an important feature of its operation. The development of the more formal information system should in no way be allowed to impede or restrict the operation of this informal communication system.

The Plan of the Book

The following text is a discussion of the design and implementation of an organizational information system based on the broad principles already outlined. The material is divided into a number of chapters focusing on the ideas touched upon in the preceding introductory discussion:

Chapter 2: A review of modern concepts in organizational direction and management—in this review, the organization is treated as a system incorporating a number of subsystems (of which the information system is one) and interacting with the environment within which it operates.

Chapter 3: A discussion of organizational decision making and of the information requirements of the various decision processes.

Chapter 4: This chapter covers the basic design of the first component of the overall system, the internal information system.

Chapter 5: A detailed discussion of the nature of strategic information, where it can be sought and how it can be interpreted and used.

Chapter 6: A treatment of the design of the second major component of the overall system, the strategic information system.

Chapter 7: A review of the benefits and costs of introducing and implementing an overall organizational information system and of the manner in which it can be evaluated.

Summary

Most modern organizations have a system of one sort or another to handle the information they need. This information system may be elaborate or relatively simple, formal or informal in nature. In recent years, the idea of implementing an information system that is specially designed to support managerial activities has gained increasing acceptance. The tasks of such a system are to acquire, process, transmit, and retain the information needed in decision making and transaction processing at all levels of the organization. The information system required by an organization can be compared with the information system contained in the human body. Some of the basic characteristics of the human system provide insight into the manner in which an efficient organizational information system can be designed.

The early information systems developed by organizations were concerned almost entirely with financial and accounting functions. When first introduced into general use, computers were used primarily to undertake the considerable clerical and data processing tasks associated with financial and accounting functions. Modern information system design, on the other hand, is based on the idea that support must be provided to a wide range of managerial activities. Despite some early mistakes and disillusionment, there are now encouraging signs that modern information systems can provide significant benefits in the management of an organization. It appears, however, that significant benefits can be derived only from those systems developed and implemented with a high degree of cooperation between specialists and managers.

Information required in the management of an organization arises both in the organization itself and also in the environment in which it operates. An exact definition of the word information in this context is not simple. In the organizational context information might best be described as recorded experience that is or can be used in decision making. This recorded experience can take many forms, ranging from sets of values of well-defined parameters to descriptive material in newspapers or technical articles. The amount and value of information drawn from any particular material depends upon the situation in which it is to be used. Different amounts of information can be extracted by different individuals from the same material. The amount and the value of information that can be extracted does not necessarily increase with the amount of material. Both the amount and value of information derived from a given body of data decrease if the individual interpreting it becomes overloaded. The process of interpretation of raw data is frequently obscured by irrelevant content.

A modern organizational information system has two major components. One component is concerned with the activities of internal administration, regulation, and control. The second component is concerned with supporting more strategic activities such as the charting of future directions for the organization. Both major components contain elements designed to carry out the basic tasks of acquisition, use, retention, and transmission of information. These elements include sensors, processing facilities, memory devices, and communication channels.

The human information system is of interest both as a model for and as a component of the organizational information system. The human information system has a high capacity for pattern recognition and identification of items in context. However, the human system has many deficiencies when considered in terms of the requirements of a modern organization. These deficiencies arise mainly from the nature of short-term memory in human beings. Their limited short-term memory makes humans particularly susceptible to information overload. In conditions of overload, individuals tend to become selective in their absorption and use of material presented. Under these circumstances individuals often favor familiar material and reject unfamiliar or controversial information. Due to the deficiencies of the human system the interface between the organizational information system and the managers who use it is a most important aspect of system design and implementation.

Following are some broad initial specifications for an organizational information system. The system must (a) serve and support the managerial activities in the organization of which it is a part; (b) have components serving both the general direction of the organization and its internal regulation and control; (c) undertake the tasks of acquisition, processing, retention, transmission, and reporting of information; (d) be designed to follow the pattern and structure of management at all levels of the organization that it serves; (e) have design characteristics that are sufficiently flexible to meet the changing needs of management; (f) have outputs designed to meet the information requirements and information processing capabilities of managers at all points that the system serves; and (g) not restrict the informal passage of information throughout the organization.

Discussion Topics

1/ Norbert Wiener draws a comparison between the human information system and the system needed to meet the information requirements of a modern organization. Do you consider this comparison useful in initial discussion of organizational information systems? What are its strengths and weaknesses? Could a reliance upon the human analogy be misleading to those engaged in information system design?

2/ It has been stated that every organization has an information system of one kind or another. Do you agree with this statement? Can you give examples of information systems that have evolved naturally in organizations?

3/ Modern computers were introduced into general use in organizations in the early 1960s. What effects did the introduction of computers have on the design and implementation of information systems? Were all these effects beneficial?

4/ What do you consider to be the proper role of a computer within an organizational information system? In which tasks would computer support be most necessary or helpful? Are there any activities in which emphasis on computer support might be undesirable?

5/ In most cases, computers were first introduced into organizations in support of accounting and clerical functions. Why do you think this occurred?

6/ How would you define information? How would you measure the amount of information in a given body of material? How can the value of a particular piece of information be assessed? Do you agree that the amount and value of information derived from a given body of material depends upon the individual receiving the material and the situation in which that individual is operating? If so, what effect should this factor have on information system design?

7/ It is suggested in this chapter that an organizational information system should consist of two major components: the internal information system; and the strategic information system. What are the managerial activities at various levels that these two system components must support? What are the essential differences between these two major components?

8/ Although the human information processor has the capability to perform prodigious feats of recognition of patterns and items in context, the human processing system also has some noteworthy deficiencies. How do these characteristics affect information system design? In light of these deficiencies, what points should be given special consideration by those in charge of the design of interfaces between the information system and the manager?

9/ R. L. Ackoff discussed five assumptions commonly made by designers of information systems that he felt were unjustified ("Management Misinformation Systems," *Management Science,* vol. 14, No. 4, December 1967). Comment on each of these assumptions, stating whether you agree or disagree with Ackoff.

10/ Do you think that the broad specifications for an information system described at the end of the present chapter provide a framework for avoiding some of the pitfalls described in Ackoff's article? Are there any other broad specifications that you might add?

11/ Comment on the statement that the role of an information system is to support decision making at all levels of an organization. Do you think that this statement correctly describes the role of an information system?

12/ Select an organization with which you are familiar and analyze the types of decisions that are made in the organization. How is information provided to those who have responsibility for these decisions at the present time? Do you think sufficient information of the right type is provided now? How would you set about determining the adequacy of available information in a real-life situation?

CASE WORK

1/ List the characteristics of the human information system and compare these with their counterparts in modern organizations.

2/ Describe in detail the information system that existed in an organization observed in historic times. For some ideas, see Dvornik, F., *Origins of Intelligence Services,* Rutgers University Press, 1974; and Starr, Chester G., *Political Intelligence in Classical Greece,* Lugdini Batavorum, E. J. Brill, Leiden, Netherlands, 1974. In your answer emphasize the distinction between the internal and the strategic components of these systems.

3/ Terrance Hanold has described his experiences in introducing a specially designed information system into his organization ("An Executive View of MIS," *Datamation,* November 1972). Read the article and list (a) points that you would consider important if you were engaged in a similar implementation; (b) points that you consider to be contrary to some observed modern practices; and (c) any differences in approach that appear to result from the fact that a senior manager, rather than a computer or "information systems" specialist, was in charge of implementation.

2

The Direction and Management of the Organization

Introduction

Two of the initial specifications for an information system developed in Chapter 1 are (a) the system must serve and support the activities involved in the direction and management of the organization of which it is a part and (b) the design of the information system must follow the pattern and structure of the management activities that it serves. A thorough study of the processes by which an organization is directed and managed is, therefore, an essential preliminary to the work of design and implementation of an information system. The purpose of this chapter is to provide a basis for such a study.

The approach will be to view an organization as a complex system, composed of a number of components or subsystems. One of the tasks of organizational management is the integration and coördination of the efforts and activities of these components toward the accomplishment of the organization's overall objectives. The organization in question may itself be merely a component of a larger system, which is composed of other organizations and elements competing for opportunities and resources. The work of charting future directions for the organization and of managing its interaction with these organizations and elements is another important task of management. Different managerial styles and structures are appropriate to the various types of environment and activities in which an organization may find itself. All these aspects of management are explored in this chapter in terms that will be found useful in the later discussion of information system design and implementation.

Some Basic Systems Concepts

A system is a set of interrelated elements called components or subsystems.[1, 2] The essential characteristics of a system derive from the relationships between its various elements. The boundaries of the system can be defined as the limits within which these relationships are meaningful. However, the strength or weakness of a relationship is not something that can ordinarily be defined in specific terms. The definition of any particular system and of its boundaries may therefore be somewhat arbitrary. The characteristics attributed to a system often depend on the perceptions of the individuals involved. The perceptions of individuals with different information, experience, and judgement may vary greatly.

Systems exist on a number of different levels. At a lower hierarchical level, each of the subsystems might be considered to be a complete system in its own right. Then again, at a higher level, the original system might be regarded only as a subsystem of an even more comprehensive set of elements. Hierarchical chains of this nature are familiar in daily life. They appear in almost all forms of human activity. There is no logical end to the process of dividing systems into components.[3] In practice, however, the process is carried no further than is necessary for the considerations at hand. The process of division into components is usually stopped at the level of some basic and elementary component beyond which little further insight would be gained.

The interaction between the components of a system is a major determinant of the system's overall behavior. The components interact both by observing one another and by actively exchanging in-

[1] von Bertalanffy, L., "General Systems Theory," *General Systems,* vol. 1, 1956, pp. 1–10.

[2] Boulding, K. E., "General Systems Theory," *Management Science,* vol. 2, 1956, pp. 197–208.

[3] Churchman, C. W., "An Approach to General Systems Theory," in M. Mesarovic, ed., *Views on General Systems Theory,* J. Wiley, 1964, pp. 173–175.

formation in one form or another. Systems and their components also observe the environment in which the system operates and exchange information with other systems. The nature of this information exchange ultimately determines the behavior of the system within its environment.

A system may be classified as simple or complex, depending on the nature of the relationships between its subsystems. A system may also be described as deterministic or probabilistic in terms of the predictability of its behavior.[4] A deterministic system is one in which the components interact in a perfectly predictable way, as in a well-balanced machine. A probabilistic system is one about which insufficient information is available to allow a precise prediction of its future behavior. Most modern day organizations must be regarded as probabilistic, rather than deterministic systems.

Systems may also be classified in terms of their behavior in reaction to an internal or external event.[5] Three types of systems displaying very different behaviors are described below, listed in increasing order of complexity:

1/ *A state-maintaining system* is a system designed to maintain a particular state under a range of internal or external conditions. It reacts in only one way to any internal or external event. It reacts to a different degree to any one of a series of events and it always reacts in such a way as to maintain the same state or outcome. The thermostat and the governor of an engine are state-maintaining systems.

2/ *A goal-seeking system* can respond differently to internal or external events under either different or unchanged conditions in order to produce a particular desired outcome. A goal-seeking system has various forms of behavior at its disposal and may often be able to achieve the same outcome in a number of different ways. The system may even learn over time how to produce the desired outcome more efficiently. However, the system is not able to change its goal as a result of experience.

[4] Beer, Stafford, *Cybernetics and Management,* English Universities Press, Second Edition, 1967, pp. 12–19.

[5] Ackoff, R. L., "Towards a System of Systems Concepts," *Management Science,* vol. 17, no. 11, July 1971, pp. 661–671.

The automatic pilot of a modern airplane is an example of a goal-seeking system.

3/ *A purposeful system* is a goal seeking system that is able to produce a variety of outcomes under a number of different conditions. This type of system can change its goals as a result of experience or can change its methods of obtaining a particular goal. A purposeful system can, therefore, change ends as well as means. A human being can be regarded as a good example of a purposeful system.

Systems theory provides a framework within which general propositions can be formulated. These general ideas can then be applied to various kinds of systems and to different levels in the same system.[6] Such propositions can be used as a basis for comparisons and analogies between parts of a system that are similar in general operation but serve different functions. The operation of subsystems of different sizes and at different levels can also be analyzed within the framework of systems theory in the hope of drawing conclusions that are of general applicability.

The use of systems theory is not without a number of disadvantages, however. First of all, the theory is a rather abstract and general approach to the study of operations. For this reason, it may not appeal to the practical manager concerned with the detailed aspects of a job. There is a danger, also, that a methodology that facilitates comparison and analogy between operations of different sizes and at different levels may conceal essential differences in these operations. These possible disadvantages must be kept in mind in the course of the following discussion of the organization as a system.

The Organization as a System

A modern organization can be considered to be an example of the purposeful system defined earlier.[7, 8] Most such organizations have

[6] Ramstrom, Dick, *The Efficiency of Control Strategies,* Almquist and Wiksell, 1967, pp. 34–38.

[7] Ackoff, R. L., "Towards a System," *op. cit.,* pp. 669–670.

[8] For a contrary view see N. S. Peery, Jr., "General Systems Theory Approaches to Organizations: Some Problems in Application," *Journal of Management Studies,* Oct. 1975, pp. 266–275.

more than one purpose. Much of the activity of an organization consists of converting available resources (such as money, person-hours and materials) into output of one sort or another in order to achieve its objectives. The output may be in the form of goods or services or a mixture of both of these.

An organization consists of a number of purposeful components, each of which may constitute a system in itself at a lower level than the organization as a whole. The basic component in an organization is usually the individual staff member. Each component normally serves a number of purposes, some of which may not coincide exactly with those of the organization. However, membership of the various components in the organization implies that they have at least one purpose in common. The components can be regarded as members of a coalition formed with the object of fulfilling their common purpose or purposes.[9]

The components of an organization observe each other's behavior and interact by communicating with each other by one means or another. The interaction between the components determines the behavior of the organization as a whole. If one of the components ceases to take part in this process of interaction and communication, it ceases, for all intents and purposes, to be a part of the organization. The organization extends only as far as the limits of communication between its components.[10] The boundaries of an organization depend therefore on the nature of the communication links between its components. The cohesiveness of an organization depends upon the strength of these links and the degree to which the purposes of the components coincide with the purpose of the organization as a whole.

The charter or founding papers of an organization usually contains a statement of its purpose. This statement can be used as the basis for defining the following:

1/ *Objectives* of the organization—the outcomes that the organization desires to achieve over an indefinite future time period;

2/ *Goals* of the organization—the steps towards achieving its

[9] Cyert, R. M., and J. G. March, *A Behavioral Theory of the Firm,* Prentice-Hall, 1963, pp. 26–38.

[10] Wiener, Norbert, *Cybernetics,* The MIT Press, paperback edition, 1965, pp. 157–161.

objectives that the organization desires to accomplish within a given time period;

3/ *Activities* of the organization—the courses of action that the organization intends to pursue in order to achieve its goals and objectives.

Once the activities of the organization have been chosen, it is necessary to arrive at a functional division of the effort required to carry out these activities. The work of deciding on this division of effort is one of the major tasks involved in the internal management of an organization. The division of effort can be made in terms of four factors:

1/ *Specialization*—each division is responsible for a specific category of operations such as finance, personnel, sales, or distribution of products;

2/ *Program of activities*—a number of specializations are combined into a program, group, or task force designed to achieve a particular portion of the common goals and objectives of the organization;

3/ *Territory*—used typically in a geographically widespread organization, the operations in a particular area are grouped together and treated as a separate program of the organization;

4/ *Time*—differentiation is made between short-term and long-term activities.

In a modern organization, the division of effort between the components is often made in terms of a combination of the above factors.

Division of effort among the components of an organization is a natural consequence of the complexity of modern-day operations. This division also results from the fact that any individual or group of individuals has a limited span of surveillance. Once this limit is reached, it is natural that responsibilities should be split up between the available components. This process, often referred to as *differentiation,*[11] leads in turn to a tendency among those to whom responsibility has been delegated to specialize, concentrating on the one aspect of

[11] Lawrence, P. R., and J. W. Lorsch, *Organization and Environment,* Graduate School of Business Administration, Harvard University, 1967, pp. 7–18.

the organization's activities with which they are concerned. Those who specialize naturally see the organization more in terms of their own area of interest and, therefore, have less in common with individuals working in other areas.

The process of differentiation often results in substantially different viewpoints and motivations among the individuals and components working within an organization. This phenomenon can often be observed in terms of (a) differences among individuals and components arising from differing interpretations of the particular goals and objectives of the organization; (b) different orientations regarding time factors and different periods of peak concentration of effort; (c) differences in the style of interpersonal relations on the part of individuals in different specialities; and (d) a tendency for individuals and components to place different values on outcomes, to institute different control procedures in the conduct of their work, and to develop different formal reporting procedures. The different viewpoints and motivations in an organization are often the cause of considerable tension and conflict between the various component groups.

The process of differentiation is necessary to the accomplishment of the work of the organization. Differentiation must, however, be accompanied by a second process referred to as *integration*. The purpose of integration is to enhance collaboration between individuals and components in the organization. Collaboration is essential to the achievement of an organization's goals and objectives. The purpose of integration is not to weld all components of the organization into a standardized and monolithic whole. The purpose is rather to encourage and foster the necessary communication and interaction between the components of an organization. At the same time, the integration process should not discourage the variety of interests and approaches that differentiation demands.

Integration is an essential task in the internal management of an organization. Insomuch as integration is primarily concerned with communication and reporting, the information system is a vital component in support of this activity.

The Organization and Its Environment

The boundaries of an organization are defined by the limits within which its components interact in pursuit of a common purpose. The space outside these limits is called the *environment* of the organization.[12] The environment may contain other organizations with similar or different purposes. The environment may also embrace conditions, phenomena, and events that affect the behavior of organizations within it and determine the feasibility of future objectives and courses of action. For example, economic factors in the environment surrounding an organization may constitute a recession and this may have an effect on its future plans and activities.

The extent of the environment of an organization depends upon the degree of its interaction with the other elements that it encounters there. An organization having few external contacts can be perceived as existing in a very limited environment. On the other hand, an organization with very strong external contacts exists in a very extensive environment. The total environment of an organization can be thought of as a system at one level higher than the organization itself. In this higher level system, the organizations in the environment are the components. The boundaries of the environmental system are defined by the strength of the interaction between its component organizations.

A typical situation involving a number of organizations is shown in Figure 2-1. The organization A is shown within its environment in the top-left part of the diagram.

The boundaries of organization A are depicted as irregular but relatively well-defined. The boundaries of its environment are shown hatched to indicate that they are somewhat arbitrary, depending, at least to some extent, on the perceptions of those involved in organization A. The environment of A contains two other organizations, C and D, with which A has some interaction. Another organization, B, is shown in the lower right of the diagram in its own environment. The environments of organizations A and B are shown as separate to indicate that the interactions between the two organizations are weak or nonexistent. The linkage between the two environments is therefore weak. If the interactions between A and B became stronger, each would become part of the other's environment. In this case, the hatched boundary in Figure 2-1 would encompass both organizations.

The interaction between an organization and its environment consists of (a) observations by the organization of the conditions in the environment; (b) observations of the behavior of other organizations

[12] Smith, P. B., *Groups within Organizations,* Harper and Row, 1973, pp. 60–64.

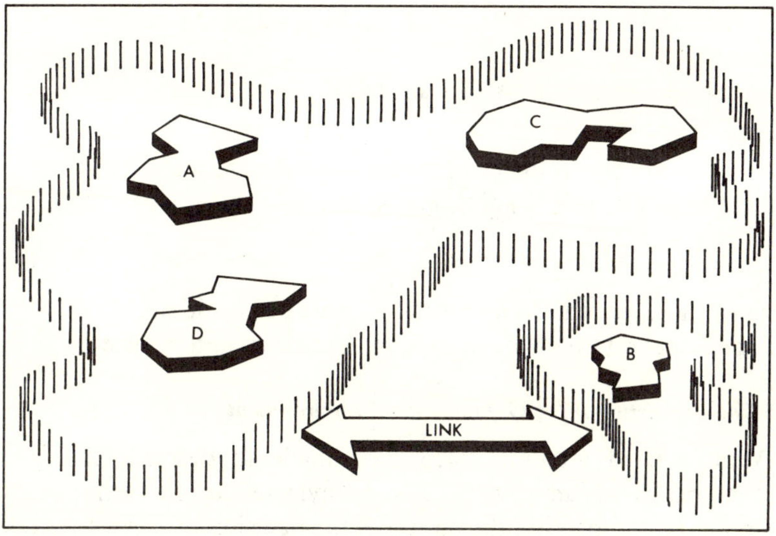

Figure 2.1. Organizations and Their Environment

in the environment; and (c) exchanges of messages and other communications between the organizations in the environment. Each of these categories of interaction comprises an exchange of information between the organization and its environment.[13] These exchanges can properly be regarded as being within the purview of the organizational information system.

It is interesting to note that it is possible to speak of the environment within the organization itself.[14] At one stage lower in the systems hierarchy, the components of an organization can be regarded as systems in their own right operating in an environment consisting of the organization of which they are part. The interactions between the components within this environment are the internal communications among the parts of the organization. These exchanges of information are those that have been considered conventionally as the area of operation of the internal organizational information system.

[13] Dill, William R., "The Impact of Environment on Organizational Development," in S. Mailick, and E. H. Van Ness, eds., *Concepts and Issues in Administrative Behavior,* Prentice-Hall, 1962, pp. 94–109.

[14] Duncan, R. B., "Characteristics of Organizational Environments and Perceived Environmental Uncertainty," *Administrative Science Quarterly,* vol. 19, 1972, p. 314.

The interactions and information exchanges that are important to an organization can be summarized as follows:[15]

1/ Those within the particular organization itself
2/ Those between the organization and its environment
3/ Those between the environment and the organization
4/ Those within the environment that are observed by the organization

Each of these information exchanges must be considered in the design and implementation of the organizational information system.

The Characteristics of the Organizational Environment

A number of attempts have been made to describe the overall characteristics of an organizational environment in terms of such attributes as complexity, the nature of the decision processes occurring in the environment, homogeneity, and rate of change.[16, 17, 18] The simplest adequate description divides the range of environmental conditions in which an organization might find itself into four categories.[19] Organizations experience one or more of these types of environment during the course of their operations. The exact types of environment experienced by an organization depend upon the nature of its activities. The four types of environment are described briefly as follows:

Type of Environment	Description
1. *Placid randomized*	A static environment, in which the benefits and disbenefits that an organization can experience are randomly distributed. In an environment such as this, organizations are able to survive

[15] Emery, F. E., and E. L. Trist, "The Causal Texture of Organizational Environments," *Human Relations*, vol. 18, 1965, pp. 21–32; reprinted in F. E. Emery, ed., *Systems Thinking*, Penguin Books, 1969, pp. 241–257.

[16] Lawrence, P. R., and J. W. Lorsch, *Organization, op. cit.*, pp. 23–54.

[17] Thompson, J. D., *Organizations in Action*, McGraw-Hill Book Company, 1967, pp. 70–73.

[18] Jurkovich, R., "A Core Typology of Organizational Environments," *Administrative Science Quarterly*, vol. 10, no. 3, 1974, pp. 380–394.

[19] Emery, F. E., and E. L. Trist, "Causal Texture," *op. cit.*, pp. 246–249.

include (a) the relative power of the participants to influence the particular situation under consideration; (b) standards of behavior expected of the participants dealing with the problem; (c) patterns of authority within and between organizations; (d) patterns of membership in trade associations, professional societies, and similar social groups; (e) commitments resulting from past actions or associations; and (f) any laws, policies, guidelines, or precedents that may govern or affect interaction between the participants.

2/ *physical, economic, human engineering, or other technological elements*—those factors that may restrict the range of courses of action available to the participants. Such restricting factors include any characteristics of organizations or available resources that may limit the actions that could be taken to resolve a decision problem immediately at hand.

3/ *natural phenomena and events*—those occurrences that may affect the future environment in which the courses of action selected by the participants will be implemented. Natural phenomena and events can be thought of as belonging in two different categories: (a) truly natural events in which there is no discernible human involvement and (b) "quasi-natural" events and phenomena which result from a combination of truly natural occurrences and the activities of individuals and organizations not directly involved in the particular decision problem or activity under consideration.

Given practical circumstances, the information gathered describing the participants and elements of the environment is never truly complete. Individuals operating in turbulent organizational environments will therefore always experience some degree of uncertainty. Furthermore, conditions of incomplete information may cause different individuals to arrive at widely disparate perceptions of the characteristics of other participants and of the other elements of the environment. This uncertainty factor, which can have a major effect on organizational decision making in turbulent environments, is examined in detail in the next chapter.

Managerial Activities

The management of an organization coordinates all those activities designed to ensure the fulfillment of the following goals: (a) appropriate interaction between the organization and its environment; (b) achievement of organizational objectives to the greatest extent possible; and (c) most efficient use of available resources in the pursuit of organizational objectives. The activities involved in management have been discussed at length in other literature. Henri Fayol was the first to discuss the functions of management in terms of (a) planning; (b) organizing; (c) commanding; (d) coordinating; and (e) controlling.[24] F. W. Taylor, a contemporary of Fayol, was concerned with "scientific management" and with the efficiency of workers in production processes.[25] Max Weber and other eminent sociologists stressed the importance of leadership and various aspects of individual and social psychology in their formulation of a theory of management.[26] More recently, a framework for the study of management activities has been advanced by Robert N. Anthony.[27] Within this framework managerial activities are classified under three headings: (a) strategic planning; (b) management control; and (c) operational control.

Strategic Planning

Strategic planning is defined by Anthony as the process of "deciding on objectives of the organization, on changes in these objectives, on the resources used to attain these objectives, and on the policies that are to govern the acquisition, use, and disposition of these resources." Strategic planning often has long-range implications and considerable time is often required to put long-range plans into effect. On the other hand, strategic plans and decisions may sometimes be concerned with extremely short-term effects, particularly when unexpected phenomena and events arise requiring immediate changes in objectives or allocation of resources.[28] Recent government actions banning certain classes of insecticide and food additives provide ex-

24 Fayol, Henri, *General and Industrial Management* (translation from the original French), Pitman, 1949.

25 Taylor, F. W., *The Principles of Scientific Management,* Harper and Row, 1911.

26 Weber, Max, *The Theory of Social and Economic Organizations,* Oxford University Press, 1947.

27 Anthony, Robert N., *Planning and Control Systems: a Framework for Analysis,* Graduate School of Business Administration, Harvard University, 1965.

28 Ansoff, H. Igor, "Managing Strategic Surprise by Response to Weak Signals," *California Management Review,* vol. 18, no. 2, Winter 1975.

amples of unexpected events affecting the strategic planning of the firms involved with producing or using the banned items.

Strategic planning is concerned primarily with the organization's interaction with its environment. Strategic planning is concerned with the choice of objectives and future courses of action that are believed to be consistent with the relationship between the organization and its environment. The aim of strategic planning is to establish and maintain a set of relationships between the organization and the environment fulfilling three basic requirements: (a) the relationships established should enable the organization to pursue its objectives; (b) such relationships should be consistent with the capabilities of the organization; and (c) the relationships should be responsive on a continuing basis to changes in the environment.[29] Although conditions in the environment are of primary concern in strategic planning, the characteristics and capabilities of the component subsystems of the organization and the relationships between these subsystems are also of great importance to the strategic planner.

The determination of goals and objectives is a major part of strategic planning. It can be thought of as essentially the process of defining the desired relationships between the organization and its environment.[30] Conditions within the environment exercise some degree of control over this process of setting goals and objectives, often providing great obstacles for the organization to overcome. Some organizations are so dominated by their environment that they are able to exercise virtually no free will in the setting of their goals and objectives. Examples of such organizations can be found in public utilities (such as commuter services) that find it very difficult to cover costs while satisfying all public demands within the confines of externally mandated rate structures. At the other end of the spectrum, large commercial enterprises often successfully dominate their environment and mould it to suit their purposes. The largest proportion of organizations fall somewhere in between these end points on the spectrum. For most organizations, strategic planning and the setting of goals and objectives involve a degree of compromise with their environments. Insomuch as the environment is dynamic and sometimes

[29] Ansoff, H. Igor, "The Concept of Strategic Management," *The Journal of Business Policy,* vol. 2, no. 4, 1972, pp. 2–7.

[30] Thompson, J. D., and W. J. McEwen, "Organizational Goals and Environment: Goal Setting as an Interaction Process," *American Sociological Review,* vol. 23, 1958, pp. 23–31.

subject to turbulent change, strategic planning is a continuous process involving both short-term and long-term considerations.

The strategic planner must become involved with two major concerns: (a) to determine the strategic change required in his organization as a result of changing conditions in the environment and (b) to build an organizational structure that is responsive to change. This task of building an organizational structure entails the allocation of available resources to the appropriate organizational activities and the assignment of appropriate tasks to the available individuals and groups.

Certain characteristics of the organization, its immediate circumstances, and past history often prevent ideal allocation of resources and personnel. The following characteristics often present the greatest obstacles to optimal allocation: (a) deficiencies in existing physical facilities and their capabilities; (b) an unwieldy organizational power structure; (c) the extent to which individuals can be influenced by rewards and penalties; (d) unproductive standards of behavior expected and sanctioned within the organization; and (e) inadequacies in the extent and effectiveness of the organizational information system.

The extent to which strategic planning and management are effective in an organization is largely determined by the characteristics of the individuals comprising the organization. Four individual characteristics appear to have the greatest effect in this respect: (a) attitude toward change and risk-taking; (b) skill in interpersonal relationships; (c) work skills with respect to strategic activities; and (d) the motivation to apply the necessary skills and attitudes.[31]

Management Control

The internal regulation and administration of the organization is accomplished through management control. Management control is defined by Anthony as "the process by which managers assure that resources are obtained and used effectively and efficiently in the accomplishment of the organization's objectives."

Management control is intimately linked to strategic planning. Management control strives to implement the objectives and allocation of resources established in the strategic planning process. Its purpose is to ensure that the resources allocated to accomplish the ob-

[31] Ansoff, H. Igor, "The Concept of Strategic Management," p. 6.

jectives of the organization are used effectively and efficiently. Effectiveness in this context is defined in terms of accomplishment of desired objectives. Efficiency is measured in terms of the amount of resources necessary for the full or partial accomplishment of a particular goal or an objective. It is possible, but not desirable, to be highly efficient while achieving only a low degree of effectiveness. It is possible, also, to be effective without necessarily operating at a high level of efficiency. The ideal, in practice, is a high degree of both efficiency and effectiveness.

The dividing line between management control and strategic planning is often indistinct. Both activities are concerned with what may be called planning. However, the planning aspects of management control are concerned with detailed budgeting and allocation of resources rather than the more strategic tasks of setting future objectives and directions for the organization. Some management control activities are structured, periodic and regular. These activities follow prescribed procedures whereas strategic planning is often irregular and unstructured. Management control is concerned with action within prescribed policies, whereas strategic planning involves the formulation of the policies themselves.

Five primary tasks are involved in management control: (a) allocation of resources to specific activities; (b) preparation of budgets covering both the expenditure of resources and the expected achievement of goals and objectives; (c) observation of results achieved in return for resources expended; (d) evaluation of these results; and (e) modification of activities and resource allocation in accordance with the evaluation of results. Completion of these tasks is facilitated by the availability of reliable and well-understood data concerning the expenditure of resources and the achievement of goals and objectives. These data are collected and processed in standard form throughout the life of the activities to which they refer. The data concerned arise primarily within the organization and are, therefore, the responsibility of the internal information system that supports the internal regulation and control processes.

Data that arise in the management control process are often useful in strategic planning. Once a store of consistent, historic data has been built up, it is possible that it can be used in exploring the relationships between the important parameters concerned with the operations of the organization. Relationships that are revealed in this way are usually no better than simplistic representations of the overall result of complex interactions. Put together in a model, however, such relationships may be useful in providing background information for use in some of the "What if?" questions that arise in planning situations. For example, historic data may provide a guide to such questions as "What would be the effect on profit of closing down plant A?" or "How would an increase in unemployment affect the cost of welfare in this city?" Answers to such questions might also be useful in organizational activities other than planning. For example, such information might be useful in the settlement of industrial relations disputes. The value of such data and simple models derives more from their ability to indicate general trends rather than to forecast exact results. The possible usefulness of such trend indications in strategic planning activities underscores the interdependence between the internal and the strategic components of the information system.

Operational Control

Operational control is defined by Anthony as "the process of ensuring that specific tasks are carried out effectively and efficiently." Operational control focuses on individual tasks rather than an entire range of activities. Operational control is concerned with a single task at a time; for example, the distribution of products or the collection of accounts receivable. Management control, by contrast, is concerned with the interaction between production, personnel, finance, and various other facets of the overall operation. Operational control deals with specific details of a particular operation. Management control is concerned with summary data covering a wide range of operational and administrative activities.

Operational control usually bases its activities upon a well-understood and completely specified model of the particular operation under consideration. The objective of operational control is to ensure that the operation proceeds according to the specifications laid down in advance. The control system must contain a method of monitoring the operation so that deviations from specifications can be detected and remedial action initiated.

Operational control is most familiar in the realm of industrial production processes. However, with the introduction of computers into organizations, many routine administrative processes can be considered in the same operational control terms previously used to describe production processes. As a preliminary to this operational control type treatment, the administrative tasks are broken down i their component parts and specifications are prepared providing complete details of the transactions and operations to be accomplished by each component part. These specifications form the basis for computer processing and support of the task. In some of the more complex administrative and operational tasks, mathematical models are introduced to further increase efficiency.

Styles of Management

Individuals involved in the management of organizations exhibit a wide range of managerial styles. Two typical and contrasting styles have been identified and termed *incremental* and *entrepreneurial.*[32]

The incremental style is oriented toward the maintenance of an equilibrium state both within the organization and between the organization and its environment. The incrementalist avoids initiating radical change. If change is encountered, the incrementalist will often take steps to minimize the effects of the change. If movement away from an existing situation becomes necessary, the incrementalist initially searches for courses of action that will achieve conditions that are only marginally different from the status quo. Movement is achieved by a succession of incremental steps, each succeeding step being undertaken after a review of the effects achieved by the previous step.[33]

In contrast, the entrepreneurial style seeks change rather than attempting to suppress and minimize it. The entrepreneurial manager anticipates threats and opportunities. He seeks advantage by striving to be the first to adapt to any change in the environment of his organization. Courses of action selected by an entrepreneurial manager tend to be bold and wide-ranging. His activities place great emphasis upon creativity.

Contrary to popular impressions, the incremental style of management is encountered widely in a large proportion of business enterprises. Also, the incremental approach is dominant in most, if not all, nonprofit organizations, including those at all levels of government

[32] *Ibid.*, p. 2.

[33] Braybrooke, D., and C. E. Lindblom, *A Strategy of Decision,* The Free Press, paperback edition, 1970, Chapter 5.

and public service. Incrementalism is adopted in a firm in order to enhance effective use of resources and promote efficiency. In nonprofit organizations, it is often utilized to maintain the status quo, both internally and between the organization and its environment.

The entrepreneurial style of management is adopted when change is desirable. This style is frequently observed in nonprofit organizations in the early stages of their development when much creative work is needed to delineate objectives, activities, and organizational structures. Once this initial work has been completed, managerial style tends to move towards the incremental. Entrepreneurial behavior may often reappear as the dominant style in times of crisis.

Entrepreneurial behavior is observed much more frequently in business enterprises. This is possibly due to the fact that the very existence of many competitive organizations is continually at stake. Over a wide range of organizations in both the public and private sector of the economy, however, incremental behavior in management is by far the more common. This is no doubt due to the fact that situations that call for the incremental style of management predominate in all kinds of organizations, despite the increasing turbulence in the modern environment.

The incremental and entrepreneurial styles of management can be analyzed with reference to the three categories of managerial activities discussed earlier in this chapter. Strategic planning normally requires the entrepreneurial approach. Individuals involved in strategic planning should be those who seek change and are not averse to risk. Strategic planners should be skilled in taking initiative and in leading others in new directions as should be the managers involved in entrepreneurial activities.

At the other end of the spectrum, operational control most frequently benefits from the incremental approach. The objective in operational activities is to preserve the status quo and protect the operation from change so that maximum efficiency can be achieved. The manager involved in operational control should be cautious in the face of risk and uncertainty and skillful in ensuring that internal and external changes do not affect the efficiency of his or her particular operation. When changes are necessary the incremental manager will implement them slowly and carefully.

The individual engaged in management control should adopt a style embodying a mixture of incremental and entrepreneurial behavior. He or she needs to accept the changes required due to modifications of strategic plans and to incorporate these changes into the operations and activities under his or her control. Once this is done, however, the manager must protect his or her operations from irrelevant changes in the organizational environment and ensure that they proceed efficiently according to plans and specifications.

The Organizational Structure

There are a number of factors that influence the structures, tasks, and administrative mechanisms necessary to integrate and control the activities of an organization. A number of these factors have been subjected to intensive study. The primary areas of previous study include the following: (a) the technology with which the organization is involved; (b) the size of the organization; and (c) the nature of the environment within which the organization operates. Both J. Woodward [34, 35] and C. Perrow [36] have presented arguments that the design of an effective organizational structure is dependent on the characteristics of the technology with which the organization is involved. Data published by P. M. Blau suggest that increases in size generate greater structural differentiation within organizations.[37] Environmental complexity and uncertainty has a major effect on organizational structure.[38] The greater the complexity of the environment, the greater is the need for components of the organization to deal directly with the environment. Furthermore, the greater the uncertainty experienced by the organization as a result of variations or turbulence in the environment, the greater is the need for an adaptable organizational structure capable of continual redefinition.

There is an important relationship between organizational structure and the process of strategic decision making.[39] This relationship de-

[34] Woodward, J., *Industrial Organization: Theory and Practice,* Oxford University Press, 1965.

[35] Woodward, J., ed., *Industrial Organization: Behavior and Control,* Oxford University Press, 1970.

[36] Perrow, C., *Organizational Analysis: a Sociological View,* Tavistock Institute, 1970.

[37] Blau, P. M., "The Formal Theory of Differentiation in Organizations," *American Sociological Review,* vol. 35, April 1970, pp. 201–218.

[38] Lawrence, P. R., and Lorsch, J. W., *Organization, op. cit.*

[39] Child, John, "Organization Structure, Environment and Performance," *Sociology* (The Journal of the British Sociological Association), vol. 6, no. 1, 1973, pp. 1–22.

rives from the fact that one of the outputs of strategic planning is the configuration of the organization. This configuration must be both feasible within the constraints imposed by the existing power structure and consistent with the nature and scale of the activities that are planned. In organizations in which little change is planned, the organizational structure can be expected to remain essentially the same over long periods of time. In those organizations needing to adapt continually to changing circumstances, changes in the organizational structure can be expected to occur very frequently.

The structure of an organization determines the distribution of power in an organization. It determines also the channels along which information concerning the progress of activities and the degree of achievement of stated goals and objectives must be passed. In organizations in which change in strategic objectives is slow, the structure needed to achieve these objectives can be expected to closely resemble the formal, published organizational scheme. When change is rapid, a new working structure, sometimes involving task forces and working groups, may often be introduced to meet the new requirements. In such cases, the existing organizational chart may have relevance only to the more routine, unchanging activities. The old organizational scheme may be virtually superseded by a new structure dictated by recently introduced activities and operations.

Summary

An organization can be regarded as a large and complex system comprising a number of components or subsystems. The essential characteristics of this system derive from the relationships between its components. The organization itself may be a component of a larger system that consists of a number of other organizations existing in the same environment. The boundaries of this larger system may be somewhat arbitrary. Boundaries are determined by the strength of the relationships between the component organizations. The interaction between the components of a system is a major determinant of its overall behavior. The most complex systems are considered purposeful in that they can change goals and objectives as well as a result of experience as well as changing means to achieve objectives. Organizations are among the most purposeful of systems.

The charter or founding papers of an organization usually contains a statement of purpose from which objectives, goals, and activities can be ascertained. Once this has been done, it is necessary to arrive at a functional division of the effort required to carry out the selected activities. This process (called differentiation) often results in differences in the orientation, specialization, attitude, values, conduct, and procedures of the individual members of an organization. Differentiation must be accompanied by a process of integration designed to enhance the collaboration and communication between the individuals and components of the organization.

An organization operates within an environment. Interactions and information exchanges both between the organization and the environment and within the environment are important to the organization, as are information exchanges within the organization itself. The environment of an organization may be static and relatively unchanging. On the other hand, it may be subject to rapid and unpredictable change, producing the set of conditions that have been labelled "turbulence." Turbulence may arise not only from fluctuations in the natural elements of the environment but also may arise as a result of interactions between organizations operating in the environment. The effect of environmental turbulence is to increase the uncertainty under which the organization must operate. The elements of the environment consist of the organizations that operate within the environment, called participants, and an assortment of relevant social, technological and natural factors. Collection of information on these elements of the environment is an important task of the information system.

The management of an organization concerns itself with the interaction between the organization and its environment, the establishment and achievement of objectives, and the efficient and effective use of available resources. Management activities may be classified conveniently under the headings: (a) *strategic planning*—activities relating to the setting and revision of objectives, and the acquisition, use, and allocation of resources; (b) *management control*—those functions relating to the effective and efficient use of resources in the accomplishment of the organization's objectives; and (c) *operational control*—those activities directed toward ensuring that specific tasks are carried out effectively and efficiently. Individuals involved in management exhibit styles ranging from incremental to entrepreneurial. The incremental style is by far the most common, being best suited to operational control. The entrepreneurial style is most often found in strategic planning. Management control usually requires a mixture of both types of behavior.

The structure of an organization depends upon such factors as its size, the technology with which it is involved, and the nature of its environment. The demands of strategic planning and decision making are a major determinant of organizational structure. These factors determine the distribution of power in an organization and also dictate the channels through which a major portion of the organization's information must flow. In slowly changing organizations, these channels are much the same as those shown in the organization chart. In organizations where change is rapid, new working structures may be introduced and existing organizational charts may lag considerably behind the actual distribution of information and authority.

Discussion Topics

1/ N. S. Peery, Jr., (*Journal of Management Studies,* October 1975, pp 266–275) maintains that the practice of viewing organizations as systems "overemphasizes growth and shows little appreciation for intra-organizational conflict, diversity of values, and political processes within organizations." Do you consider these criticisms valid? What is your opinion of the application of systems theory to organizations?

2/ What type of functional division of effort do you favor in an organization? Would you generally favor division by specialty, by activity, by territory, by time, or by a mixture of all of these? What factors would influence you in your choice of a system for division of effort in a practical case?

3/ What are the dangers of placing too much emphasis on differentiation in an organization? To what extent can organizational integration compensate for any disadvantages of differentiation? What are the practical steps that are involved in integration and what are the most effective of these?

4/ Comment on the statement that the extent of the environment of an organization depends upon the interaction between its components. How does this compare with Wiener's statement that an organization extends only as far as there extends an effectual transmission of information? (*Cybernetics,* 1965, paperback edition, pp 158–159)

5/ Individuals in different organizations may have different perceptions of the environment in which they are jointly engaged. How might this difference affect the interactions between the organizations and the process of setting goals and objectives in each of them?

6/ What are the practical manifestations of the existence of a number of subsystems within an organization creating, in effect, an environment within the organization? How might such internal factors affect the behavior of the organization in its external environment?

7/ Do you think that organizational environments are becoming increasingly turbulent? If so, what do you think are the major reasons for this increasing turbulence? What steps can a manager take to protect his internal operations and activities from the effects of this external turbulence?

8/ Does the classification of managerial activities under the headings strategic planning, management control, and operational control appear satisfactory in your view? Would you prefer a different categorization and, if so, what would it be?

9/ What are the strengths and weaknesses of the incremental and entrepreneurial styles of management? Is some behavior of each style necessary in all organizations? In which organizational activities do you see each of the two styles as essential? Can one individual exhibit behavior of both styles to meet the demands of different managerial activities?

10/ What do you consider to be the major factors determining organizational structure? How does the actual working structure compare with the formally drafted organizational chart in conditions of rapid change? What difficulties might differences between the charted structure and the actual functioning structure cause in practical situations?

CASE WORK

The Delta Corporation is a manufacturer of garden equipment and implements. Their main product lines consist of small machines for soil preparation, hand tools, garden furniture, and related accessories. About 80 products are manufactured in the corporation's plants and supplied on a wholesale basis to retail outlets throughout North America.

The head office of the Delta Corporation is in Winnipeg, adjacent to its largest plant. Two smaller plants are operated, one in Vancouver and the other just outside Montreal. The Winnipeg plant supplies a wide area in the central part of the continent. The Vancouver plant serves the northwest and the Montreal plant supplies the east and northeast.

In 1977, Delta acquired (as a wholly-owned subsidiary) a company called Gamma Inc., a manufacturer and distributor of similar products, located in South Bend, Indiana. Gamma had been a major customer for some time. In the final year before acquisition, Gamma purchased 47 percent of the output of the Winnipeg plant for distribution in the United States. Gamma also manufactures products that were thought, at the time of acquisition, to provide a good complement to the Delta lines both in Canada and in the United States. Plans for manufacturing Delta's products in the Gamma plant (and vice-versa) have been under consideration for some time.

Gamma has not yet been integrated into the structure of the Delta Corporation. The Delta-Gamma combine employs 2,303 persons, distributed at the present time as follows:

Head Office	210
Winnipeg Plant	930
Vancouver Plant	215
Montreal Plant	421
Gamma Inc.	527

The labor force is unionized. One international union represents the production personnel at all plants while another represents the secretarial, clerical, and junior management personnel.

The sales revenues of Delta increased sharply and consistently from 1958 to 1976. In 1958, when the company was founded and the Winnipeg plant was the only manufacturing facility, annual sales totalled about $1.5 million. In 1976, just prior to the acquisition of Gamma Inc., annual sales revenue was $83 million. With an increasingly large sales base to carry plant overhead, market research, and fixed management costs, the Delta profit margin, based on sales in dollars, increased from 5.4 percent in 1958 to 7.3 percent in 1976. Since 1976, however, sales have levelled out while labour and overhead costs have increased disproportionately. Furthermore, sales revenue per employee that stood at $16,000 in 1958 and increased to $45,000 in 1976 has dropped back to about $38,000 at the present time.

The president of Delta has noticed the downward trend in profitability and has been trying to discover the causes for it from his own observations. Undoubtedly, a part of the cause is the state of the economy. However, the president has noticed some other factors that may also be contributing to the decline. He has, therefore, appointed a team of middle- and senior-level managers (of which you are one) to investigate and report on measures that should be taken to meet the present situation.

The president's directive to the team has been studied and it has been decided that the following questions need to be answered before any courses of action can be recommended:

1/ What are the characteristics and elements of the environment in which Delta and Gamma are operating?

2/ What should the goals and objectives of the combined Delta and Gamma organizations be while operating in this environment?

3/ What activities of Delta and Gamma will contribute most to the securing of these goals and objectives? What constraints may limit the achievement of the goals and objectives?

4/ Is the present company organizational structure appropriate to these activities, goals, and objectives? What should the major components and sub-systems of a combined Delta, Gamma organization be as viewed from a systems point of view? What should be the major interactions between these subsystems?

You are asked to prepare answers to the above questions as a contribution to the work of the team. If the preceding description does not provide you with enough information to answer these questions, feel free to add details of your own in order to enhance your answers.

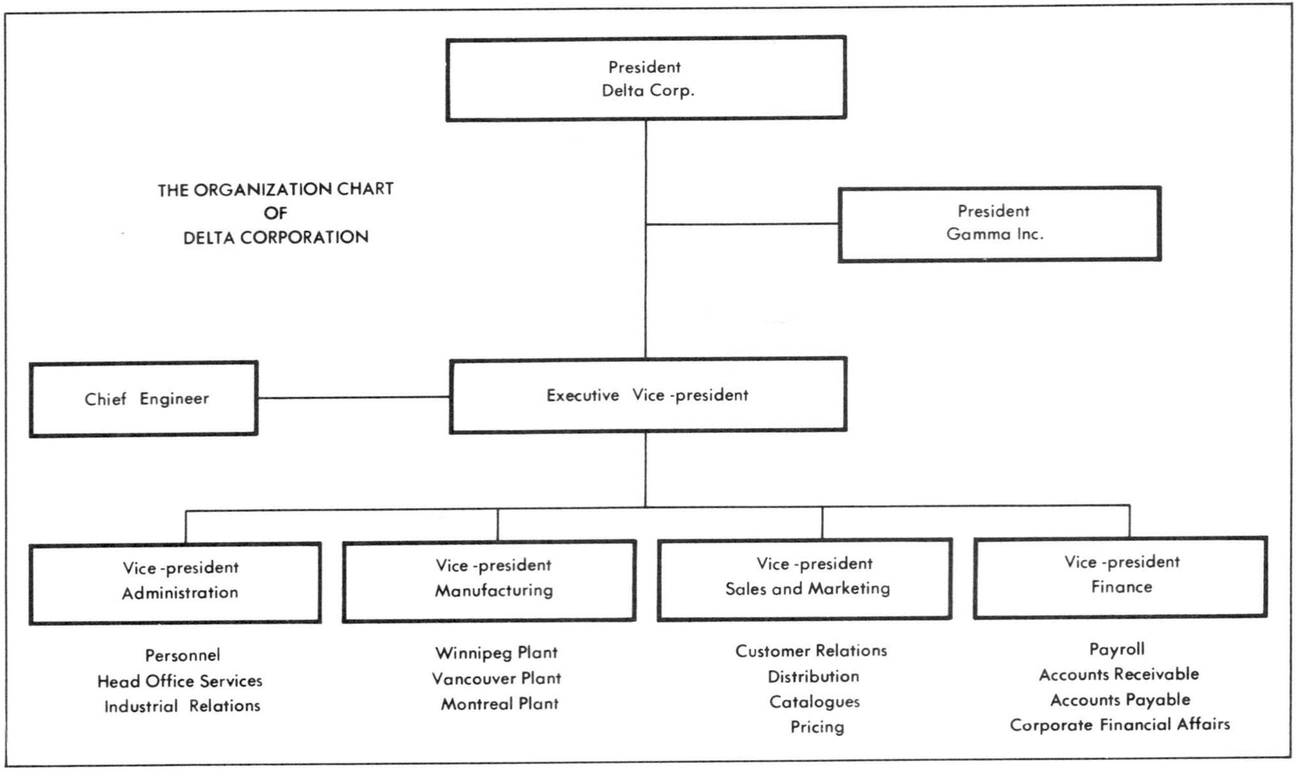

The Organization Chart of Delta Corporation

3

Decision Making in Organizations

Introduction

Decision making is one of the most important tasks of managers and administrators in modern organizations. Dealing with decision problems of one sort or another consumes a large proportion of the time available to members of an organization. At least one prominent author has taken the position that decision making is synonymous with management.[1]

The essence of decision making is the formulation and selection of alternatives. In most cases, the alternatives are concerned with the various ways of proceeding from an existing situation to one that is judged to be more preferred. Effective decision making requires that the choice among alternatives be made only after consideration of as much relevant information as possible. The acquisition and presentation of this relevant information is a major task of the organizational information system. The information system, therefore, is vital to the decision-making activities of the organization. By the same token, knowledge of the nature and pattern of decision making in an organization is essential in the design and implementation of its information system.

[1] Simon, Herbert A., *The New Science of Management Decision,* 2nd ed., Prentice-Hall, 1977, p. 39.

This chapter is devoted to a discussion of organizational decision making. The chapter begins with a description of the decision-making process. This process is illustrated through the discussion of a series of steps starting from the first encounter with a decision problem and ending with the eventual resolution of the problem. A distinction is then drawn between (a) decision problems that are well understood and that can be resolved by means of a standard procedure and (b) those problems for which a more flexible approach involving a greater degree of human judgement is necessary. Finally, organizational procedures for dealing with these two types of decision problems are described in detail, as a preliminary to placing them in the context of the organizational information system in the chapters that follow.

Steps in the Decision Process

Descriptions of the process of resolution of decision problems that are encountered in modern organizations abound in the literature. One such description that has provided a basis for development of decision-making procedures for many years divides the process of resolution into three phases:[2]

Intelligence—the environment inside and outside the organization is searched for conditions requiring a decision and information is gathered with respect to those conditions;

Design—the available courses of action are determined and analyzed to determine their relative values as solutions to the decision problems that have been detected;

Choice—an available course of action is selected that is designed to convert the present, less-desirable situation into a future situation judged to be more desirable.

These three phases of the decision-making process do not have clear-cut boundaries, nor is it intended that they be applied in rigorous sequence. In actual practice, they often need to be undertaken concurrently rather than in the strict order shown. Moreover, resolution of a particular problem may require a number of passes through each of these phases.

This model of the decision-making process can be developed further

[2] Ibid.

by a breakdown of the tasks that must be undertaken in each phase, as follows:[3, 4]

Intelligence

(a) *Perception and formulation of the problem*—the identification of a decision problem and the distinguishing of its main characteristics

(b) *Construction of a model of the problem*—a model provides a vehicle for estimating the possible outcomes of a decision problem over a wide range of possible conditions[5]

(c) *Determination of appropriate quantitative measures of costs and benefits*—uniform measurement systems facilitate comparisons between the alternate ways of resolving the decision problem

Design

(a) *Specification of available courses of action*—possible courses of action are identified and clearly formulated

Choice

(a) *Estimation of the outcomes from available courses of action*—the effect of the implementation of each course of action is assessed in terms of the measures of costs and benefits specified earlier

(b) *Establishment of a criterion for choice between outcomes*—rules are established by which outcomes can be related to the objectives of the party making the choice

(c) *Resolution of the decision problems*—on the basis of an acceptable criterion a choice is made from among the available courses of action

As before, it is not intended that these steps be taken in exactly the

3 Eilon, Samuel, "What is a Decision?," *Management Science,* vol. 16, no. 4. December 1969.

4 Radford, K. J., *Managerial Decision Making,* Reston Publishing Co., 1975, pp. 12–19.

5 Little, J. D. C., "Models and Managers: the Concept of a Decision Calculus," *Management Science,* vol. 16, no. 8, April 1970, pp. B466–485.

order shown, nor is this outline intended to preclude the repetition of all or some of the steps as may be necessary during the process of resolution.

Types of Decision Problems

Decision problems that arise in modern organizations can be thought of in two broad categories:

1/ Completely specified (or specifiable) problems—problems that can be solved by the straightforward application of a series of steps similar to the three phase system that has just been discussed. Decisions that can be treated in this way are primarily those that occur repeatedly in exactly or nearly the same form. As a result of this repeated experience, the characteristics of a particular decision problem eventually become well known and a routine procedure for its resolution can be devised. Decisions of this type were originally called "programmed" by Herbert A. Simon.[6] However, because the procedure adopted constitutes a complete specification for dealing with the particular problem at hand, these decisions have more recently been described as "completely specified."[7]

2/ Nonspecifiable problems—for which no completely predefined and routine procedure for resolution is applicable. This type of decision has been called "ill-structured,"[8] "unstructured,"[9] and "nonprogrammed." The more complex of the decision problems in this category arise in strategic planning. Such problems have been termed "wicked" problems, as opposed to the "tame" variety that submit to resolution by a routine procedure.[10] No clear winner emerges from the contest for a name

[6] Simon, Herbert A., "The New Science of Management Decision," reprinted in R. M. Cyert and L. A. Welsch, eds., *Management Decision Making,* Penguin Books, 1970, pp. 13–16.

[7] Radford, K. J., *Managerial Decision Making,* pp. 21–25.

[8] Simon, Herbert A., "The Structure of Ill-structured Decision Processes," *Artificial Intelligence,* vol. 4, 1973, pp. 181–201.

[9] Mintzberg, H., D. Raisinghani, and A. Théorêt, "The Structure of Unstructured Decision Processes," *Administrative Science Quarterly,* vol. 21, June 1976, pp. 246–274.

[10] Rittel, H. W. J., and M. M. Webber, "Dilemmas in a General Theory of Planning," *Policy Sciences,* vol. 4, 1973, pp. 155–169.

for this class of decisions. The author prefers the names *non-completely specified* or *nonspecifiable,* primarily because they stress the fact that no complete, routine procedure is available for the resolution of a decision of this nature.

Completely-specified decision processes can be found in most organizations in applications such as payroll, accounts payable and receivable, inventory control, order processing, and product distribution. Once the procedure for resolving a completely-specified decision problem has been agreed upon, repeated occurrences of the problem can be resolved in exactly the same manner according to the routine procedure. Repeated resolution of a problem of this type is often undertaken automatically and at high speed. There is, therefore, no opportunity for interpretation of or disagreement with the specification at the time of each resolution. Any proposed modifications to the specification must be discussed parallel to the ongoing resolution process and incorporated, as appropriate, into the specification that is used for later operations.

A decision may be nonspecifiable for one or more reasons.[11] For example, the problem involved may be new and unique, so that there exist no previous experiences upon which a complete or partial specification can be based. On the other hand, there may be insufficient information available at the crucial moment to allow the decision makers to arrive at a complete understanding of the problem. A significant characteristic of decision problems of this type is that no course of action can be proved to be the "best" solution to a particular problem. Courses of action that are selected in such decision situations are usually remedial measures rather than final solutions to the problem. These courses of action are selected primarily because the person responsible thinks that they are the best available responses to the problem in the time available for making the decision.

In dealing with decision problems that cannot be completely specified, it is often possible to identify a part of the problem that can be treated according to a routine procedure. For example, consider the task of selecting an individual to fill a vacant position from among a large number of applicants. The original roster of applicants can often be condensed to a short list by a routine comparison of each applicant's qualifications with those required for the position. A series of interviews is then conducted with those remaining on the list. During

[11] Radford, K. J., *Complex Decision Problems: an Integrated Strategy for Resolution,* Reston Publishing Co., 1977, Chapter 1.

these interviews matters that cannot be conveniently included in the original, structured specifications can be explored. The final decision is made using the information obtained in both phases of the selection process. The basis of the final decision is not wholly a routine procedure, but rather relies upon the judgement, intuition, and experience of those involved. Problems of this sort are often called "partially-specified." They can be regarded as a subcategory of the nonspecifiable variety of decisions.

The distinctions between the two primary types of decision problems is illustrated in Figure 3-1. In this diagram, completely-specified decision processes are found at one end of a continuum. The exact location of a problem in the continuum depends on the degree to which the problem can be treated by an agreed procedure. The position of a particular decision in the continuum does not necessarily remain fixed. For example, as more information becomes available and as more experience is gained regarding applicable methods of resolution, a partially-specified decision process may move closer to the completely-specified end of the continuum.

Completely-Specified Decision Processes

Most, if not all, of the completely-specified decision processes in an organization are concerned with routine administrative and operational tasks and relate to the managerial activity of operational control. The specification for each of these decision processes may consist of a string of simple, essentially clerical tasks that, taken together, represent a complicated administrative or operational procedure. The simplest of these procedures are called *transactions*.[12]

Transactions are the processes that are necessary to ensure that such basic tasks as the issuing of checks, the recording and filling of orders, the administering of a pension plan, and the ordering of spare parts into inventory are accomplished. Transactions exist in every functional area of an organization. Transaction processing not only ensures that numerous routine tasks are undertaken but also provides much of the information required for effective operational and managerial control of the organization.

Some completely-specified decision processes make use of complex models representing administrative or operational tasks. In such cases,

[12] Davis, Gordon B., *Management Information Systems: Conceptual Foundations, Structure and Development,* McGraw-Hill, 1974, pp. 255–282.

RANGE OF DECISION PROBLEMS

Completely Specified	Partially Specified	Nonspecifiable
1. Specification of decision process agreed in advance of resolution.	1. Only a part of the decision process can be specified.	1. Decision process cannot be specified in advance.
2. No managerial involvement at time of each resolution.	2. Manager makes final resolution using results from specified portion and his experience, judgement and beliefs.	2. Manager resolves each problem on the basis of his experience, judgement and beliefs.
3. Repeated resolutions with same data produce same result.	3. Two different managers may reach different conclusions.	3. Two different managers may reach different conclusions.
	Examples (for an Electric Utility)	
a. Customer billing.	a. Operational balance of supply and demand of electric power.	a. Manner of financing capital projects.
b. Control of nuclear power generating station.	b. Fault-finding in operational network.	b. Relations with local and state authorities.

Fig. 3.1. Types of Decision Problems

the specifications consist of sets of mathematical statements, rather than strings of simple clerical tasks. In other cases, the specifications may combine a mathematical model with an administrative or operational procedure. Mathematical techniques developed in operations research have proven very successful in providing the means for selecting optimal solutions to certain well-defined problems. Such techniques have found greatest application in areas such as product distribution, production scheduling, inventory control, and queueing problems.

In modern organizations, most, if not all, completely-specified decisions are computer-supported. The specifications in use at any time comprise an internally consistent model of the process of resolution upon which the necessary computer programs can be based. The fact that a particular problem can be resolved repeatedly using the same set of specifications provides the ideal conditions for computer support of the decision process. Completely-specified decision processes can, in many ways, be regarded as analogous to the decisions involved in process control in industrial production.

Systems designed to support completely-specified decision processes are quite naturally labeled "completely-specified systems." The tasks that are undertaken in a completely-specified system consist of:

1/ *Data input*—in which data relevant to the decision process is gathered from sources both internal and external to the organization;
2/ *Data edit*—in which the data gathered are checked for consistency before being fed into the system;
3/ *Processing*—in which input data are processed according to the specifications that have been prepared in advance;
4/ *Output*—in which the hard-copy output (such as checks or invoices) required as a product of the particular process is prepared;
5/ *Additional data output*—which entails the production of data and information useful to other similar systems or to higher levels of management.

A schematic diagram of a completely-specified system is shown in Figure 3-2. In this diagram, pertinent data from both internal and external sources enter the system at the right, through the data edit function. Output from the process is shown at the bottom of the diagram.

Two important functions within the completely-specified system are shown at the top and the left of the diagram—the *monitor* and the *interface*. The *monitor* represents a means by which the manager responsible for the operation of the system can ensure that it is running in accordance with specifications. A built-in component of the particular specifications provides and displays information on the progress of the operation for use by the manager in charge. There may be certain limits or thresholds in the process beyond which operations

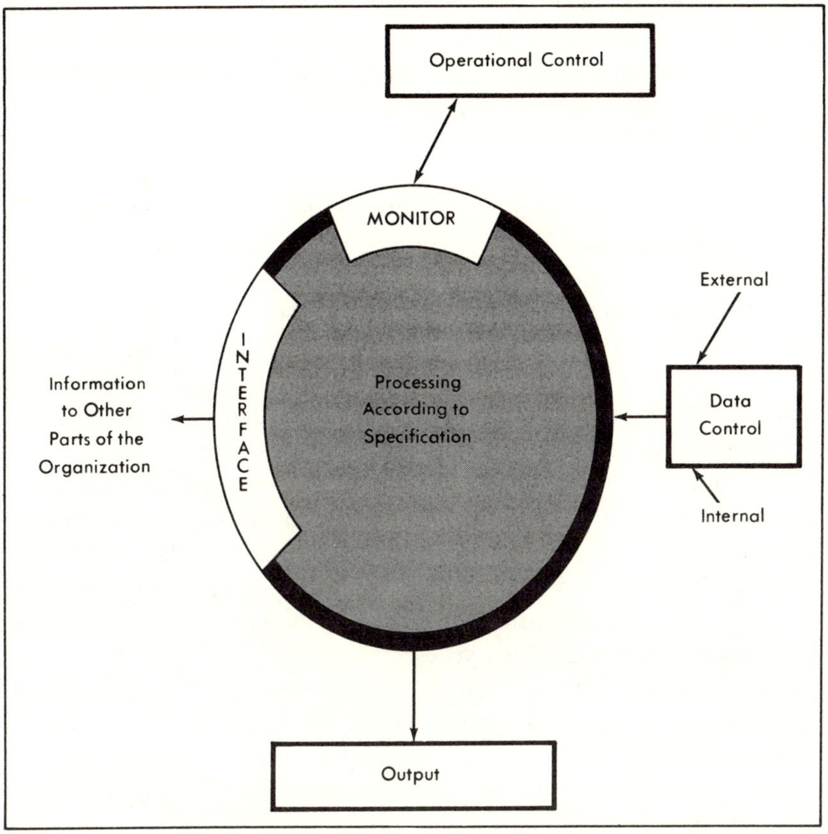

Figure 3.2. Schematic Diagram of a Completely-Specified System

would not be satisfactory. Data available at the monitoring station can be used by an operator to diagnose the cause of any anomaly or any violation of the specified thresholds.

The monitor can also be used to initiate the necessary remedial action. The monitor in an administrative or operational system can be regarded as serving a function analogous to the control panel of a power station or similar industrial facility. Data presented at the monitor may be used for periodic reviews of the efficiency of the process and may also provide an indication of the applicability of the specification to the administrative or operational task under existing circumstances.

The greatest proportion of the data and information processed by a completely-specified system remains within the system itself for use in support of the routine function that it serves. However, some of the data generated by the system may be of interest to other functions and to other levels of management in the organization. For example, a completely-specified system designed to produce invoices in an accounts receivable function contains information on amounts that have been owing for different periods of time. This sort of information is of interest to those engaged in management control.

Data and information originating in the system that are required by other parts of the organization are made available at the *interface*. Most of this output is made available in summary rather than detailed form. For example, payroll information forwarded to another department may be concerned with the total amount paid in wages over a given period to a given group of individuals rather than referring to the amount of each pay check. The amount of data at the interface is therefore small compared with the total amount of data within the completely-specified system. However, there is relatively more information contained in interface data and it is, therefore, of greater importance in managerial activities.

Not all completely-specified systems are completely automatic in their operations. It is, of course, possible to operate such a system entirely manually. A manual system is not likely to be very efficient however, especially if rapid, accurate, and repetitive processing is required. Many completely specified systems do contain portions that are operated manually. However, in such cases, the individuals involved in the operation rarely work in a completely-specified fashion. Such individuals usually make minor judgements that no one has been able to efficiently incorporate into the overall specifications. Such partially manual systems can be regarded as occupying a position a small distance from the end of the continuum occupied by the completely-specified decisions encroaching somewhat into the region of those decisions that are partially-specified.

Decisions That Cannot be Completely Specified

Decisions that cannot be completely specified include both those that can be partially specified and those for which there is a total lack of specification or structure. Decision problems that cannot be completely specified have one or more of the following characteristics:[13]

- Only limited information is available regarding the decision problem. In some cases, only symptoms have been identified and there exists no actual complete description of the problem;
- The individual or organization encountering the decision problem may have more than one objective and some of these objectives may conflict with one another. In such circumstances, there may be difficulty in deciding on an acceptable basis for the choice between alternate courses of action. For example, a municipality considering a proposal for a new industrial site might find the objective of improving local employment opportunities in conflict with the policy of minimizing the loss of valuable farm land;
- More than one participant involved in the decision situation may have the power to influence the choice between alternatives. In the example concerning the choice of an industrial site, the participants might be the municipality itself, the proponents of the industrial site, local contractors, and local citizens' groups;
- There may be disagreement between or within participant groups regarding the priority to be assigned to various objectives as well as disagreement concerning methods of measuring progress towards achieving the chosen objectives;
- The problem under consideration may be interlinked with other concurrent problem situations. Choices made in one area often have repercussions in others.

Managers involved in non-completely-specified decision situations form subjective opinions concerning the nature of the problem and the manner in which the problem should be resolved. It is possible that two different managers, each acting in accordance with his or her perceptions of the problem, could come to diametrically opposed opinions regarding the desirable course of action in a particular problem.

In the absence of a standard procedure for resolution of wicked problems, responsible managers conduct a search for information

[13] Radford, K. J., *Complex Decision Problems,* Chapter 1.

using whatever time and resources are available to them. Each manager performs this intelligence-gathering function in his or her own way. The final choice of a course of action is often made using judgement and intuition rather than a formal procedure such as is used for resolution of a more routine problem.

Decisions that cannot be completely specified arise in both management control and in strategic planning situations. In management control a relatively great amount of relevant processed data is likely to be available to the manager responsible for the decision. These data are available at the interfaces of the administrative and operational systems with which the management control problem is concerned. For example, a manager involved in making budgetary allocations to two or more plants normally has summary data available concerning the efficiency of the plants and production processes, the present and anticipated demand for the products, and on various aspects of production cost. The manager's decision is made by combining this output from completely-specified systems together with information gleaned from other sources.

Decisions involved in strategic planning are generally far less structured than those made at the management control level.[14] It is highly unlikely that a set of predetermined and explicit responses to a strategic decision situation would exist in an organization. In fact, the initiation of a strategic decision process is very often a matter of chance.[15] The most complex of the nonspecifiable decision problems arise in strategic situations in which two or more participants have different and conflicting objectives. Situations such as this often involve competition between individuals or organizations in an external environment. Such wicked decision problems may also arise within an organization in which there is competition between groups in the internal environment of the organization.

In strategic decision situations of this nature, the participants can be envisaged as contemplating courses of action that they could take to improve their individual positions. A number of different future outcomes, or scenarios, could result from the implementation of the courses of action contemplated by those involved. Each participant has a perception of these possible outcomes and an order of preference

[14] Mintzberg, H., et al., "Structure," op. cit, p. 246.

[15] Segev, Eli, "Triggering the Strategic Decision Process," *Management Decision,* vol. 14, no. 5, 1976, pp. 229–238.

between them. Usually the preference orderings of the participants are different. The resolution of the decision problem depends upon determining which of the possible future outcomes is ultimately acceptable to all of the participants and upon which they will all eventually agree. Such a situation is illustrated in Figure 3-3.

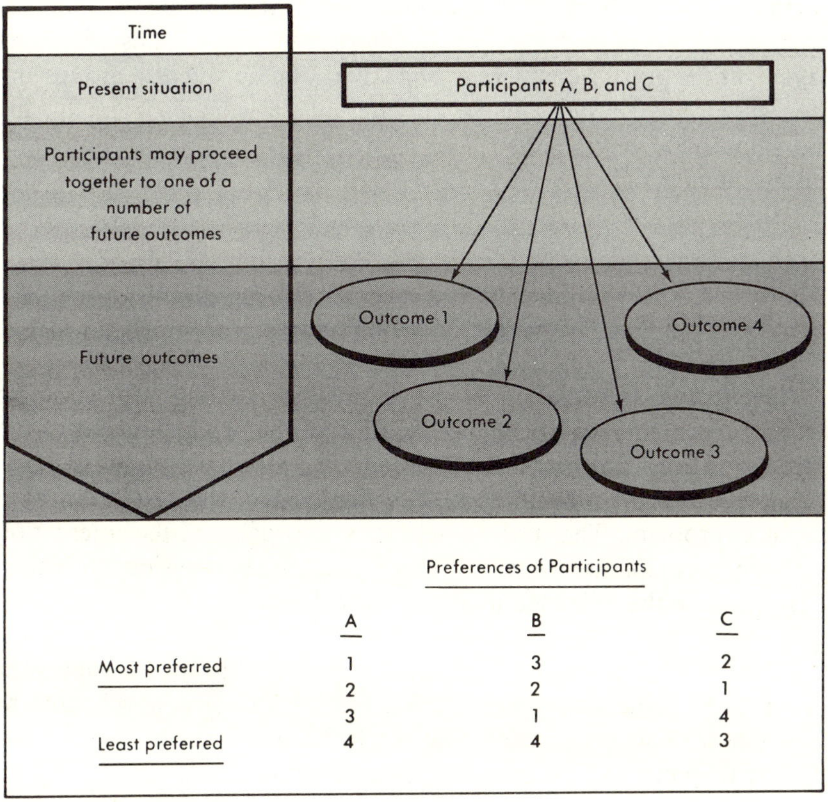

Figure 3.3. Participants and Future Outcomes

In the situation illustrated in Figure 3-3, not all of the participants are able to obtain the outcome that they most prefer. Selection of the actual outcome comes about only after a process of communication, negotiation, and bargaining between the parties during which information is exchanged between the parties in a number of ways. This process of selecting an outcome may take place in many stages.

The resolution of the problem occurs when one or more of the participants decides to agree to an outcome that was not originally his most preferred. A participant normally accepts a less preferred outcome because he or she eventually prefers the acceptance of an outcome that was originally considered less desirable to the continuation of the confrontation or dispute. One of the most potent factors in the resolution of a problem of this nature is the relative ability of the participants to influence the eventual choice of outcome.[16] A similar process of resolution occurs when different interest groups within an organization pursue conflicting objectives. These interest groups are then essentially participants in an internal decision problem having the same basic characteristics as a problem involving a number of autonomous entities.

Organizational Procedures for Dealing with Strategic Decision Problems

An effective formulation of procedures for dealing with strategic decision problems requires a modification of the original model of the decision process put forward by Simon. The modified model is based on a redefinition of the three phases involved in the resolution of a decision problem. The new model takes into account the interaction between participants, a major feature of complex decision problems. The phases in the redefined model are as follows:[17]

- *Information gathering*—information relevant to the decision situation is gathered by each participant. This information is used to review courses of action that might be available to each of the participants and to construct possible future scenarios;
- *Strategic analysis*—possible future outcomes that could result from the implementation of courses of action by the participants and their individual preferences for these outcomes are studied;
- *Interaction*—the participants communicate in a way that often involves negotiation and bargaining. In the course of this inter-

[16] Ibid., pp. 115–116.

[17] Radford, K. J., "Decision Making in a Turbulent Environment," *Operational Research Quarterly*, Vol. 29, 1978. Atkinson College, York University, November, 1976.

action, information is exchanged in an attempt to reach an agreement concerning mutually-acceptable outcomes.

These phases of the resolution of a strategic decision problem are illustrated in Figure 3-4.

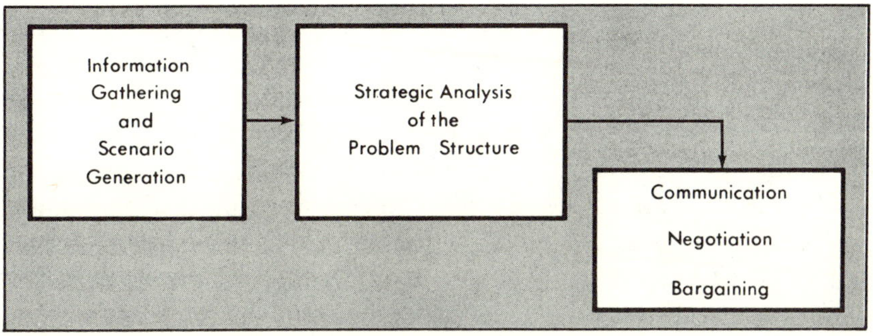

Figure 3.4. Three Phases of Resolution of a Complex Decision Problem

The communication, negotiation, and bargaining phase is shown displaced down the page to indicate that it usually takes place after the strategic analysis and is separate from it while information gathering and strategic analysis often occur simultaneously.

Strategic decision problems are seldom resolved in a single run through the three phases shown in Figure 3-4. Resolution of such problems is usually a continuing process during which information is gathered and reviewed continuously and in which a series of reassessments of the strategic structure of the problem is made as additional information becomes available. Communication with the other participants may also occur at a number of separate instances over a period of time. During this whole process, the manner in which the participants perceive the problem and their preferences for outcomes may change. Natural events may occur that affect the courses of action available to participants, their preferences for outcomes, or their relative power to influence the outcome.

It is interesting to note that the participants in a decision problem generally have access to different amounts and types of information at any given time. However, as the continuous process of resolution unfolds and communication between the participants in one form or another occurs, their perceptions may draw closer together. This drawing together is the primary objective in the process of resolution.

Unless it occurs, the resolution of the decision problem will not be facilitated and the possibility of an eventual outcome least desired by all participants is considerably increased.[18, 19]

A representation of the continuing resolution process from the point of view of one participant is shown in Figure 3-5. In this diagram, time is depicted as unfolding from top to bottom and the three phases of the process of resolution are spaced across the page. Information gathering and assessment leading to perceptions of the problem and to the formulation of courses of action is shown as a continuous bar to the left of the diagram. It is represented in this manner to emphasize the continual role of information gathering in the decision process.

The central part of the decision process diagram is shown under the heading "strategic analysis" represented as a series of frames indicating periods of concentrated consideration of the problem. In actual organizational activities, these frames might represent sessions of a task force charged with consideration of the problem, portions of regular management meetings devoted to the particular problem, or merely periods of time during which a single decision maker devotes his attention to the problem. The strategic analysis frames are shown dotted at the top and bottom of the diagram to give the impression of a continual process of consideration. The portion shown in full lines is only a segment of the process selected from the whole for the purposes of illustration.

Arrows from the information-gathering-and-assessment bar to the strategic analysis frames denote that there is a regular flow of new information and perceptions into the strategic analysis. The distances between strategic analysis frames are variable to emphasize that these considerations need not (and in most cases, should not) be at fixed intervals. In more urgent circumstances, the frames might be expected to move closer together and in less urgent cases to move further apart in time.

A more complete representation of the total decision process is shown in Figure 3-6. In this diagram, the activities of a number of participants are combined. The strategic analysis sessions of the various participants are shown by a vertical series of frames in each case. The input of information and perceptions from the participants' individual information gathering and assessment activities is indicated

[18] Stoessinger, John G., *Why Nations Go to War,* St. Martins Press, 1974.
[19] White, R. K., *Nobody Wanted War,* Doubleday, 1968.

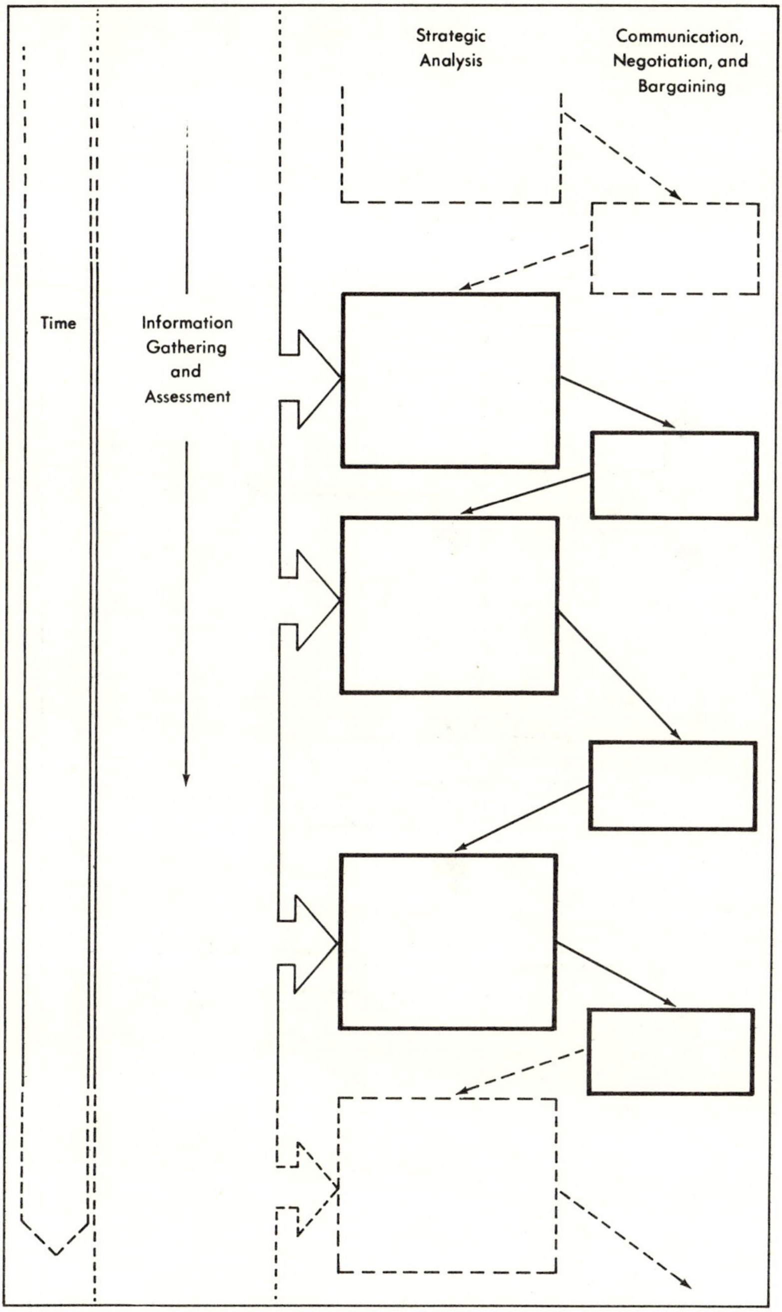

Figure 3.5. Diagrammatic Representation of Treatment of a Complex Decision Problem by One Participant

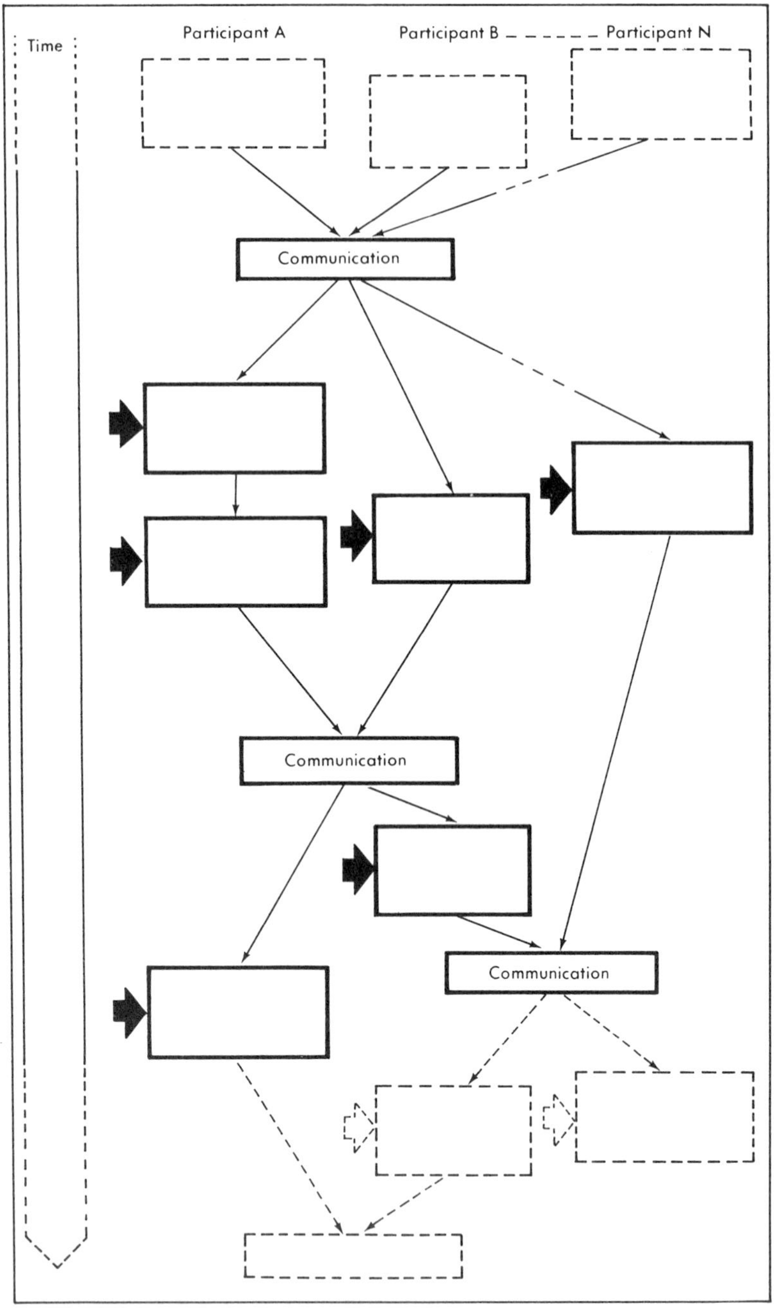

Figure 3.6. Model of a Complex Decision Problem Showing More Than One Participant

by the arrow head to the left of each frame. From time to time, the participants communicate with one another concerning their perceptions of the problem or with regard to any actions or moves that they have decided to take as a result of their strategic evaluations. This exchange of information is represented in Figure 3-6 by boxes labelled "communication."

Not all the participants are necessarily involved in any one exchange of information. A participant may decide for tactical or other reasons to communicate certain information to only a selected few of the participants that are known to him or her. Other participants may be deliberately excluded or their participation in the problem may be unknown to the initiator of the communication. In cases in which the information is imparted more widely, such as by a public statement, the statement may go unnoticed or be ignored by one or more of the participants. A further elaboration of the representation of the decision process in Figure 3-7 shows the relationship between a number of concurrent, linked decision problems.[20]

The portions of the decision process with which we are most concerned in this text are those referring to the acquisition, interpretation and transmission of information. Some of the information that is used in the resolution of strategic decision problems originates within the organization and is concerned with its internal operations. This information is acquired and processed by the organization's internal information system, which is discussed in the next chapter. Other information necessary to the resolution of strategic problems is of a less quantitative nature and originates both inside and outside the organization. Responsibility for handling this information rests with the strategic component of the overall information system, which is the subject of discussion in Chapters 5 and 6.

Summary

Decision-making is one of the most important tasks of managers and administrators. The essence of decision-making is the formulation of alternatives and the choice between them. The information system provides support to the decision-making process by acquiring, processing, and presenting information that provides a background and basis for this choice.

[20] Radford, K. J., op. cit., *Complex Decision Problems,* p. 157.

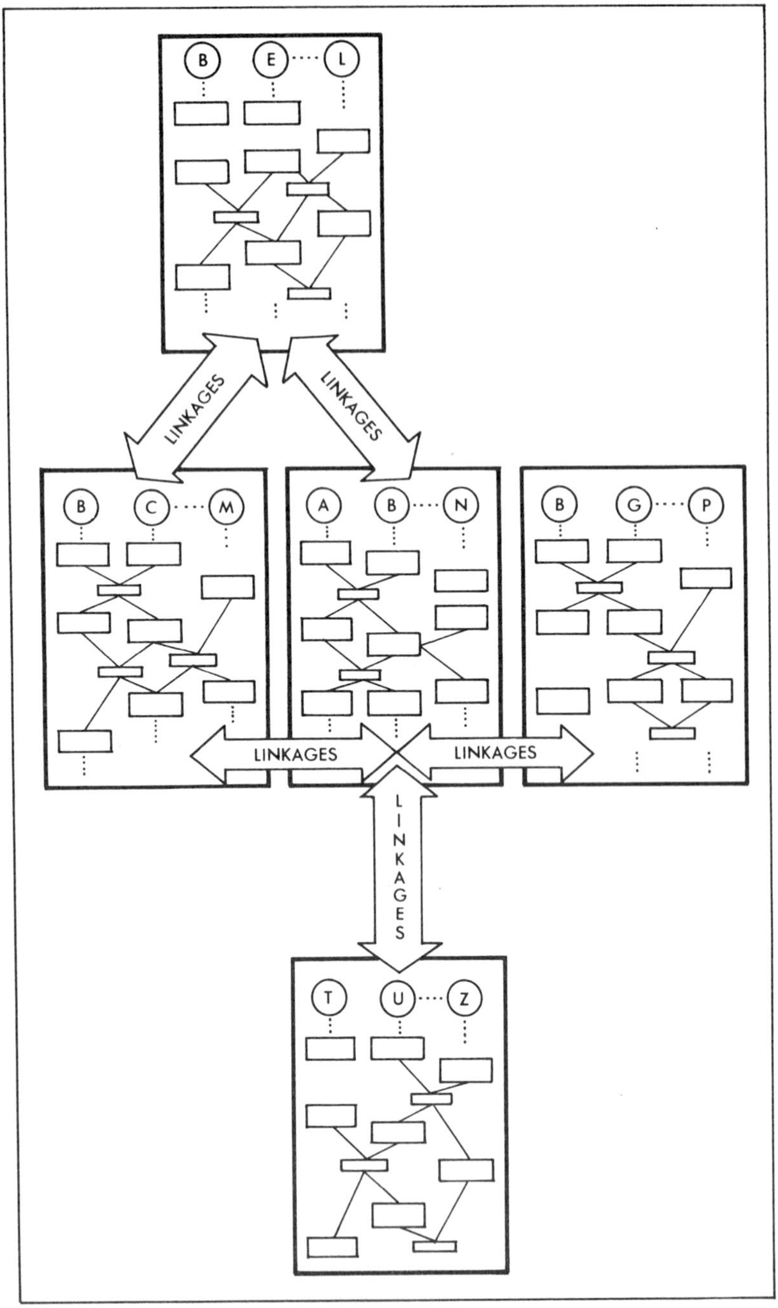

Figure 3.7. Diagram Showing Horizontal and Vertical Linkages Between Problems

The decision-making process has been thought of as consisting of three broad phases: *intelligence*—the search for conditions calling for a decision; *design*—the formulation of appropriate courses of action; and *choice*—the selection from among available courses of action. These three phases can be broken down further into a number of steps. When a decision problem becomes familiar and well-understood, it is often possible to adopt a routine procedure for its resolution consisting of an agreed-upon progression through the necessary steps. Decision problems of this type are termed "programmed" or "completely-specified." Programmed decisions are encountered in modern organizations in many recurrent administrative and operational activities. Other less completely understood decision problems are such that a specification can be devised for only a part of the process of resolution. Under such circumstances, the final choice is made by the individual responsible, using the available information along with his or her own judgement, intuition, and experience. In yet other cases, usually encountered at the higher more strategic levels of the organization, not even a partial specification of the decision problem is available. Decision problems such as these are called unstructured, nonspecifiable, or judgemental.

Decision problems that arise in modern organizations can be organized into a continuum ranging from the completely-specified to the nonspecifiable decision problems. The extreme cases occupy the end positions on the continuum while the partially-specified decisions lie in between. The position of a particular decision in the continuum does not necessarily remain fixed. As more information becomes available, a partially-specified or nonspecifiable decision may well move towards the completely-specified end of the continuum.

Completely-specified decision processes range from relatively simple administrative and operational transactions to processes requiring complex mathematical models. Completely-specified decisions are supported in practice by systems that undertake the following tasks: data input, data edit, processing according to specification, and output. Completely-specified systems such as these incorporate two important components that have been labeled the *monitor* and the *interface*.

The monitor consists of a display of information that allows the individual in charge to ensure that the process is working according to the specifications. Data available at the monitor also allows the efficiency of the process to be assessed. The design and implementation of modifications to the process necessitated by changes external to the system are likely to be the responsibility of the manager in charge of the area in which the monitor is located.

The interface is the location at which any information concerning the system that is required by other parts of the organization is presented for distribution. Most such information is in summary form. Not all completely-specified systems are completely automatic in their operation. However; in modern organizations the greatest proportion of such processes are computer-supported.

Most completely-specified systems are concerned with the management activity of operational control. Data and information presented at the interfaces of these systems are utilized in management control and occasionally at the level of strategic planning. The decisions arising in these latter activities are usually such that they cannot be completely specified. The more complex of these decisions involve the multiple and conflicting objectives of a number of participants having differing potential to influence the final outcome. Such situations are made more complex by the fact that they may be interlinked with other concurrent situations. The resolution of such problems is a matter of determining which of a number of possible outcomes is acceptable to all participants and which is, therefore, the outcome they will all agree to bring about. In such circumstances, not all participants may obtain their most-preferred outcomes, but each may have decided to settle for a less-preferred outcome rather than continue the dispute.

The organizational procedures for dealing with complex, strategic problems are based on three phases. These are modification of the procedure mentioned earlier, as follows: (a) information gathering; (b) strategic analysis; and (c) interaction. Resolution of such strategic decisions is usually a prolonged procedure. Perceptions of the problem and of possible outcomes may change as more information becomes available supplementing the limited information usually available in the early stages of the process of resolution. The information system therefore plays a crucial role in the strategic decision process.

Discussion Topics

1/ Do you agree that management is synonymous with decision making? Can you name any managerial activities that do not involve decision making?

2/ How can a manager be sure of diagnosing a decision problem correctly on the basis of the available evidence? What are the penalties attached to an incorrect or delayed diagnosis?

3/ Decision making is easier when quantitative measures of costs and benefits are available. Specification of such measures may be more readily achieved in profit-making organizations. Is profit necessarily the only measure of benefit in such an organization? Under what circumstances are proxy measures of benefit and cost useful and applicable in either profit-making or nonprofit organizations? What are the dangers of hasty or overenthusiastic use of such alternative measures?

4/ What are the major categories of constraints experienced by organizations in the search for feasible courses of action in a given decision situation? What are the limitations likely to result from the constraints in each of these categories?

5/ Criteria used in the choice between alternatives must relate to the objectives of the organization or the individual making the choice. How can such a criterion of choice be selected in cases where multiple and conflicting objectives exist?

6/ We have spoken in the text of a continuum of decision problems. Where on this continuum do you think the greatest *number* of decisions arising in organizations would be placed? What sort of decisions are these? Where on the continuum does the greatest number of different *types* of decisions exist?

7/ What sort of data and information would you expect to find at (a) the monitor and (b) the interface of a completely-specified system? What is the essential difference between these functions? Why are both functions necessary and what might happen if one or the other of them was omitted in the system design?

8/ Can you think of any decisions in which no portion of the problem is specifiable? Would you agree with the statement that all decision problems that cannot be completely specified can be at least partially specified? What aspects of a complex decision problem are most susceptible to specification?

9/ What effect does the relative power of a participant have in the resolution of a complex decision problem? If one participant attempts to exert his power to obtain an outcome he most prefers, what will be the most likely effect on the other participants? If they accept an outcome that is less preferred by them, do their basic preferences change?

10/ What are the essential differences between the resolution of a completely-specified decision problem and the resolution of one in which there are a number of participants with conflicting objectives? Is it possible to arrive at a "best" solution for the latter sort of problem and, if so, what does a "best" solution entail?

11/ Resolution of complex decision problems is a continuous process. What implications does this statement have for the design and implementation of the strategic component of the information system?

12/ What are the likely sources of the information needed in the resolution of strategic decisions? To what extent is the information available at the various system interfaces concerning the internal operation of an organization likely to be useful in resolution of strategic decision problems?

CASE WORK

1/ Amalgamated Electric is a manufacturer of electric fans of all types. Its models range from small household exhaust fans to the heavy industrial type. Each fan consists essentially of a motor, fan blades, and a housing. These components are manufactured at Amalgamated's plant, which also includes an assembly shop. Orders come into the plant through a small administrative unit located in a building adjacent to the production and assembly shops. Before a customer's order is passed on to the plant, his credit rating is checked and the content of the order is verified. This is done by comparing the characteristics of the items ordered with those in a standard catalogue. If an anomaly is found, it is checked with the customer. If no irregularities are found, the order is passed to the plant manager.

When an order is received at the plant, the items it contains are broken down into their component subassemblies and parts. Purchase orders are prepared for any items not in stock. The necessary production and assembly work is scheduled and a delivery date is calculated. Trucks are reserved for delivery. Production and assembly then proceeds and status reports on each item in the order are issued at regular intervals. The production and assembly shops have a job ticket system. The job ticket contains each employee's identification, base rate of pay for the job, and the time spent on the job. The job ticket is used for payroll preparation and, together with materials and overhead costs, for cost accounting. Invoices from suppliers are checked and paid by the administrative unit. When the order is filled, an invoice is prepared and the transaction is included in a status report on accounts receivable made at regular intervals.

The above is only a bare outline of Amalgamated's administrative and operational procedures. You can add additional details from your own experience and imagination. As an exercise, give the following information concerning Amalgamated Electric in as much detail as time permits:

- the titles and the broad functions of the completely-specified systems that exist, either actually or potentially, in Amalgamated's administrative and operational activities
- for each such specified system give a brief description of
  - (a) the input data sets from both internal and external sources
  - (b) the editing and checking routines applicable to these data sets
  - (c) the processing required for these data
  - (d) the paper (or other tangible) output of the system
  - (e) the information required at the monitor
  - (f) the information required at the interface

2/ As an additional or alternative exercise, suppose that you work for a municipality and that you have been asked to do a preliminary survey of the existing and potential completely-specified systems within its administrative and operational activities. Your survey is to include the following departments:

1/ police, including Motor Vehicle Act violations administration

2/ parks and public recreation facilities, including the municipal zoo and other attractions for which an entrance fee is charged

3/ license bureau, responsible for issuing licenses for dogs, taxis, bicycles, etc.

4/ social assistance, covering all forms of welfare and other assistance to those in need

5/ property assessment and taxes

6/ finance, covering all operations in which municipal funds are involved

7/ personnel, including all services for the employees of the municipality.

Prepare a list of the titles and broad functions of the completely-specified systems that you are likely to detect in your survey. Include as much detail as you can devise in the areas listed as (a) through (f) in the previous exercise.

4

The Internal Information System

Introduction

The internal component of the information system supports the internal management and administration of the organization. It coordinates and integrates information available at the interfaces of the completely-specified systems. The internal information system sorts this information and provides it in an easily understood form to those involved in management control and, to some extent, those involved in strategic planning. The basic role of the system is to facilitate and enhance the flow of internal information within the organization of which it is an integral part.

The internal information system consists of a number of parts: [1]

- *The completely-specified systems*—which have already been described in detail;
- *The common data base*—which acts as a store for data and information used in more than one part of the organization;
- *The management reporting system*—which provides periodic and timely reports to those engaged in management control of the organization;

[1] Radford, K. J., *Information Systems in Management,* Reston Publishing Company, 1973, Chapter 5.

- *The information retrieval system*—by means of which data and information that has been stored can be retrieved on a demand basis;
- *The data management system*—which arranges and controls the flow of data and information among the various parts of the organization.

A diagram illustrating the relationship between the parts of the internal information system was published by the author in 1973.[2] The diagram is reproduced here as Figure 4-1. The completely-specified systems are shown in Figure 4-1 as circles around the lower periphery of the diagram. These systems support the managerial activity of operational control. They are the basic building blocks upon which the whole design and implementation of the internal system is based.

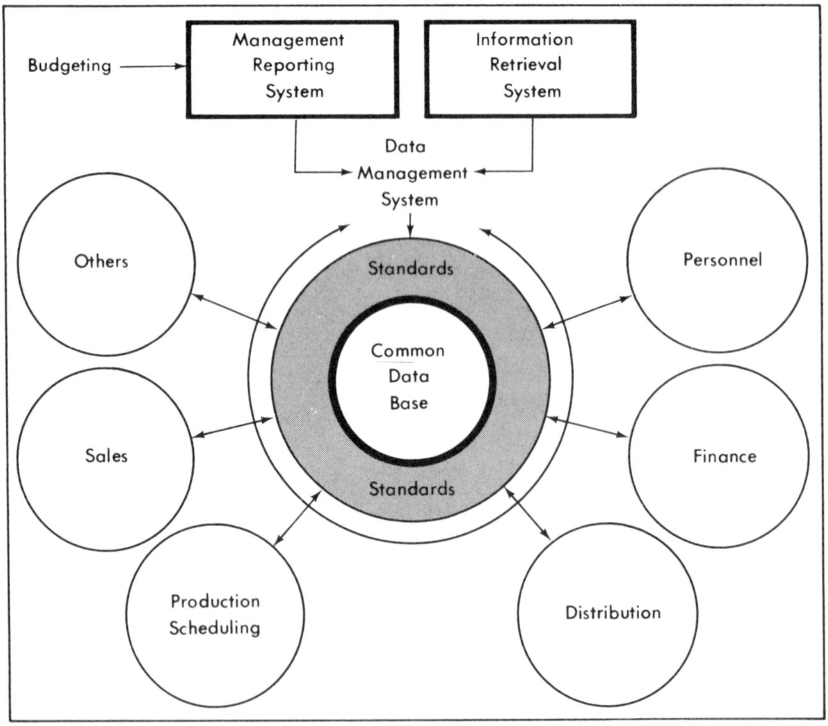

Figure 4.1. Basic Design Diagram for the Internal Information System

[2] Ibid., p. 56.

Most of the data vital to the routine administrative and operational activities of an organization exists and remains in these completely-specified systems. Much of the information necessary for higher-level decision making results from the summarization and aggregation of this original mass of basic data. A detailed description of the characteristics of the completely-specified systems was given in Chapter 3 and it will not be repeated here. The reader is asked to refer to that description or to other accounts of the design and implementation of these systems elsewhere in the available literature as necessary in the course of the following discussion.[3, 4]

Summary data and information from the completely-specified systems appear at the individual interfaces and are transferred into the common data base. This data base acts as a central repository and exchange facility containing information needed by two or more components of the internal system. Data and information entering the common data base must be in a standard form that can be understood and used by all parts of the organization. This standardization requirement is represented in the diagram by the hatched area that surrounds the common data base.

Reports required for effective management control are compiled from data and information that are contained in the common data base. Reports such as financial statements that are needed at regular intervals are assembled by the management reporting system. This system deals only with reports that are to be presented in a previously-designed format on a regular and periodic basis. Other information needed in management control but not included in the structured, periodic reports can be provided to managers on demand by a specially designed information retrieval system. The flow of data and information throughout the internal information system is controlled by the data management system. The function of the data management system is to link together the various parts of the internal information system and to ensure its smooth operation.

The design shown in Figure 4-1 can be used as the basis for the construction of an internal information system for either a whole organization or a segment of the organization. If parts of an organiza-

[3] Davis, Gordon B., *Management Information Systems: Conceptual Foundations, Structure and Development,* McGraw-Hill, 1974, Chapter 10.

[4] Blumenthal, Sherman C., *Management Information Systems,* Prentice-Hall, 1969.

tion are geographically separated or semiautonomous in operation, it may be desirable for each such part to have its own information system. In such cases, however, communications between the various parts of the organization are greatly facilitated if each internal system adopts the same basic design and adheres to the same standards regarding the data it contains. In fact, the amount of formal communication between the parts of an organization in such circumstances varies in direct proportion to the degree of standardization achieved between the various internal information systems.

The components of the internal information system are now discussed in greater detail.

The Common Data Base

The common data base is the heart of the internal information system. It contains information that is vital to the internal regulation and control of the organization. The common data base also contains the information needed for the construction of a store of consistent data and information concerning the past activities of the organization. A store of this nature is of great use in strategic planning and policy making.

Data and information in the internal information system can be conveniently referred to in terms of *data sets*. A data set is a collection of pieces of data and information that have been grouped together by virtue of some common attribute or association. For example, data sets might contain the personal records of employees, lists of parts in an inventory, or production records over a period of time. Such data sets are the modern-day counterparts of the files and other forms of record keeping in widespread use before the introduction of automatic data processing.

The data and information processed by a completely-specified system comprises a large number of data sets. Data sets pertinent to only one completely specified system usually remain in that system throughout their useful lifetime, much in the same way that an internal file would not generally move out of the office in which it is used. However, some of the data sets that exist in a completely specified system may need to be made available to other related systems or parts of the organization. Such data sets are designated *common data* and are considered to be members of the common data base. Data sets of this nature that are generated in a completely-specified system appear at the interface and are then transferred to the common data base, from which they can be retrieved by other parts of the system as required.

The formal requirement allowing a data set to be designated a member of the common data base is that it be required in exactly the same form by two or more parts of the system.[5] Membership in the common data base implies that the data set is to be used in the same standard form throughout the organization. The work connected with establishing and maintaining the standard forms for common data base members is a vital part of the implementation of an internal information system. This task includes (a) establishing a standard representation for each of the data sets that are to be made members of the common data base, (b) obtaining agreement from the various users regarding these standard forms, and (c) ensuring that the standard forms are observed in day-to-day operations. Only a small proportion of the data sets in the completely-specified systems need to be established as common data. The majority of the data sets in these internal systems never need to be used outside their own system and are not, therefore, subject to the rigorous procedure of standardization that is necessary for members of the common data base.

A distinction must be made at this stage between the *logical* and the *physical* attributes of a data set. A logical attribute of a data set arises from its relationship to data sets in other parts of the information system. Membership in the common data base is, therefore, a logical attribute by this definition. In contrast, the location in which a data set is stored is a physical attribute of that data set. Figure 4-1 is a logical diagram showing the operating relationships among the component parts of the internal information system. No attempt is made in this diagram to show the relative physical positioning of the components of the system. Similarly, membership in the common data base does not necessarily imply that the data set involved must be stored in any particular location.

The physical location in which a member set of the common data base is stored is usually decided on the basis of ease of access, transfer, and use of the data involved. If these considerations so dictate, common data sets may be stored in two or more physical locations in the internal system. For example, a common data set used in two completely-specified systems may be stored in each of these systems.

[5] Radford, K. J., *Information Systems, op. cit.*, p. 62.

However, in such cases, the format and content of the data set is identical in each of the locations in which it is stored. Furthermore, the content of such a data set in each location is updated in exactly the same fashion and at the same time at each of the storage locations.

The Design of the Data Base

Important considerations in the design of the data base arise from the differences in perspective between the user and the information systems specialist. The user's primary concern is with the availability of the data in a form appropriate to the decision problems immediately at hand. The technical specialist must provide the most efficient means for the storage and retrieval of the data as is possible within the constraints imposed by the physical characteristics of the available equipment and techniques.

The user generally views data in terms of its *information structure*. The data user naturally thinks of data almost entirely in terms of how it can be applied in his or her work. His or her approach to the organization of data is logical in that the approach is concerned with the logic of data application. The user does not normally think of data in physical terms related to the mechanics of storage. Information structures, as envisaged by the user, can be classified as being hierarchic or associative.[6]

A *hierarchic* structure is one that relates data sets in terms of a superior-subordinate connection. For example, an invoice in an accounts receivable file bears a subordinate relationship to the record of the customer to whom it is addressed. At the same time, the invoice bears a superior relationship to the items that it contains describing the merchandise that the customer has ordered or received. Hierarchic relationships of this type may exist through a number of levels. In contrast, an *associative* relationship between data sets exists when different data sets share one or more elements in common. For example, two invoices addressed to the same customer would both contain the data element identifying the customer, or a particular item might appear in the invoices associated with a number of different customers.

The technical specialist, on the other hand, is concerned primarily with the physical characteristics of the data and of the locations in which the data is stored. He or she must meet the needs of users for

[6] Davis, Gordon B., *Management Information Systems, op. cit.*, pp. 290–292.

fast and effective retrieval of information. At the same time, the specialist must design the data base so that it can operate at an acceptable level of efficiency. The major concerns of the technical specialist are as follows:

1/ *Data descriptors*—each data set and each element of the data set must be identified by a nontechnical description that is meaningful to users of the data base. These descriptors must be unambiguous. They must include all characteristics of the particular piece of data and at the same time remain reasonably compact.

2/ *The data base directory*—the data descriptors must be incorporated into a directory that provides users with a comprehensive guide to the content of the data base. Construction of a directory of this nature is essential if the users are to become familiar with the store of information at their disposal. The quality of the data base directory and the efficiency with which it is kept up to date are major factors determining the extent to which the data base can be put to use within an organization.

3/ *The retrieval procedure*—once the nontechnical data descriptors have been chosen and the directory has been constructed, a procedure that enables users to retrieve information from the data base must be devised. This procedure must be readily understandable by the users and must provide access to the data in as uncomplicated a manner as possible. The retrieval system must also incorporate a means of safeguarding the confidentiality of items in the data base, so that only individuals with a valid need to know can retrieve the available data.

4/ *The technical descriptors*—in addition to a nontechnical, user-oriented description, each data set and each element must have a technical descriptor. This technical descriptor is used in the design and operation of the data base system. Technical descriptors include such items as (a) the length of the data element and whether its length is to be fixed or variable, (b) the nature of the data element, whether it is to be numeric or made up of letters, (c) the format in which the data in the element is expressed, (d) the coding of the data, and (e) the degree of confidentiality of the data.

5/ *The data manipulation routines*—these routines are the procedures by which collections of data are assembled and disassembled in the data base. In practice, such routines are embedded in the complex computer software by means of which the data base is operated. The nature of the routines necessary in a particular organizational data base depends primarily on the type of editing, retrieval, and updating procedures that it is necessary to apply to the data in the base.

6/ *The data file structures*—the nature of the data manipulation routines is a major factor in determining the type of file structure to be used for the storage of data in the base. The most fundamental decision in data base design concerns whether the file structures are to be serial, random, or a mixture of the two.[7] This decision must take into account not only the efficiency of operation of the data base but also such factors as storage cost, retrieval time, and ease of maintenance of the data base.

Technical design of the data base involves a number of compromises.[8] One of the most important of these compromises concerns the conflict between the desire for immediate access to information related to a particular problem and the need to operate the data base in as efficient a manner as possible. On the one hand, the most efficient mode of operation is usually one in which a high proportion of the output is in prestructured form. On the other hand, user requirements often demand facilities for random and unstructured enquiry of a type that is expensive to provide. The resulting compromise system usually incorporates some capability for each of the modes of access into the final design.

The Structure of the Data Base

The data base for the internal information system of a modern organization is a large and complicated entity. Its physical structure is difficult to imagine because its elements and data sets are often spread throughout a number of storage devices. For our purposes at this moment, however, let us envisage the data base in the form of a large, irregular mass of cells, not unlike an asymmetric honeycomb.

[7] Ibid., pp. 292–312.

[8] Head, Robert V., *Manager's Guide to Management Information Systems,* Prentice-Hall, 1972, pp. 55–56.

Each cell can be thought of as the location in which a particular element of the data base resides.

An element of the data base can be in one or the other of the following forms or in a mixture of both:

- *Numerical data*—concerning matters such as the number of hours worked on certain projects, the amount of resources used in production, the cost of overhead items in the various activities of the organization, the current value of the assets of the organization's pension plan, and quantitative results achieved in production or other activities;
- *Non-numerical data*—consisting of such items as the names and addresses of staff members and customers, catalogues of items produced and purchased, and lists of other details that are used primarily in processing day-to-day operational transactions.

Nonnumeric items, such as letters of the alphabet, require more storage space in automatic data processing systems than do numbers. Practical considerations in the design of a data base, therefore, favor the replacement of nonnumeric items by numerically coded equivalents to the greatest extent possible.

A significant portion of the content of the common data base consists of data generated as a direct consequence of the administrative and operational activities of the organization. For the most part this portion of the data base content contains information concerning the resources expended by the organization in pursuit of its goals and objectives along with information concerning the results obtained from these expenditures. The data sets involved originate in the completely-specified systems and summaries of this data are required by those engaged in management control. These summaries are forwarded, therefore, from the completely-specified systems via the interfaces into the data base.

A second category of information often found in a common data base does not originate within the organization. This information pertains to the environment in which the organization is operating. It may refer, for example, to the demography of a particular region, to a competitor's share of the market, or to the general trend of the economy. Such information may be either detailed or general in form. Information of this nature may also be of interest to those involved in activities other than management control. Such information may, for example, be of considerable use in strategic planning. There is, therefore, an important link between the common data base in the internal information system and its counterpart in the strategic system serving the planning and policy making activities of the organization. This link between the data bases of the two major components of the overall information system is discussed in greater detail in Chapter 6.

Each cell in the data base is associated with a descriptor describing the characteristics of the information it contains. These descriptors are assigned when the data base is constructed and remain fixed unless the overall design is changed. As operations proceed, however, the data and values that are placed in the particular cells will vary, much in the same way as the reading on the odometer of an automobile changes as it moves along the road. Some of the variation in the data cells may be regular and progressive as in an odometer. Other changes may be irregular, reflecting variations in the conditions that the organization experiences. The data stored at any particular moment will, taken together, reflect the state of the organization's activities at that particular time. At the next instant, however, the data indicated in the cells and the state of the organization may be different.

The Historic Store

In most organizations, it is desirable to retain a record of past operations and conditions. This can be done by examining the content of the common data base at regular intervals and recording this information in a permanent form. By this means, an historic store of data concerning past operations of the organization can be built up. A store of this nature is often an invaluable source of information for use in planning and related activities. In creating the historic store, it is important to take precise note of the data descriptors applicable to each of the elements at the time that each historic record is entered into the store. Data descriptions tend to be changed with time. It is unwise to rely on the memories of staff members for the conversion of past data to present day specifications. If data descriptors are changed, the new and old specifications should be carefully documented, as should be the method of conversion between them. If possible, previously stored data are converted to the new descriptors at the time that the change is made. The historic store is reviewed continually and portions that are judged to have lost their relevance are discarded. This procedure, which is normally followed in dealing with other forms of storage, prevents the cost of the historic store from becoming too high.

There is another compelling reason for arranging to record the contents of the data base at regular intervals. Recently-taken records provide a basis for restarting the operation of the information system should the current contents of the data base be lost or destroyed in a system failure. As a precautionary measure, the recorded contents of the data base are often removed to a location distant from the site of current operations. Such a precaution virtually eliminates the possibility that both the current and the recorded data could be destroyed simultaneously. Most of the recordings made in precautionary measures of this sort are discarded as they become obsolete. Only those that are to become part of the historic store are retained past the time of their immediate usefulness as a back-up to the operational system.

Administration of the Common Data Base

Many of the data sets that exist in the internal information system are of interest only in that portion of the system in which they reside or originate. The small proportion of all the data sets that become members of the common data base do so by virtue of their broader application in the management of the organization as a whole. It is natural, therefore, that the common data base and the data sets it contains should be administered by an agent working on behalf of the whole organization, rather than an individual responsible for only a part of the operation.

In most modern organizations in which the common data base concept is adopted, responsibility for the data base and its contents is assumed by a "data base administrator." The responsibilities of the data base administrator include (a) building the common data base from the existing semiautonomous files in the organization; (b) maintaining a current directory to the common data base; (c) ensuring that the standards relating to membership in the common data base are maintained; (d) arranging for the continual updating and editing of the data in the common data base; and (e) ensuring the confidentiality and security of the data base.

Constructing the Common Data Base

At the start of the construction of a common data base, it is often found that a substantial proportion of the data sets most likely to be included are already in a suitable standard form. For example, much of the financial information in most organizations is in a form appropriate for immediate incorporation into the common data base. This phenomenon is in most part due to the past efforts by those involved in accounting in introducing standard data definitions and descriptions. Some of the personnel information in a modern organization may also be in similar readily usable condition. Such information in these and other categories that is required in the common data base can often be admitted with little or no modification of existing definitions and formats. A substantial body of data may, therefore, be available immediately as a start toward building the common data base. However, subsequent augmentation of the data base may not be achieved quite as easily.

Inclusion of a data set in the common data base requires that responsibility for routine administrative procedures with regard to that data set (including editing and updating) be formally ceded to the data base administrator. This individual then uses his or her authority to ensure that the data set is maintained in a manner beneficial to the organization as a whole. In actual practice, however, administration of many of the data sets in the common data base is often delegated back to those responsible for the part of the organization where the data sets originate. Little difficulty is normally experienced in cases where responsibilities and administrative procedures with regard to a data set are clear cut and well understood.

Much more difficulty is likely to arise in situations in which two or more individuals are administering data sets that are essentially the same with each claiming primary responsibility for the particular data within the organization. In such circumstances, one or the other may not readily agree to relinquishing control over the data. Hostility, conflict, and bad feeling can result if a situation such as this is not handled with tact and understanding. On the other hand, the principle of the common data base is at stake in such circumstances. The small proportion of the data in an organization that is basic to communication between its various parts must be administered by a single authority. Considerable effort may be necessary to obtain agreement between those involved in individual cases of dispute over particular data sets. However, agreement in cases such as this is vital. If agreement cannot be reached by negotiation a solution must be mandated as a last resort by reference to higher authority. The intimate relationships between data, administrative procedures, and the concerns of individual staff members in such circumstances provide compelling reasons in favor of the gradual formation of the common data base. Imposition of a newly constituted data base without regard for the fabric of the organization that surrounds the data is a potent recipe for disaster in the implementation of an internal information system.

When the common data base has been established, it is necessary to maintain the quality of the data that it contains. This involves continuous monitoring to ensure that the standards and administrative procedures related to the data base are being observed. Unless this is done, the quality of the data base soon deteriorates and individual managers lose faith in the concept. The inevitable consequences in these circumstances are that separate stores of information are established for individual use in different parts of the organization and that communication within the organization diminishes.

Advantages of the Common Data Base Approach

The concept of a common data base that has just been described is a relatively recent development in the literature of information systems. Much of the early work in this area concentrated on individual systems but failed to give recognition to the interrelationships between data sets in their various applications.[9] More recently, however, it has been recognized that the key to a successful and efficient internal information system is an integrated data base of the type described above.[10] It provides the following major advantages over other approaches to the handling of organizational data:

- The common data base approach facilitates interrelationships between both the basic functions and activities in the organization and the completely-specified systems that support them.
- The common data base approach provides that data sets in different parts of an organization that refer to identical matters are in a standard form. Comparisons in terms such as cost and performance in a particular time period between the parts of the organization are therefore greatly facilitated.
- The approach provides that only information used in two or more

9 Head, Robert V., *Manager's Guide, op. cit.,* p. 23.

10 Hannold, Terrance, "An Executive View of MIS," *Datamation,* November 1972.

parts of the organization needs to be standardized. Implementation of even this reduced amount of standardization is often quite costly. However, it is much less of a task than the often-advocated introduction of totally redesigned systems in which *all* data set designations and formats are changed.

- The common data base can be built up gradually as more and more candidate data sets are considered for membership. This gradual approach greatly reduces the possibility of system collapse during implementation.

The common data base approach is not without its problems. Many managers and administrators who have grown accustomed to control of data in a semiautonomous specialist environment may object strenuously when "their" data is transferred to the common data base. Another related source of difficulty is that the routine editing and updating of a particular common data set cannot be undertaken efficiently in more than one location. If two or more individuals have been accustomed to carrying out these tasks themselves, one or more will be required in the future to receive edits and updates from another part of the organization. This may generate friction and jealousies, especially in organizations in which no preparatory program of training and reorientation has been undertaken. These difficulties are by no means insuperable. However, they can cause considerable delay and inefficiency during the implementation of the information system. Methods by which some of these problems can be overcome or their effects reduced are discussed in a later section of this chapter.

The Management Reporting System

The management reporting system is the component of the internal information system in which periodic and prestructured reports are prepared for distribution to management. The material from which these reports are constructed originates mainly in the completely-specified systems. When a particular data set is required for the compiling of a management report that data set automatically becomes a member of the common data base. The particular data set thus appears at the interface of the completely-specified system in which it originates and is passed to the management reporting system in standard form via the common data base. As with data sets in the other component systems, data sets of interest solely to the management reporting system can be stored within the management reporting system, if such localized storage is felt to be more efficient and economical.

Periodic and prestructured reports generated by the management reporting system normally fall into four categories: (a) reports showing the expenditure of resources (such as money, person-hours, and raw materials) to date, comparing these figures with the amounts budgeted for expenditure in that particular time period; (b) reports relating to results achieved, for example trends in production or amount of work completed; (c) combinations of expenditure and production figures into statements concerning the efficiency of the operations surveyed; and (d) statements concerning the overall effectiveness of the work done toward the achievement of the organization's objectives. These four types of reports have their counterparts in one form or another, in all organizations.

The reports prepared in the management reporting system usually include those data that have been found from experience to be required periodically by those involved in management control. There is no absolutely certain method of determining the exact nature of the reports required by a new activity or organization. However, the type of reports already in use both inside and outside the organization provide a starting point in a study of the output needed from the management reporting system in a new implementation.

It is a good idea to gather all available relevant reports into a composite whole as a first step in the design of a new system. A composite report of this nature is a good basis for the discussions with managers needed to determine their needs for information in the management control activity. It is often difficult for these individuals to state their needs in definitive form.[11] Discussion of existing reports, however, often leads to suggestions regarding omissions and superfluous data.

Managerial suggestions can be incorporated into a new experimental format produced in parallel with existing reports. Ample opportunity should be given to managers to criticize the new format during this parallel operation period allowing them to suggest additions or deletions. Throughout this period, the existing format usually re-

[11] Daniel, D. Ronald, "Management Information Crisis," *Harvard Business Review*, September–October 1961, pp. 99–101.

mains the official reporting system. At some future time, after sufficient time has been allowed for development, modification, and adaptation of the suggested new format, a decision is made by senior management adopting the modified new format as the official formal reporting system for the organization. The new format continues to be developed after the changeover to accommodate the changing needs of the organization. It may be desirable in some cases to carry out the implementation of a new reporting procedure level by level in the organization, rather than all at once for the organization as a whole. In such circumstances, it is usually better to start at the topmost levels of the organization and work downwards. The existence and acceptance of the new system at the higher levels makes the task of implementation throughout the entire organization easier.

The Information Retrieval System

Not all of the information necessary for management control is contained in the periodic and structured reports provided by the management reporting system. These reports contain only information that has been found from experience to be useful when provided on a continual basis. It is natural that managers should require additional information from time to time. This additional information may be new and unrelated to that provided in the regular reports. It may, on the other hand, consist of new interpretations of information already reported.

The information retrieval system allows managers to obtain specific information from within the internal system on demand to augment the data furnished by the management reporting system. The purpose of this system is to provide managers with the means to retrieve information that they regard as necessary to the investigation of previously unexplored aspects of the problems that they face. The keys to the successful use and adoption of the retrieval system are (a) the establishment and maintenance of a comprehensive directory of the contents of the common data base and (b) the availability of simple and efficient procedures for retrieval of the information.

The information retrieval system is shown as logically communicating with the common data base in Figure 4-1. It is shown this way because much of the information demanded by managers through this system is already contained in the common data base. There are occasions in practice, however, when managers require data from the files held in a completely-specified system that have not yet been admitted to the common data base. In such circumstances, a request for such information is good reason to consider placing the information requested in the common data base as soon as possible. Meanwhile, the data requested can logically be considered to move from the completely-specified system in question through the common data base to the originator of the request. Note that the information retrieval system is not concerned with the information needed in operation control. The majority of this latter information is provided at the monitors of the completely-specified systems.

Resolution of many of the decision problems that arise in management control requires a knowledge of information not generated within the organization. Such information originates in the environment of the organization and is included under the general heading of "strategic" information. This heading refers to such matters as the activities and characteristics of other participants in the decision problems at hand and to the social, technological, and natural aspects of the environment. This information is contained in a strategic data base which, in mature information systems, is an equal partner of the common data base. The information retrieval system provides access to both data bases and, therefore, forms a link between the internal and the strategic components of the overall information system. The strategic component of the system is discussed in detail in Chapter 6 and the role of the information retrieval system as the link between the two components is explored further at that time.

The Data Management System

The data management system is the name applied to the collection of technical support services that together maintain, protect, and operate the internal information system. In most modern information systems, these support services are provided by a complex collection of computer software referred to by names such as "the operating system," "the information management system," and "data base support." The data management system serves a number of functions listed below: [12]

[12] Head, Robert V., *Manager's Guide, op. cit.,* Chapter 4.

- Updating the data in each of the storage locations serviced by the system;
- Transferring data sets from the interfaces of the completely-specified systems to locations where they are required;
- Deleting data sets that have become obsolete or superfluous to the operations of the organization;
- Structuring the storage of data sets in the system in a manner that facilitates the most efficient operation of the system;
- Arranging for the detection and correction of errors in the technical handling of the data sets. These errors may arise as a result of mistakes by individuals or may be caused by machine malfunctions during transmission or processing of data;
- Servicing the requirements of the management reporting and information retrieval systems for data sets stored in the overall system;
- Providing for the security of the system and protecting the confidentiality of the data it contains;
- Providing backup systems for the recovery of the information in the system should operations cease as a result of a major machine malfunction.

Technical details of the software required to carry out these tasks are the responsibility of information systems specialists charged with the technical design and maintenance of the system. Individual managers, particularly those charged with overall supervision of the information systems, will often take considerable interest in technical factors to assure themselves that the support services provided by the data management system specialists afford the users the most efficient access to the data contained in the internal information system.

Information Flow in an Organization

One of the major purposes of the internal information system is to facilitate and foster flow of information through formal channels within the organization. While fulfilling its formal function, the information system often stimulates informal communication at the same time. However, its prime concern is with the formal passage of information between the parts of the organization that need to communicate in the course of their day-to-day activities. The greater proportion of that communication is usually in the "vertical" direction, representing information flow from lower to higher levels in the organization, and vice versa. Nevertheless, some percentage of the necessary communications is in the "horizontal" direction, among individuals and offices at roughly the same level in the organizational hierarchy.

Information generally flows in organizations along two specific sets of paths: between individuals and offices having the same specialized function, such as personnel, sales, accounting, or production; and between responsibility centers set up to carry out specific tasks or projects. The overall flow of information in a modern organization can usually be seen to consist of a combination of the above types. The dominant flow in any particular organization is determined by the style of management adopted by the organization and the structure of the authority and reporting procedures that have been set up to serve that style of management.

In many organizations that are not subjected to continual change, the emphasis is often placed upon generating information flow along specialized functional lines. The usual information flow in an organization where the specialist functions are predominant is illustrated in Figure 4-2. In this example, which resembles a conventional organization chart, most of the formal flow of information is in the vertical direction. Information from the specialized functions is combined for the purposes of management control primarily at the level of the president or director. Horizontal flow of information at all levels is usually for liaison purposes only. The information system design corresponding to this type of management structure is a single diagram of the sort illustrated in Figure 4-1. In these circumstances the circle marked "Finance" at the lower right of the diagram can be envisaged as a series of nested systems carrying out specialized financial functions at the various levels of the organization. Information is passed between these systems in such a manner that data relating to the organization as a whole appears at a financial system interface at the level just below that of the president. This information is then passed into the common data base, combined with other functional data, and incorporated into management reports at the topmost level.

By way of contrast, organizations that are required to face constantly changing conditions often set up responsibility centers to deal with specific tasks as they arise. These responsibility centers are, in fact, miniature organizations themselves. They incorporate many specialized functional activities within their own management structure.

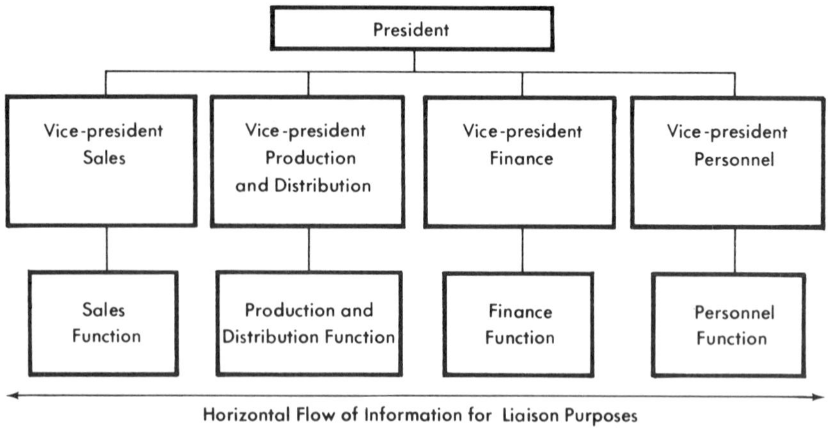

Figure 4.2. Information Flow by Specialist Function

The emphasis in an organization consisting of a network of responsibility centers is placed upon expediting information flow between the centers. The information passed is interfunctional in nature rather than being related to separate specialized functions. Communication between the specialist functions working in the various responsibility centers is correspondingly less.

An example of the information flow in an organization entirely structured by responsibility centers is illustrated in Figure 4-3. In this diagram, three responsibility centers are shown, each reporting to senior management for Tasks A, B, and C respectively. The tasks are themselves broken down into components, such as A_1, A_2, and A_3. The information system diagram corresponding to this form of management structure is shown in Figure 4-4. In this information system design, specialized functional data is collected at the interfaces of the completely specified systems serving the specialized functions in each of the responsibility centers. The information is passed from the interfaces to a common data base for the responsibility center. Reports based on a combination of data from each function are used in the management control of the responsibility center. Formal communications within the organization consist of exchanges between the common data bases in the various centers. As mentioned earlier in this chapter, data exchanged between common data bases in the responsibility centers must adhere to the standards set for the overall organizational data base.

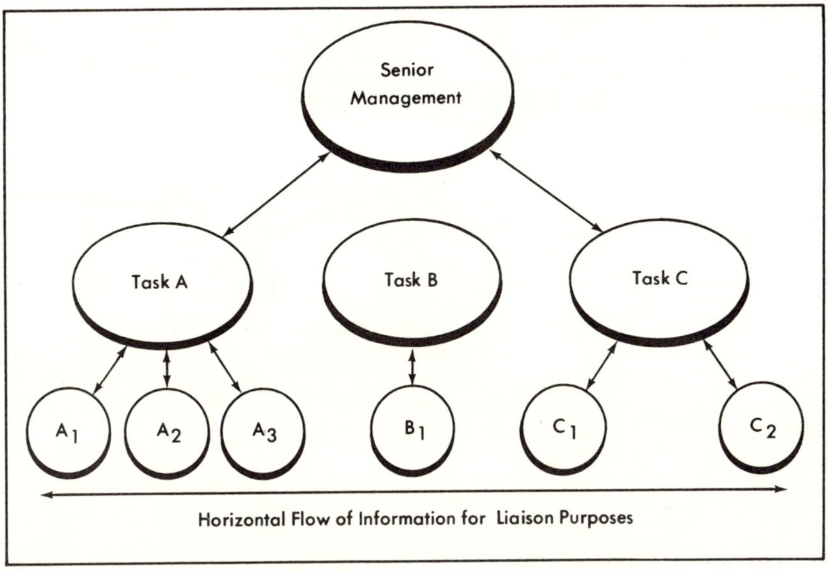

Figure 4.3. Information Flow by Responsibility Center

In actual practice, the information flow in most organizations combines the two situations described above, and illustrated in Figures 4-2 and 4-3. The design diagram for the average internal information system can, therefore, be expected to resemble that shown in Figure 4-4 with the added feature that some communication occurs between the specialized functions within the responsibility centers. The degree and amount of this communication depends upon the particular management structure adopted. Flow of information between specialist functions can be envisaged in Figure 4-4 by imagining hierarchical communications links between the circles representing specialized functions at the same level and at higher and lower levels in the organization.

Dispersion of the Data Base

It has already been noted that not all data sets that are members of the common data base necessarily reside in the same physical location. Indeed, it may be desirable, in practice, to store data in more than one location in order to facilitate access by different parts of the organization. However, no matter where a member data set of the common

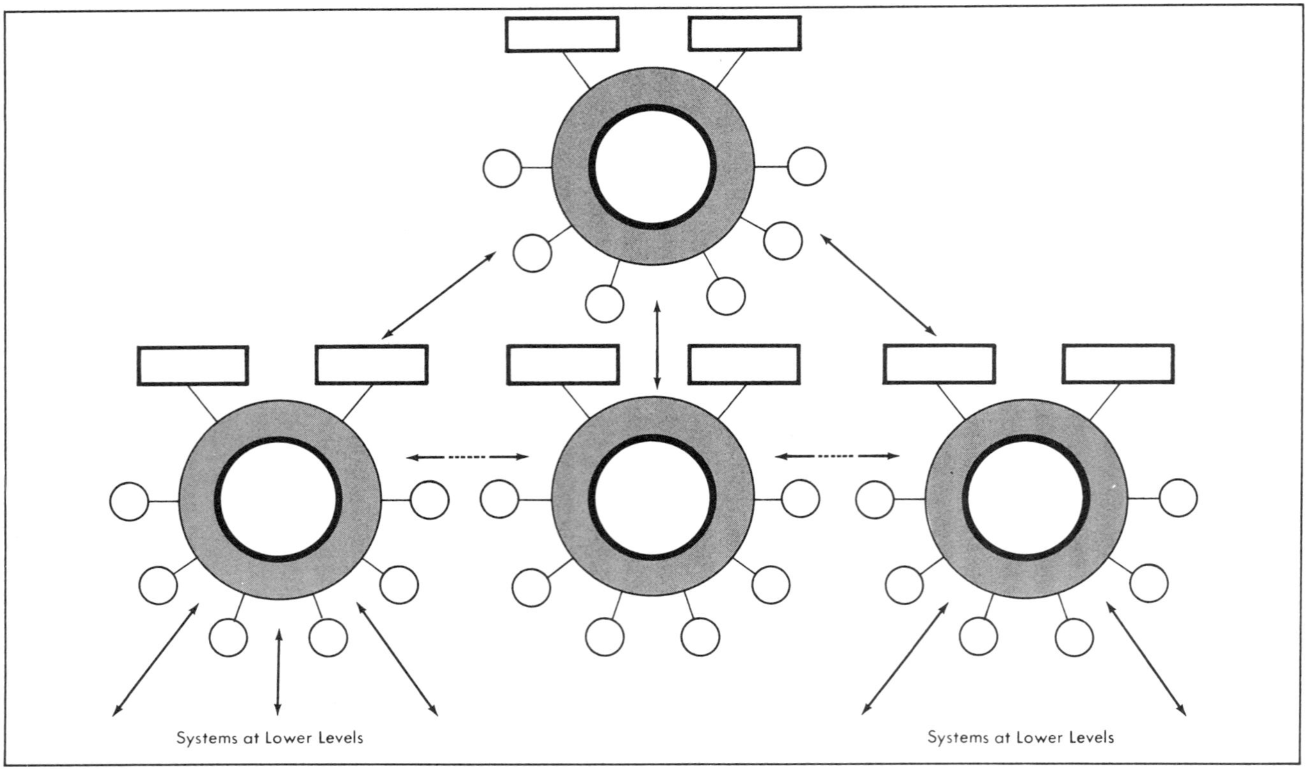

Figure 4.4. Basic Internal Information System Design Diagram

data base is stored, it is always represented in exactly the same standard form.

The data base is clearly a significant factor in formal communications between the various parts of an organization. For example, in an internal system such as that illustrated in Figure 4-4, a substantial portion of the formal communications between the responsibility centers is made up of exchanges between the data bases at the various locations. Note that these communications occur not only between those in the direct line of authority between levels in the organization, but also between centers at the same level.

The overall organizational data base may, therefore, be hierarchical in nature. The fact that any particular data set is always stored in the same form regardless of its location in the organization considerably enhances communication between the responsibility centers. In fact, the greater the degree of standardization achieved between the contents of the data base stored in the various locations, the greater is the potential for formal communication between the responsibility centers concerned.

Aggregation and Uncertainty Absorption

At the lower levels of an organization, there exists a mass of data, stored mostly in the completely-specified systems. Individual items in this mass of data generally have a specific and limited significance. Each datum refers only to a small portion of the activities of the whole organization. Although one such item may on occasion take on great importance, their relevance as individual items exists almost exclusively at the level at which they originate. Data and information that are passed to higher levels usually represent summaries of items that exist at a lower level. As such, these summaries are of greater significance to the organization as a whole. The process of summarization is essential to good data management.[13] It is necessary to avoid placing an information overload on managers at the higher levels. However, summarization involves two processes in which information can be lost. These processes are known as *aggregation* and *uncertainty absorption.*

Aggregation occurs when two or more pieces of data are combined to form a new quantity. For example, the expenditures within two

[13] Ackoff, R. L., "Management Mis-information Systems," *Management Science,* vol. 14, no. 4, December 1967, p. B148.

parts of an organization for a certain activity may be combined to obtain the total expenditure of the organization for that activity. No information is lost if both the aggregated and unaggregated data are retained. There is a tendency, however, to discard the original data once the aggregated value has been obtained. If this is done, the separate items cannot be retrieved at a future date to be used in decision problems in which the aggregated value does not provide sufficiently detailed information.

Aggregation of data is necessary throughout the internal information system. It occurs, for example, in preparation of the data sets that must appear at the interfaces of the completely specified systems. Aggregation occurs when management reports from two lower levels are combined into a higher level report. It is important, however, to guard against any loss of information by making provision in the design of the information system for the retention of basic data until such time as it can be reasonably assumed that the data has no conceivable future use. Such retained data can be regarded as part of the historic store of information in the organization, as discussed earlier in this chapter.

Uncertainty absorption is the somewhat awkward term used to describe the effect arising from summarization of data. Uncertainty absorption occurs when inferences are drawn from a body of data and the inferences, rather than the body of data itself, are communicated.[14] A trivial example of this phenomenon occurs during aggregation of data, when the sum of two or more values (the inference) is reported rather than the original values themselves. An important type of uncertainty absorption may occur when the form of the message to be passed is not completely specified. In these circumstances, the information transmitted by the initiator of a message may be his or her perceptions of the meaning of a particular group of data. In such a case, the personal views and judgements of the initiator may be incorporated, consciously or unconsciously, into the information reaching the recipient.[15]

The potential for uncertainty absorption is important in the design of the internal information system in that it underlies the necessity for clear and unequivocal definitions of the meaning of the variables

[14] March, J. G., and H. A. Simon, *Organizations,* Wiley, 1958, p. 165.

[15] Ference, Thomas P., "Organizational Communications and the Decision Process," *Management Science,* vol. 17, no. 2, October 1970, pp. B83–96.

represented by the data sets and data elements in the system. If definitions are not universally known and accepted, interpretation differences may arise and uncertainty absorption may occur.

The occurrence of uncertainty absorption is much greater in the strategic information system, in which information is much less quantitative and much more open to interpretation by the individuals who deal with it. The effect of uncertainty absorption upon the transmission of information will be taken up again in Chapter 5, in which the background of the strategic information system is described.

Implementation of an Internal Information System

There are two considerations that take precedence over all other matters in the initial planning and implementation of a new internal information system.[16] These considerations are (a) the nature of the information system that already exists in the organization and (b) the choice of a basic system design that can act as a guideline throughout the process of implementation.

Every organization has an information system of one form or another. This existing information system may be well developed and sophisticated in its operation or it may be rudimentary and undeveloped. However, whatever its state of development, the existing system is an integral part of the organization at the time when the introduction of an improved internal information system is contemplated. Components of the existing system may be incorporated into the newly planned internal information system. A program for documenting and cataloguing the system already existing in the organization is, therefore, a logical first step in the implementation of its replacement.

A second and equally important initial step is the choice of a basic design to be followed in the implementation. Early selection of a design, such as that illustrated in Figure 4-4, prevents the haphazard and inefficient growth of the system. A process of implementation that is not guided by a basic design may have an undesirable disruptive effect upon the whole organization. Lack of a basic design may also lead to an escalation of estimated costs as the unforeseen effects of an uncoordinated implementation process emerge. Once a basic design for the new internal system has been proposed, discussed, and

[16] Radford, K. J., *Information Systems, op. cit.*, Chapter 6.

modified to meet the needs of the organization, it is adopted as the basic blueprint governing all aspects of the conversion from the existing situation to the new system.

The next step in the initial stages of the implementation process is to determine the extent to which the existing internal information system meets the requirements laid down and agreed upon in the newly adopted overall design. In some cases, where the existing system is well developed and relatively sophisticated, the modifications required to meet the new design may be minor. In other cases, where only a rudimentary internal system exists, the work of conversion may be much more extensive. Documentation and cataloguing of the existing system in terms of the chosen basic design allows the relationship of each existing component to its counterpart in the new system to be established. By a thorough analysis of the existing system, the extent of the modifications required to bring each component of the existing system into line with the standards laid down by the new design can be determined. A detailed plan can then be developed outlining the process of transition from the existing system to the new system without any major disruption of the work of the organization. This implementation plan should include a statement establishing priorities for implementing the various parts of the new system, an estimated schedule for the implementation, and provisional estimates of the costs of the conversion. This statement can form the basis for a presentation to the senior management personnel describing the goals, benefits, costs, and methodology of the implementation. Approval of the plan, modified as necessary to account for management requirements and any financial constraints, can be the signal for the implementation to begin.

A Modular Approach to Implementation

There has been considerable discussion in recent years concerning the relative merits of implementation plans that call for a total replacement of all components of the internal system all at once as opposed to those that are based upon a gradual, step-by-step improvement of the system. The "total system" approach has, at times, resulted in a considerable disruption of the work of the organization concerned. This disruption has occurred especially in cases in which the introduction of the new system was carried out over a very short span of time. Most authorities now agree that a gradual approach in which successive modules of the system are introduced over a more prolonged period of time is likely to prove more acceptable in modern organizations. This gradual approach provides insurance against major disruptions during the implementation of the system. At the same time, gradual implementation allows the various parts of the organization enough time to adapt to changes in the system as they occur.

The steps in the modular approach to implementation are shown in Figure 4-5. Following adoption of a basic design and documentation of the existing system in a form consistent with that design, attention can be turned to the completely-specified systems. These systems contain the data mass from which the content of the internal information system is drawn. It is natural, therefore, that the process of implementation and conversion should start with these completely-specified systems. The methods and procedures that can be used in the design and implementation of completely-specified systems have been treated fully in existing literature and need not be repeated here.[17, 18, 19, 20] However, the importance of the interface and monitor components of these systems must be stressed. Provision for these components is sometimes overlooked in the rush to produce an operational system in the shortest possible time.

1. Adoption of a basic overall system design
2. Documentation and cataloguing of the existing internal information system in a form consistent with the selected design
3. Redesign and progressive replacement of the completely specified systems
4. Gradual compiling of the common data base
5. Redesign and replacement of the management reporting system
6. Introduction of an information retrieval system

Figure 4.5. Steps in the Implementation Process

Maintenance of the interface component is the key to the process of redesign and replacement of completely specified systems. Successive revisions of these systems can be introduced without disturbing

[17] Davis, Gordon B., *Management Information Systems, op. cit.*

[18] Blumenthal, Sherman C., *Management Information Systems, op. cit.*

[19] Murdick, R. G., and J. E. Ross, *Information Systems for Modern Management,* Prentice-Hall, 1971.

[20] Lucas, Henry C. Jr., *Computer-based Information Systems in Organizations,* Science Research Associates Inc., 1973.

the logical flow of information within the system as long as the requirements for data flow at the interface are met. It is necessary, of course, that the data sets available at the interfaces of the new systems conform to common data base standards.

Gradual augmentation of the common data base is another feature of the progressive, step-by-step approach to implementation of an internal information system. As the completely-specified systems are redesigned, various data sets are considered for admission to the data base. The gradual approach allows careful assessment of the qualifications of each data set for common data base membership. This approach also provides time for studying any administrative procedures connected with the data sets that will need to be modified to make them consistent with the administration of the new data base. Redesign of the management reporting system can proceed at the same time as the construction of the common data base. As the implementation of the new system gains momentum, the creation of the information retrieval system can be considered.

As with many such processes, the steps shown in Figure 4-5 are not necessarily undertaken in rigorous sequence. Some of these steps may run concurrently. Furthermore, the order of implementation need not be exactly as indicated. A complete implementation process often consists of a series of phased repetitions of all or some of these steps. However, each step is essential to the process and a complete implementation of an internal information system necessarily involves each of them.

Operations using the new system need not await the completion of implementation. Once the basic system design has been adopted and conversion of existing components has been started, operation of the system can often conform to the new concept very rapidly. It may, however, require a considerable period of time to convert all parts of the system to the new mode of operation. Furthermore, once initial implementation is completed, it is likely that another round of progressive improvements will be found to be desirable. Achievement of a completely satisfactory system conforming to the basic design is usually a continuing process requiring many months if not years, rather than a task that can be completed once and for all in a short period of time. The elapsed time required in any particular case may vary greatly depending on the complexity of the implementation, the amount of manpower and resources available, the acceptance of the project within the organization, and the skills of those taking part.

In using the modular approach to system implementation, new components are continually replacing the components previously in operation. In these circumstances, it is prudent to allow for a period during which the existing components and the replacement components operate in parallel. During this period, the new system can be thoroughly checked and its capabilities compared with those of the system which it is replacing. The existing system is continually available during this period in the event that, for any reason, the replacement is found to be unsatisfactory. Parallel operations of this type undoubtedly increase the implementation cost of a new internal information system. However, this extra cost can be regarded as insurance against disruption of the system in the event the new components being introduced prove unsatisfactory.

The Role of Managers in the Implementation

The role of managers in the implementation of an internal information system cannot be overemphasized. The formal information system in any organization is a vital part of the communications system used by managers. It is necessary, therefore, that any modification of that system be discussed thoroughly with management before the conversion starts. The views of managers must be incorporated to the greatest possible extent in the overall plan. The support of senior management and the continual participation by senior individuals in the design and implementation of a new system are factors essential to the success of the project.

The success of the implementation of an internal information system is also dependent upon cooperation and communication between managers and information systems specialists.[21] Managers generally have a thorough knowledge of the operations of the organization and of the intricacy of the administrative tasks and decision processes involved. The information systems specialists usually have little detailed knowledge of these organizational matters. Their skills lie in the field of design and implementation of computer-supported systems. The successful combination of these diverse skills ensures that all aspects of the tasks required for implementation will be considered.

Generally speaking, it is best that the planning and implementation

[21] Exton, William Jr., "The Information Systems Staff: Major Obstacles to its Effectiveness and a Solution," *Journal of Systems Management,* vol. 21, no. 7, July 1970, pp. 32–36.

of a new system be placed under the overall direction of a manager in the organization rather than an information specialist. Managers understand the day-to-day problems of the organization. If the managers selected to work on the project are future candidates for senior positions in the organization they will already have, or be able to obtain the authority to make any necessary commitments. Managers will be materially interested in the success and practicality of the system because they will be required to work with it in the future. Their involvement will tend to induce their subordinates to actively assist in the implementation. Furthermore, when the managers return to their normal work after directing the implementation, they will continue to assist in the future development of the system.[22]

Constant communication and cooperation between managers and systems specialists is necessary to assure proper attention to organizational, behavioral, and human factors in the design of the system. Unless this cooperation exists, the design may tend to ignore the needs of users. Input and output characteristics of the system may be determined with very little thought being given to the human characteristics of those who need to use them. Managers working in the organization have a responsibility to insist that human and organizational factors are taken into account during the design and implementation of the system.

Some managers are hesitant to assume implementation responsibility if they lack detailed knowledge of the technical aspects of computer supported systems. However, experience has shown that competent managers can acquire this knowledge very quickly. It is, moreover, much easier for a manager to acquire a working knowledge of these technical matters than it is for an information systems specialist to obtain the detailed knowledge of the organization possessed by the manager.[23] In recent years, an ideal type of person to direct the work of implementation has begun to become available. These uniquely qualified people are those who started work in the computer support activities of the organization and have risen by virtue of ability to the ranks of senior management.

Nomination of a manager to the overall direction of the project does not lessen the importance of the information systems specialists

[22] Martino, R. L., "Task Force Selection and Training," Management Development Institute, Wayne, Pennsylvania, p. 12.

[23] Dearden, John, "MIS is a Mirage," *Harvard Business Review*.

in the work of design and implementation. Their role, however, should be to support the managers involved, concentrating on introducing the computer systems and techniques required by management.

Computer Support for the Internal System

In the past, the approach to the subject of computer support for an internal information system has often been characterized by the suggestion, "Let's get a computer in and build the system around it." [24] This approach was sometimes encouraged by computer specialists who saw the acquisition of a computer as a means of increasing their status and progress in the organization. Times have changed somewhat and it is now generally recognized that it is impossible to accurately specify the needed computer support until a detailed design for the system has been written.

Once the information system has been devised, a decision must be made to determine whether computer services will be provided by an in-house computer or computers or by an external service bureau.[25] In many cases, this decision can be made independently for each of the completely specified systems and for the services necessary to support the management reporting system, the information retrieval system, and the operations of the common data base. Recent developments in minicomputers make it possible for many of these systems to be served by their own small computers rather than by a large central computer.

Introduction of minicomputers brings computing capability back to the location of the system being served, as was the case in the days before the general introduction of large computers into organizations. This development has the added advantage that computer support again comes under the administrative responsibility of the managers in charge of the individual systems. Decisions with regard to computer support can be taken individually for each system on the basis of individual costs and efficiency of operation.

Security and Confidentiality of the System

The internal information system contains information that is vital to the operation and well being of the organization that it serves. The

[24] McKeever, James M., "Building a Computer-based MIS," *Journal of Systems Management,* vol. 20, no. 9, September 1969.

[25] Radford, K. J., *Information Systems, op. cit.,* pp. 110–116.

physical security of the computer installations and devices is therefore extremely important. Security can be enhanced by measures to minimize or prevent damage due to fire, flood, power failure, civil disorder and other similar occurrences. It is also necessary to maintain strict control over access to the processing facilities and to the places where data sets are stored. Rigorous screening of those who are allowed access to the facilities and data is advised. Special procedures that allow the reconstruction of the data and information in the system at any given time are also recommended.[26] This reconstruction can be done using the contents of historic stores located in areas geographically separated from the normal operational area.

Methods are available to ensure the confidentiality of data sets not intended for general distribution within the organization. These methods are the equivalent of the lock on a filing cabinet or a safe in a nonautomated office. These methods consist of special computer techniques that provide access to data sets only by use of key procedures similar to the combination needed to open a safe. These procedures can be made available to those with a need for the protected information and can be changed easily from time to time to maintain the confidentiality of the data.

The Impact of the Implementation on the Organization

The internal information system contains the main channels of formal communication in an organization. It deals with data and information that are vital not only to the organization's continued operation, but also, to a great extent, determine the contributions, status, and progress of the individual members of the organization. The work of redesigning the internal information system often causes reconsideration of the patterns of management and decision making in the organization that it serves. It is natural, therefore, that the design and implementation of a new system should have a major impact at all levels of the organization.

The implementation of a new internal information system is intended to bring about a greater availability of consistent data concerning the internal activities of the organization expressed in a standard and well-understood form. Another objective of such a system is the automation of those decision processes that can truly be

[26] Chu, Albert L. C., "The Corporate Achilles Hill," *Business Automation,* February 1, 1971.

completely specified. The intention is that managers should be freed from the details of these routine decision processes, so that they can then turn their attention to the more complex problems of management control and strategic planning.

The implementation of a new information system may, however, be seen by some as a step towards reducing the role of managers in the decision process and decreasing the role of human judgement in the affairs of the organization. These reactions may arise from a number of situations and perceptions.[27] The move towards more standardization of data may cause managers to feel restricted or to feel that they have less room to maneuver. They may feel less able to question the validity and meaning of data. They may withdraw from communication and possibly withhold information from the system in an attempt to enhance their power in the organization by producing their personal information only at a vital stage in the decision process. Those who have previously exercised authority by withholding certain information may feel that their status in the organization has been reduced. Others may feel that ambiguity is essential to the process of management and that the greater degree of standardization of data reduces this necessary ingredient of their work. Some may have the impression that their performance in their job is likely to be assessed in primarily quantitative terms. A small proportion may be engaged in activities that are, to some extent, in conflict with the objectives of the organization as a whole. They may feel that a move to increase the flow of data in the organization will reveal this aspect of their operations.

All of the above reactions may contribute to the growth of resistance to the design and implementation of a new internal information system. This resistance may be expressed more by those who feel inadequate or unqualified to work with the new system and the related management methods. For example, some managers, who have reached a stable position in the organization consistent with their qualifications and needs, may have become used to expending effort mainly to maintain that position. They may have diverted part of their interest and energy to activities outside the organization rather than concentrating their efforts upon seeking new and greater responsibilities in their work. To such persons, the apparent need to acquire

[27] Argyris, Chris, "Management Information Systems: The Challenge to Rationality and Emotionality," *Management Science,* vol. 17, no. 6, February 1971, pp. B275–292.

new skills in order to maintain their position in the organization may be perceived as being beyond their present capabilities and a threat to their status quo. The result is resistance to the design and implementation of the new system as a measure of defense against its apparent consequences.

Resistance to the system as a threat to the status quo is most often found in older organizations that have over the years lost direction and force and have become less and less effective. In many such cases, staff members and groups in the organization turn to performing tasks that they do well or particularly like, rather than concentrating on those tasks that might make the organization more effective. A proposal to implement an information system in an organization of this nature may be interpreted as a direct threat to the survival of the staff members and groups involved. On the other hand, in a younger organization, interpersonal communication is often very good and staff members usually closely identify with organizational objectives. The need for a formal information system may not be recognized in such cases. Nevertheless, the introduction of an information system early in the life of an organization can be a major factor in maintaining its momentum and resisting any deterioration with time.

Methods of dealing with resistance from staff members consist almost entirely of regular communication regarding matters connected with the design and implementation of the new system. Activities such as periodic briefings on plans and updates on programs do much to reduce the uncertainty in the minds of those who may be affected by the developments. Programs of education and information work well up to the point at which people begin to see each other as a threat.[28] Reduction of conflict after this point can be achieved only by communication and compromise. Successful implementation of the internal information system requires an increased commitment by members of the organization concerned to deal with the interpersonal problems that are likely to arise.

Summary

The internal component of the information system serves the internal management and administration of the organization. Its basic role is to facilitate and enhance the flow of information to managers in the

[28] Ibid.

organization of which it is an integral part. The internal information system consists of (a) the completely-specified systems (b) the common data base (c) the management reporting system (d) the information retrieval system; and (e) the data management system. These components are linked together by the flow of information between them. The diagram (Figure 4-4) illustrating this flow represents the basic design diagram for an internal information system.

The completely-specified systems are the primary building blocks of the internal information system. Data sets that are used by two or more of these systems are designated common data. They have the attribute of membership of the common data base. Wherever they appear in the system, they must conform to standards that are set up by the common data base administrator on behalf of the organization as a whole. The common data base approach is advantageous in that important data sets are always represented in the same format and have the same meaning in every part of the organization. Interrelationships between different functions in the organization are therefore facilitated, as are comparisons of cost and performance between different responsibility centers.

Adoption of the common data base approach may cause some initial problems, particularly in terms of managers' perceptions of their responsibilities for administration of data that they have controlled in the past. However, these difficulties can be overcome by careful attention to design and implementation procedures. The advantages derived from the establishment of a body of consistent data central to the operations of the organization normally outweigh the effect of any such difficulties.

Technical design of the data base involves a compromise between the users' desires for immediate access to the information it contains and the technical requirements of efficient operation. This compromise is obtained in practice by the provision of regular and periodic reports in prestructured form (provided by the management reporting system) complemented by the ability to obtain unstructured data on demand (through the information retrieval system). A record of past operations is maintained by the establishment of an historic store of data, consisting of a series of recordings of the content of the data base taken at regular intervals. The practice of storing the contents of the data base regularly during operations is an important safeguard against the loss of organizational information due to system failure, fire or other similar disaster.

The greatest part of the content of the common data base consists of data concerning the resources used by the organization in pursuit of its goals and objectives and the measures relating to the achievement of these goals and objectives. This content consists of both numeric and non-numeric data. The prime use of this data is in operational and management control. The common data base may, however, also contain information arising in the environment of the organization that would be useful in strategic planning. There is, therefore, an important link between the common data base and the data base in the strategic component of the information system.

Administration of the common data base is supported by the data management system. This is normally a complex computer software package that provides facilities for the handling, processing, and transfer of data within the internal information system.

Information flow in an organization may be through either formal or informal channels. The internal information system is concerned with the formal part of this flow. The formal information flow may be in the "vertical" direction between hierarchic levels in the organization or in the "horizontal" direction between individuals and offices at roughly the same level. Information often flows between individuals and offices with the same specialized function. It may flow also between responsibility centers through the formal authority structure. In practical cases, the flow of information usually consists of a mix of both of these, dictated by the style of management adopted in the organization. The flow of information in any particular organization can be illustrated by a combination of two diagrams representing the flow between specialist functions and responsibility centers. This combined diagram can act as a basic model for the internal information system.

At the lower levels of an organization there exists a mass of data, each item of which has a limited and specific significance. As information flows from the lower to the higher levels, it tends to become increasingly summarized and gain in informational content. In this summarization process, individual data elements are aggregated and cannot be recovered in the original form unless steps are undertaken to store them individually as part of the historic store. Aggregation of data can, therefore, result in loss of information. To avoid this loss, unaggregated data should be stored until it is judged to be of no further use.

Aggregation is related to another phenomenon called "uncertainty absorption." This is said to occur when inferences drawn from a body of data are communicated, rather than communicating the body of data itself. The concept of uncertainty absorption is important in the design of an internal information system in that it underscores the necessity for clear and unequivocal data definitions. Uncertainty absorption is of great importance also in dealing with the communication of opinion and other qualitative information, where the views and perceptions of the initiator of a message may be incorporated consciously or unconsciously into its contents.

Before embarking on the installation of an internal information system it is necessary to prepare an overall design, which can form the basis for all work concerning the new system. The first step in implementation is to catalogue and document the system already existing in the organization in terms of its overall design. The extent of the necessary modifications to the existing system to achieve the new operating concept can then be determined. Senior management must be closely involved in this and later stages of the work of design and implementation.

The basic building blocks of the internal information system are the completely specified systems. Successive versions of these systems can be introduced without effect on the logical flow of information in the organization as long as requirements for data at the interface are met. As the implementation proceeds, additional data sets can be admitted progressively to the common data base. Gradual augmentation of the data base (as opposed to an attempt at complete system replacement) provides time for a study of the administrative procedures surrounding the data sets involved. As the data base is built up, the management reporting system can be redesigned and replaced. The information retrieval system can be introduced in the later stages of the implementation.

Successful implementation is dependent above all upon cooperation and communication between managers and information systems specialists. It is usually best that the planning and implementation of the new system be under the overall direction of a manager rather than a technical specialist in computers or information systems. It is also best to leave considerations concerning computer support necessary to operate the new system until such time as a detailed design for the system has been written and agreed upon. In introducing new components during the gradual process of implementation, it is usually wise to allow for a period of parallel operation of both the new and old components in order to avoid any disruption in the event the new systems prove initially unsatisfactory. The data, information, and physical components of the new system should be afforded an appropriate degree of security and confidentiality.

The installation of a new internal information system usually has a major impact on the organization involved. Some managers may feel restricted or displaced by the new development. These feelings may lead to the growth of resistance to the new system and to its operation. Methods for dealing with such resistance consist almost entirely of the adoption of a policy of open communication and briefings concerning the objectives and progress of the new system. Such a policy is often successful in at least partially reducing resistance. However, full acceptance of the new system usually requires commitment and compromise by all concerned.

Discussion Topics

1/ The basic design diagram of an internal information system discussed in this chapter relies upon the common data base concept. Can you think of any other equally acceptable or even preferable basis for the design of an internal system? If so what would be its characteristics? If not, what are potential disadvantages of the common data base concept?

2/ The completely specified systems are the building blocks of the internal information system. To what extent can such systems remain under the semiautonomous control of functional specialists in an internal information system? What are the advantages and disadvantages of such independent management of these systems?

3/ In building a common data base, responsibility for administration of the member data sets can exist in one location only. What difficulty is this likely to cause during implementation and how might such difficulty be resolved?

4/ What would you include in the job description of the data base administrator? What experience and qualifications would you require in selecting a person for this job?

5/ The common data base can be built up progressively as the implementation proceeds. Where and how would you start this process? Make an attempt to draft some of the regulations and procedures that the data base administrator might require various systems to adopt during the creation of the common data base.

6/ How would you go about redesigning and implementing a management reporting system? Under what circumstances would you add to or delete from the content of an existing reporting system?

7/ You are charged with the responsibility of setting up the historic store of information for the organization in which you work. Write a summary of the policies and procedures that you would institute to ensure that important data sets are preserved in the store. How would you keep storage costs within acceptable limits?

8/ What information contained in the common data base is likely to be useful in strategic planning? What should be the link between the internal information system and its strategic counterpart in an organization?

9/ What is the relationship between "vertical" flow of information between responsibility centers and similar flow within specialized functions? How can the need for these two types of information flow be accommodated within an internal information system?

10/ To what extent are aggregation and uncertainty absorption necessary in an organization? What are the dangers associated with overuse of these techniques in the design of the information flow within an internal information system and how can these pitfalls be avoided?

11/ Why is it desirable to compare the existing information system in an organization with the chosen basic design before embarking on implementation? Under what circumstances would existing components be left in operation during and after an implementation?

12/ Why is it necessary that senior management be involved in the design and implementation planning of an internal information system? What can happen if this involvement is not achieved? What steps can be taken to ensure that senior management continues to be informed and involved throughout the implementation?

13/ Why should implementation of an internal information system be under the overall direction of a manager rather than being run by a computer or information systems specialist? What type of manager would you advise the head of an organization to choose to oversee the implementation job? What would be his or her main strengths and characteristics?

14/ Considerations of computer support are best left until a detailed design of the system has been written. Why is this so? What problems can arise if the design of a system is based on a preference for a particular type of computer?

15/ Suppose that you are assigned to safeguard the physical security and the confidentiality of the internal information system and the data it contains. List the steps you would take and the procedures you would implement to this end.

16/ What are the main causes of the discontent and resistance that sometimes accompany the installation of a new information system? How can the effects of such resistance be minimized? Prepare a plan for ensuring that these difficulties will have a minimum effect on the implementation of the system for which you have responsibility.

17/ What human and behavioral factors are most important in the design of an internal information system? What effects can the neglect of these factors have on the operation of the system once it is implemented?

18/ How can it be ensured that both the costs and benefits of the system are taken into account at all stages in the design and implementation of a new system? What do you feel are the major categories of cost and benefit that should be considered?

19/ How can the element of risk be minimized or eliminated in the implementation of an information system?

20/ In what ways do you think the internal information system contributes to communication within an organization? Is it possible that a new system could restrict communication? If so, how can that possibility be avoided?

CASE WORK

The Acme Merchandising Company of Canada Limited

The Acme Merchandising Company is a major fictitious company specializing in retail distribution of consumer goods in Canada and across the border into the northern United States. The company headquarters are in Toronto. Branch offices are located in 15 cities in Canada. The largest offices are in Montreal, Vancouver, and Halifax. The company employs 6,600 persons, about 800 of which are located at each of the two major branches in Montreal and Vancouver. Approximately 1,600 persons are employed in Toronto at company headquarters and in the main company distribution center.

Acme was formed two years ago by the merger of a number of small companies. The president stated at the time of the merger that, as far as possible, operations of the new company would be under decentralized control. Procedures that had served efficiently in the past would not be altered simply for the sake of change. He said, however, that he would concern himself with the efficiency of procedures for handling the very large number of monthly transactions that arose in the administration of the new company. Accordingly, he decided to authorize the design and implementation of an internal information system to ensure that these important operations could be carried out efficiently and promptly.

In a directive describing the project, the president envisaged a system in which all company accounting procedures, financial reporting budgets, facility usage, product distribution, inventory, and personnel records would be processed on a large computer located in Toronto. Regional offices would have remote terminal connections into the central computer. He reported that a firm of consultants had been hired to undertake the overall direction of the design and implementation of the new system. Members of this consulting firm would form the largest part of a project team charged with carrying out the work of converting from the existing procedures to the new system. The project would be completed within two years of the starting date. There were good reasons for the time limit in terms of other company developments. At the start, two years seemed to be plenty of time.

Minor data processing operations were already in being at the head office in Toronto and at the branch offices in Montreal and Vancouver. These operations had been developed locally and utilized a variety of equipment and techniques. Staff members from the head office and from these branches were drafted temporarily into the project team formed to implement the new system. This personnel shift caused some disruption of the ongoing operations. Complaints were received from customers. The complaints were answered in part by a publicity release about the new system and a description of its many advantages over existing procedures.

The newly formed project team set to work and spent the first three months visiting the regional branch offices. Information obtained during these visits was incorporated into a detailed description of the new system to be installed. In keeping with the policy outlined by the president, changes in procedures were to be kept to a minimum. If data from any one branch was in a form different from that in use in other parts of the company, it would be retained in that form at the branch and converted into a standard company form before being entered into the central computer. Outputs from the computer would be converted back into the local form before distribution to the branch concerned. A detailed description was presented to the president seven months after the start of the project.

The project description was accepted by the president who decided to obtain bids from manufacturers for the needed hardware. Bids were received from seven firms. Analysis of the bids showed one firm clearly superior. This firm was introducing a new line of computers which would provide a three-fold increase in processing speed at a somewhat lower cost. This firm also promised more support than the other bidders. A proposal embodying the analysis was approved by the Board of Directors and the hardware contract was signed. Ten months had passed. The equipment was to be installed in Toronto in six months time, eight months before the implementation deadline. The hardware company offered considerable amounts of free time on earlier types of computers, which were said to be compatible to the new line, for the testing of the new computer programs as they were written. With fourteen months to go, the project team began the detailed work of writing the computer programs. Somewhere around this point in time, things started to go wrong.

The work involved in converting the input data from the branch offices into a standard form was much more than had been estimated. In fact, when taking into consideration all the work of conversion, the computer that had been ordered could not handle the load. An amendment to the contract was negotiated allowing for a more powerful computer at a 35% increase in cost. Programming was a larger task than had been estimated and twelve contract programmers had to be hired at an additional cost of $420,000. After the initial setbacks, the work proceeded smoothly until new legislation was enacted that required changes in the basic financial operation of the company. Many of the programs that had already been written therefore needed to be changed.

With five months remaining before the implementation date, the senior members of the project team toured the branch offices to explain the procedures involved in changing over to the new system. They were shocked to find that very little preparation had been made in these offices. In fact, some of the branch offices were in the course of preparing new versions of their existing procedures. The project team even encountered some resistance from the local managers who said they preferred their existing methods to a new computer system of which they had very little knowledge. A hasty program of training and briefing of local personnel was prepared to counteract these attitudes.

On returning to Toronto, the project team found a letter awaiting them from the computer suppliers saying that unforeseen difficulties had delayed the software for the new computer by eight months—it would not be ready until after the implementation date. A less capable software system would be delivered with the hardware, but this would severely limit the scope of the operations that would be possible. To make matters worse, three of the senior computer programmers on the team received offers from another company at a salary that Acme did not wish to match.

With two months to go, trials were started on the newly installed equipment. Problems with converting the input data were so great that the results of trials were fragmentary and inconclusive. Only the most optimistic members of the project team thought that the system could now be made to work by the agreed implementation date. The situation was explained to the president in a long meeting. Over $1.5 million had been spent. The project team was disheartened as the required implementation date approached.

The above history is only a very brief description of the events involved in the Acme Company's experience with information systems implementation. Using your imagination to fill in any gaps in the story, write an analysis of the problems experienced by Acme and suggest how at least some of these problems might have been avoided.

5

Strategic Information

Introduction

The information contained in the internal information system is primarily concerned with routine administration and day-to-day operations within the organization. The internal information system is used, for the most part, to support the managerial activities of operational and management control. The output from this internal system was compared earlier in the text with the reports that the captain of a ship receives from the engine room, the purser's office, and other points within the ship. These reports contain information concerning the operation and administration of the ship's internal services.

There is, however, another category of information essential to the decision-making activities of an organization. This information consists of reports on both the internal and external environments of the organization. As discussed in Chapter 2, this category includes information concerning the characteristics of the participants and other elements within the external and internal environments. It is used to support the management activity of strategic planning and facilitates the choice of objectives and the selection of future courses of action. In terms of the ship analogy this information can be compared with the reports submitted to the captain by the officers and lookouts scanning the vicinity of the ship for information and developments that may require a change of course.

Information of this sort has been called "strategic intelligence" by Sherman Kent.[1] His use of this particular term reflects his background in military and political affairs. Harold L. Wilensky later referred to the same type of information in the government and industrial environment as "organizational intelligence." [2] We will use the term *strategic information* in this text; first, to stress the relationship of information of this sort to strategic planning and, second, to emphasize the distinction between strategic information and the more tactical information that forms the major part of the content of the internal information system.

The Nature of Strategic Information

Much of the background material upon which the study of the acquisition and use of strategic information in modern organizations is based is derived from military and political affairs. The question arises as to whether experience in the military and political fields is truly useful, and not misleading, when applied to the needs of organizations operating in other areas. One immediate difference between the two types of activity is that disputes between nations may have consequences that are much more grave and far-reaching than the consequences of any similar situation which the average modern organization might encounter. On the other hand, all such situations involve a conflict between the interests and objectives of the parties concerned. The major differences between disputes in the political or military arenas and those in the organizational or individual spheres involve the magnitude of the stakes and the means available to resolve the conflict. In all other aspects, the basic characteristics of the two types of situations are very similar. Accordingly, we will draw on experience from the military and political fields in the following discussion wherever it appears appropriate and desirable.

It is interesting to note in the current context that studies of the politics of ancient Greece reveal that the leaders in those times were very interested in any information concerning the political intentions of their neighbors. Matters such as the danger of war, the nature of alliances, internal divisions in competing states, and the characteristics

1 Kent, Sherman, *Strategic Intelligence,* Archon Books, 1965, p. 7. (First published in 1949 by Princeton University Press).

2 Wilensky, Harold L., *Organizational Intelligence,* Basic Books, 1967.

of the opposing leaders were considered to be of very great importance to those involved in setting the objectives and courses of action of any particular state.[3] There is also evidence that not only the capabilities and intentions of the potential opposition but also geographic information concerning roads and potential invasion routes were the subject of deliberate investigation by those involved. The considerations of interest in the competition between organizations are actually very similar. The danger of war is analogous to the possibility of increased open competition. The nature of alliances corresponds to the characteristics of the mergers and coalitions in which an organization is involved or with which the organization competes. Internal divisions among the staff of competitors and the characteristics of opposing leaders are clearly of as much interest today as they were in ancient times. By the same token, present-day organizations often carry out deliberate studies of their opposition's capabilities, marketing strategies, and potential areas of operation.

The need for strategic information in the organizational context was raised by D. Ronald Daniel in 1961.[4] He wrote concerning the need for "competitive" information, in addition to the more commonly available material generated during the routine operation and administration of an organization. The term "competitive information" was taken to include detailed information concerning the characteristics of competitors, their marketing strategies, and any innovations or unconventional courses of action that they might adopt. In a later survey of the "external" information required by managers in a number of industrial firms, the major areas of strategic information were listed as (a) current activities in the market and the competitive field, (b) pending technological developments and, (c) leads concerning possible acquisitions, joint ventures, or mergers.[5]

Strategic information can be considered conveniently in four categories:[6] (a) the characteristics of the participants in the decision situation, such as their intentions, objectives, values, and power to

[3] Starr, Chester, *Political Intelligence in Classical Greece,* Lugduni Batavorum, E. J. Brill, 1974, p. 30.

[4] Daniel, D. Ronald, "Management Information Crisis," *Harvard Business Review,* Sept.–Oct. 1961, pp. 111–121.

[5] Aguilar, Francis Joseph, *Scanning the Business Environment,* MacMillan, 1967, p. 41.

[6] Radford, K. J., *Complex Decision Problems: an Integrated Strategy for Resolution,* Reston 1977, Chapter 2.

influence the outcome of the situation; (b) social elements of the environment, including any laws, policies, precedents, or widely-held values that might influence the behavior of the participants in the decision situation; (c) technological elements of the environment, including any physical, economic, organizational, or human engineering factors that might affect the practicality of the courses of action available to the participants; and (d) natural and "quasi-natural" events and phenomena that might affect the environment of the decision situation. Quasi-natural events and phenomena are those that are essentially man-made (such as the state of the stock market at any given time) but which, for all intents and purposes, can be treated as occurring naturally.

The extent to which information of a strategic nature is gathered by an organization depends largely upon the orientation of the individuals working in the organization and the type of situation in which they are involved. Some of the above information may be available through the internal information system of the organization. For example, details of some of the technological elements of the environment may be contained in data sets within the completely specified systems or in the historic store. This information obtained through past experience in similar situations may be of use as a whole or in part within the new decision problem. The internal information system also contains a great deal of information concerning the characteristics of the organization of which it is a part. The organization's own internal information system is, therefore, a source of information on the characteristics of at least one of the participants in the decision situation under consideration.

Three basic forms of strategic information are generally gathered by an individual or an organization in the attempt to satisfy the demand for strategic information. The three forms are (a) the *basic descriptive* form, which provides a general overview of a subject drawn from past history (b) the *current reportorial* form, providing information by which the basic description of a subject can be updated in the light of current developments; and (c) the *speculative-evaluative* form, in which opinions concerning the inferences and possible implications of the current strategic information are reported.

The basic descriptive form of strategic information is essentially encyclopedic in nature. It might consist, for example, of a written survey of the characteristics of an individual, giving details of his or her past behavior, likes and dislikes, and standing within an organization. Such a survey would, no doubt, contain information regarding the objectives, values, and preferences of the individual concerned. It should be noted in passing that it is entirely ethical to make or commission studies of individuals who may be major participants (or who may represent major participants) in an important decision situation. A distinction must be drawn, however, between collection and collation of openly available information and the other less ethical or actually illegal practices by which information concerning individuals might be gathered.

Strategic information in the basic descriptive form might also consist of a description of an organization that is actually or potentially a participant in a decision situation. This description might cover such items as the financial state of the organization, its strengths and weaknesses in terms of personnel and its present and potential share of the market. On the other hand, strategic information in the basic descriptive form might describe the current state of a technological development and its applicability to the current decision situation. The exact format of this type of strategic information in any particular case would depend primarily on the style and working habits of the individual collecting the information and the desires of those for whom it is being collected. Descriptive information might take the form of an essay, or a compendium of detailed notes and data or it may consist simply of a file of clippings and memoranda.

Information collected and presented in the basic descriptive form is a record of the characteristics of the organizations, individuals, events, and phenomena described up to a given point in time. These characteristics are constantly changing, however, and the record must, therefore, be modified and augmented continuously to take account of any changes occurring after the original survey was made. Strategic information collected for the purpose of updating existing records or for establishing a record on a new development falls into the current reportorial category. Information in this form is often fragmentary. Just as one is only rarely in a position to actually see a fish jump out of the water when fishing, collectors of strategic information are seldom in the fortunate position of concentrating their attention on an area at the precise moment at which an unexpected change occurs. Available resources are not usually sufficient to cover simultaneously all areas in which changes might occur. Collection of strategic information in the current reportorial form is, therefore, more concerned with symptoms than with complete descriptions. Knowledge of the general direction of change is often as important as detailed information and may, in practice, be the only sort of information that can be detected in the limited time available before action must be taken by the participant concerned.

The speculative-evaluative form is the most complex type of strategic information. It consists of a record of the inferences drawn by an individual or individuals from information collected in the two other forms. Individuals preparing this sort of strategic information use their judgement, experience, and, sometimes, their prejudices in interpreting the "meaning" of what has been observed. The result is often in the form of an estimate of the likely future course of events. In this regard, the preparation of strategic information in the speculative-evaluative form is an activity similar to technological forecasting,[7] although this latter technique is usually associated solely with estimates drawn from quantitative data.[8]

Strategic information in the speculative-evaluative form is necessarily subjective, in that the views and opinions of the individuals preparing it are often incorporated into the information to some extent. This form is essentially communicated and interpreted information. Uncertainty absorption may have taken place during its preparation. It is necessary, therefore, that the source, date, and author of the information be attached to it, in order that these qualifying specifics may be made available to the recipient. This may aid him or her in reaching an opinion as to the information's validity and applicability to the decision situation in question. Confirmation of such information from two or more unrelated sources is an important factor in establishing the validity of the message contained and avoiding the possible consequences of taking action on unsubstantiated information and rumor.[9]

Strategic information has two general uses in organizations involved in the complex decision problems that arise in the turbulent and dynamic environment of the modern world. The first use is in problem detection. Continuous scanning of the environment for symptoms of change is essential to preventing an organization from either missing an opportunity or being caught off guard. What is required is

[7] Kent, Sherman, *Strategic Intelligence,* p. 8 ff.

[8] Martino, Joseph P., *Technological Forecasting for Decision Making,* American Elsevier, 1972.

[9] Starr, Chester, *Political Intelligence,* p. 32.

an "early-warning system" that provides information to the individuals responsible during the very early stages of formation of a decision problem.[10]

The concept of strategic planning is often taken to refer to activities over a long time period. There is, however, an equally important aspect of strategic planning that is concerned with the extremely short term. This aspect concerns the avoidance of surprise arising from a "strategic discontinuity." [11] A strategic discontinuity may arise from a sudden, unfamiliar and surprising change in the environment in which an organization is operating. Such discontinuities may, for example, be in the form of an unexpected shortage of a vital resource or a surprise move by a competitor. Changes of this nature may constitute a threat to the organization or may offer a unique opportunity. They usually precipitate a crisis of some sort. It is interesting to note in this connection that the symbol in the Chinese language for crisis is very similar to that for opportunity.

The second use for strategic information is in the estimation of (a) future courses of action available to participants in a decision situation and (b) the preferences of various participants for the outcomes that would result from the adoption of one or more of their available courses of action.[12] Much of the speculative-evaluative form of strategic intelligence used in complex decision situations is employed in the preparation of estimates of this nature. Combinations of courses of action available to participants form the possible future scenarios or outcomes. Estimation of the preferences of the various participants for possible outcomes is an essential activity in assessment of the strategic structure of a decision situation. These estimates also play an important part in the process of communication, negotiation, and bargaining that precedes resolution of the decision problem.

In order to be useful in these activities, strategic information must have certain characteristics. For example, the information must be clear, concise, and as unequivocal as possible, so that it can be readily understood by those who use it. It must be timely, inasmuch as information received after an opportunity for action has passed is

[10] Friend, J. K., and W. N. Jessop, *Local Government and Strategic Choice,* Tavistock Publications, 1969, p. 275.

[11] Ansoff, H. Igor, "Managing Strategic Surprise by Response to Weak Signals," *California Management Review,* vol. 18, no. 2, Winter 1975, pp. 21–33.

[12] Radford, K. J., *Complex Decision Problems,* Chapter 3.

worthless, at least as far as the opportunity in question is concerned. The information must be consistent and reliable, in the sense that independent observers with diverse backgrounds and experience can agree on its interpretation and evaluation. In addition, strategic information should be wide-ranging, covering as many aspects of the topic as possible and avoiding over-concentration on any one aspect at the expense of others.[13] It is not often that all the above characteristics are met in practice at the same time. However, they describe the ideal type of strategic information required to support the managerial activities in a modern organization.

The consequences of not possessing appropriate strategic information can be as disastrous for an organization engaged in business as for a country whose vital interests are attacked. The element of surprise has long been regarded as an essential part of military strategy.[14] It plays a similar role in confrontations between organizations. Neglect of the strategic information component of the overall information system is, therefore, a major reason why organizations succumb to change or are unable to take advantage of the opportunity that changing conditions offer. This aspect of the role of strategic information will be taken up later in this chapter following a detailed consideration of the sources of strategic information and its acquisition and interpretation.

The Search for Information

Study of the manner in which information is gathered in an organization has stemmed in recent years from the writings of Herbert A. Simon and others on the subject of organizational and managerial behavior in decision making.[15] In these writings, the authors pointed out the inapplicability of the model of decision making in which "economic man" is assumed to possess all information pertaining to a question in advance of the choice between alternatives. In the language of Chapter 3, many decision problems are not completely specifiable because the information available concerning them is incomplete. In these circumstances, organizational decision makers are

[13] Wilensky, Harold L., *Organizational Intelligence,* pp. viii–ix.

[14] Liddell-Hart B., *Strategy: the Indirect Approach,* Faber & Faber, 1965.

[15] March, J. G., and Herbert A. Simon, *Organizations,* Wiley, 1958.

observed to search for information that may be of assistance in the process of choice. The information sought may relate to new alternative courses of action or to those that are known to exist. The search for information continues throughout the decision-making process, within the limits imposed by the availability of time and resources. For this reason, information gathering is shown as a continuous process in the more recent depiction of the decision process illustrated in Figure 3-5. Intelligence is one of the major activities in decision making. It is a necessary accompaniment to the other components of the decision process, namely assessment of the strategic structure of the decision situation and interaction among the participants.

Observations of the behavior of those engaged in the search for information have led to a number of theories and assumptions concerning the nature of the search process.[16, 17] These may be summarized as follows:

- *Search is motivated.* The process of search for information is not normally one of routine and continuous scanning of available sources. It is, on the contrary, usually initiated upon recognition of a problem situation, stimulated by the continuing existence of that situation, and suppressed by the appearance of a real or apparent means of resolution of the problem.
- *Search is simple minded.* The initial direction of search is toward the neighborhood of the observed symptoms and the currently proposed means of resolving the situation. There is little inclination to investigate areas that do not seem to be immediately connected with the observed symptoms. Furthermore, search is often concentrated around courses of action that have long been considered desirable by members of the organization. The observed symptoms are sometimes interpreted as an opportunity to implement an already-preferred course of action.[18] When a course of action has been decided upon, search activity becomes more intensive and concentrated as the time for implementation approaches.

[16] Cyert, R. M. and J. G. March, *A Behavioral Theory of the Firm,* Prentice-Hall, 1963, pp. 79–80 and pp. 120–122.

[17] Ference, Thomas P., "Organizational Communications Systems and the Decision Process," *Management Science,* vol. 17, No. 2, Oct. 1970, pp. B83–96.

[18] For example, see the discussion of the faith held in strategic bombing in Harold L. Wilensky, *Organizational Intelligence,* pp. 24–34.

More complex search behavior is usually adopted only if the simpler process does not provide a satisfactory result. Even then, alternatives are normally investigated sequentially, rather than simultaneously. Search routines that have proved successful in the past are often used in new situations. The most intense search activities usually occur in situations where there is competition for the use of resources or facilities.

- *Search is biased.* The nature of the search process varies, depending on the special training and experience of the individuals or organizational units involved. It may be affected by the hopes and expectations of those involved or by conflicts and communication difficulties between various parts of an organization. It may also be inhibited by rules, policies, and procedures that have been set up for various purposes in the organization concerned.

The nature of the search activity under any particular set of circumstances is closely related to the personal characteristics of the individual or individuals involved.[19] For example, the intensity and duration of the search for information is often a function of the curiosity of a key individual. Symptoms of a problem situation may be assigned different interpretations by different individuals, so that the motivation of those involved to seek out information may vary. Personal desire to bring about what is perceived to be a more desirable situation may stimulate intense search activity in certain individuals. The same effect might also result from a wish to reduce the dissonance experienced as a result of observed symptoms or information that has been presented. For example, an individual receiving news that he or she regards as disturbing often initiates a search for more information to relieve his or her anxiety.

Primary Sources of Strategic Information

Strategic information that is useful in the planning and policy-making activities of an organization can be placed within one of the following four categories: (a) information openly and widely published that is generally accepted as factual by all the participants in

[19] Ebert, R. J., and T. R. Mitchell, *Organizational Decision Processes,* Crane Russak and Co., 1975, pp. 72–74.

a particular decision situation; (b) information that is deliberately provided by one or other of the participants or by an individual or agency that does not appear at the time to be a participant; (c) information that is held completely confidential by participants; and (d) information that is held confidential by a participant but that is available to those representing the participant in a particular decision situation.

Open and widely published information is available through several media, the most common of which are public documents and reports, records of activities and events, newspapers, technical and trade journals, professional publications, and magazines. Such open information may be presented and discussed at professional meetings, trade shows, or industrial conferences. It refers mainly to the technological and natural elements of the environment and, to a lesser extent, to the social elements of the environment as well. Some general information concerning the characteristics of participants may be available in publications such as brokers' research surveys, market surveys, and consultants' reports. However, many such characteristics, and in particular their intentions, objectives, and preferences, are usually held confidential by participants. The various products or services furnished by a competitor also provide an open source of information, in that they can be studied and analyzed to determine their characteristics and the means by which they are produced.

One difficulty in dealing with information published in open publications is the very great amount of such publications that exist today and the great amount of overlap in the subject matter that they contain. In North America alone over half a million papers are published in technical journals each year. The volume of reports produced by governments is probably almost as great.[20] It is not unusual to find a paper of great importance and usefulness in a journal with a theme that appears to be entirely unrelated. For example, a series of papers on gathering strategic information appears in the 1966 volume of the journal *Chemical Engineering*.[21] Abstracting services perform a useful function by reducing the amount of material that must be scanned in order to ensure reasonable coverage of modern developments. How-

[20] The President's Science Advisory Committee, Alvin M. Weinberg, Chairman, *Science, Government and Information,* U.S. Government Printing Office, 10 Jan. 1963.

[21] *Chemical Engineering,* April 25, 1966.

ever, in practical circumstances, only a fraction of the available information can be detected and only a much smaller fraction can be assimilated by those involved in a decision situation.

Some information that appears in open publications or is otherwise openly available may have been deliberately provided by a participant to further his own purposes. In such cases, provision of the information is usually a move in a process of bargaining or negotiation.[22] The information provided may be completely factual or it may contain distortions of the truth designed to benefit the participant initiating the release. The source of such information and the reasons behind its provision may not be immediately apparent. The initiator may design the release so that it appears as information normally available in open channels. He may do this in order to conceal his intentions or his interest in the subject matter.

Information held confidential by participants usually consists of (a) objectives, goals, intentions and plans; (b) details of industrial processes and unpatented designs; (c) characteristics and performance of new products and services; and (d) any other information that the participant considers potentially harmful if revealed. Confidential information of this sort may be contained in documents and records that are protected by a security system. In many cases, the security is provided by a combination lock on a safe or filing cabinet. If the confidential records are part of the internal information system, the security may be provided by access procedures designed into that system.

The contents of the internal information system of a participant provide valuable information on the present state and potential of that participant. This information may be of great importance in determining the feasibility and availability of the contemplated courses of action. It may, therefore, have considerable significance in the strategic activities of the participant. Internal barriers and divisions within a participant may prevent those responsible for strategic planning from obtaining full access to all the information available from internal sources. It is clearly to the advantage of an organization that its strategic plans be based on the best possible assessment of its current potential. Any confidentiality barriers within an organization that hamper such assessments may severely handicap the organization in strategic situations.

[22] Radford, K. J., *Complex Decision Problems,* Chapter 5.

Most authorities agree that material that is openly and widely available is the best source of strategic information in the greatest proportion of cases. Few of us ever come to take part in an espionage operation of such depth and far-reaching consequences as Ultra or to have contact with a master spy.[23] The gathering of strategic information in modern organizations is usually far less spectacular. This activity normally involves constant, detailed, and painstaking work only occasionally relieved by moments of inspiration. The task is sometimes seen as the equivalent of solving a giant jigsaw puzzle, with the pieces of the puzzle presented in random fashion. In many cases, the best sources of strategic information arise from observing the other participants, taking particular notice of their behavior in similar situations in the past.[24] Such information is seldom secret, and observations of this nature can usually be made within the limitations of ethical behavior. The temptation to investigate secret sources of information may be very great on occasion. However, considerable experience shows that the results obtained by a sophisticated analyst working with open information are usually better than those obtained by an undercover agent working with what is apparently top-secret information.[25]

Sources Used by Managers Gathering Strategic Information

In a comprehensive study conducted by F. J. Aguilar, an attempt was made to determine the relative importance to managers of various sources of information concerning the environment external to their organization.[26] A distinction was drawn between "outside" and "inside" sources of information. Outside sources included customers, suppliers, business and professional associates, bankers, merger brokers, consultants, trade shows, publications, and news media. Inside sources were described as subordinates, peers, superiors, and reports available within the organization. A second distinction was made between information communicated personally and that secured by the manager from impersonal and broadly addressed communications.

The detailed findings of this study may not have general applica-

[23] Winterbotham, F. W., *The Ultra Secret,* Dell Publishing Co., 1975.

[24] Wilensky, Harold L., *Organizational Intelligence,* op. cit., p. 72.

[25] Ibid. p. 180.

[26] Aguilar, F. J., *Scanning the Business Environment, op. cit,* pp. 94–96 and 115–117.

bility because the number and type of organizations examined was not large. However, certain of the broader findings, especially those that were supported by significant evidence, may have a general application. For example, an overwhelming majority of managers reported that personal sources of external information greatly exceeded impersonal sources in importance. This indicates that managers place a heavy reliance on their personal networks of communication. Information from subordinates accounted for about half of all the information obtained from inside sources. Such information was estimated to be about a quarter of the total received from all sources. Customers and those having no regular business relationship with the organization were found to be the two most important outside sources of information. Publications were estimated as being the most important impersonal sources of information about the environment external to the organization. Superiors and in-company reports were graded as poor sources of external information.

Other broad conclusions of the study were: (a) managers not in the mainstream of external information rely heavily on peers for this information; (b) senior managers have a high preference for personal sources of external information that are not in regular business communication with the organization; (c) subordinates were seen to be an increasingly important source of external information at each higher level in the organization; (d) the higher their level in the organization, the less managers rely upon obtaining important external information directly from publications; (e) managers in large organizations rely more heavily on internal sources for external information than do managers in smaller organizations; and (f) managers who are relatively inexperienced in their jobs rely more heavily on publications as a source of external information than do those with greater experience in their jobs.

Another interesting aspect of the study concerned whether or not the external information received by managers was solicited. The survey showed that slightly less than half of the information was solicited. Of the solicited information, more than half of it was obtained as a result of an organizational activity as opposed to a direct request by the recipient. In over half of the cases, the presentation of unsolicited information was directed at benefiting someone. The direct beneficiary was most often the recipient of the information, rather than the source. On the other hand, this condition appeared in situations where the transmitter of the information knew the recipient's interests and had some incentive to satisfy his needs. The study also showed that information from outside sources was largely unsolicited, whereas information from inside sources was mainly solicited. In addition, managers appeared to be unreceptive to information supplied by subordinates unless it happened to be the particular information that they were actively seeking at the time.

The most important lesson that can be drawn from this study is that the managers involved who were seeking strategic information placed great reliance on personal contacts and networks of communication. Less reliance was placed on formal organizational sources of strategic information. The findings of the study might well have been different if the organizations surveyed had had a formal strategic information system in operation. Nevertheless, the conclusions reported provide a picture of the situation likely to be encountered at the start of a project to design and implement a strategic information system. The findings of the Aguilar study should, therefore, be given consideration in the design of such a system.

Interpretation of Information

The processes of searching for information and of evaluating what has been gathered are inseparable. They are both intimately affected by the perceptions of the individual involved.[27] A perception may be defined as the immediate result occurring in an individual's mind upon the receipt of some information or stimulus. The process of perception consists of (a) selection or screening of information so that content considered to be irrelevant or disruptive is discarded and (b) ordering the information received in categories so that complex material can be considered in simpler terms.

The perceptions of an individual are a result of a number of factors. Among the most important of these factors are (a) the response of the individual to the information and stimuli received—response to familiar items is usually much quicker than response to unfamiliar material; (b) the nature of the individual's feelings towards the subject to which the information or stimuli refer—things for which one

[27] Shaver, Kelly G., *An Introduction to Attribution Processes,* Winthrop Publishers Inc., 1975.

[28] Ebert, R. J. and T. R. Mitchell, *Organizational Decision Processes, op. cit,* p. 76–77.

has strong feelings are normally recognized more quickly than those that are regarded as less important; (c) an individual's predisposition to a response—the predisposition may be linked both to previous experience and to current needs and expectations; and (d) the nature of the physical environment of the individual.

Perceptions may also be influenced by a number of other characteristics of the individual involved. Some of the more important of these characteristics are (a) aversity or attraction to risk; (b) the acceptable range that has been established in an individual's mind for a particular stimulus (called the "adaptation level"); (c) the goals and objectives adopted by the individual (sometimes called the "aspiration level"); (d) the motivation of the individual to achieve and succeed; and (e) the manner in which an individual thinks and conceptualizes. The process of perception is therefore highly personal and subjective. Any attempt to force ideas on an individual that are contrary to his or her existing perceptions may lead to rejection of the information concerned.

Evidence that the perceptions of individuals are influenced by preconceived ideas is particularly strong.[29] Perceptions of certain individuals tend to become stereotyped in people's minds. The effect of this stereotyping may remain impervious to contrary evidence for long periods of time.[30, 31] A number of conceptual blocks may also affect an individual's treatment of information. These blocks may include (a) *perceptual blocks*—tending to limit the areas in which new information is sought; (b) *cultural and environmental blocks*—resulting from exposure to a particular set of cultural patterns or a particular social or physical environment; (c) *emotional blocks*—arising, for example, from a fear of failure; and (d) *intellectual and expressive blocks*—resulting from an inability to generate ideas and to communicate them to others.[32] The natural result of conceptual blocks is a general diminution in the breadth of vision of an individual and a lessening in his or her creativity.

[29] Holsti, O. R., "Cognitive dynamics and images of the enemy," in J. C. Farrell, and A. P. Smith, eds., *Image and Reality in World Politics,* Columbia University Press, 1967, pp. 16–39.

[30] Wilensky, Harold L., *Organizational Intelligence,* p. 40.

[31] Stoessinger, J. G., *Why Nations Go to War,* St. Martins Press, 1974, for a discussion of the "diabolical enemy" stereotype.

[32] Adams, James L., *Conceptual Blockbusting: a Guide to Better Ideas,* W. H. Freeman and Co., 1974.

Perceptions are also affected when the individual concerned is subjected to stress. The main effects of stress over prolonged periods of time are "increased irritability, subclinical paranoid reactions, heightened suspiciousness, hostility, and increased defensiveness."[33] A mild degree of stress often increases performance and awareness. However, under intense or persistent stress, individuals often revert to more simple perceptual processes. The number and variety of stimuli to which an individual will react are often limited under such conditions. The gap between perceptions and reality tends to widen under stress. Human beings cling even more rigidly to preconceived notions in such circumstances and often act only in accordance with pre-existing premises.[34]

The behavior of those involved in information gathering and interpretation is often different when these activities are carried out in a group rather than individually. Members of groups are sometimes subjected to subtle constraints that prevent them from bringing forward information contrary to the majority opinion in the group. These constraints are often reinforced unconsciously by those in a position to give leadership.[35]

Effort Allocated in Organizations to Activities Concerned With Strategic Information

H. L. Wilensky has described four major determinants of the amount of manpower, time, and money that an organization allocates to activities concerned with strategic information.[36] These determinants are: (a) the degree to which those in the organization feel that competitive forces exist in the external environment in which it operates; (b) the internal condition of the organization; (c) the degree to which the internal operations of the organization are considered to be appropriate to its operations in the external environment; and (d) the size and structure of the organization.

[33] Milburn, T. W., "The Management of Crises," G. F. Herman, ed., *International Crises: Insights from Behavioral Research,* The Free Press, 1972, pp. 259–77.

[34] Holsti, O. R., "Crisis, Stress and Decision Making," *International Social Science Journal,* vol. 23, no. 1, 1971, pp. 53–67.

[35] Janis, Irving L., *Victims of Group-Think,* Houghton-Mifflin, 1972.

[36] Wilensky, Harold L., *Organizational Intelligence,* pp. 10–16.

The first of the four factors mentioned above is a natural determinant of the amount of effort allocated to the acquisition and interpretation of strategic information. The more an organization is engaged in decision situations in which other participants in the environment have objectives and intentions in competition with its own, the more information regarding these participants will be seen to be necessary. At the same time, strategic information concerning the elements of the environment is of vital importance under these conditions. If the members of the organization consider that it is operating in a more placid and static (Type 1 or 2) environment, the priority given to collecting strategic information is likely to be lower. This low information priority may, however, be to the disadvantage of the organization if it causes the members to overlook or ignore changes in the environment toward the more turbulent and dynamic states of Types 3 and 4.

The second determinant is concerned with the relationships between individuals and groups internally within the organization. An organization can be regarded as a coalition composed of individuals and groups of individuals. Each individual and group has objectives and goals that it is seeking to achieve, some of which may be different from, and possibly in conflict with, the goals and objectives of the organization as a whole. Membership in the organization, however, carries with it a commitment to further its goals and objectives. The need to honor this commitment may act, to some extent, to the detriment of the objectives of the member individuals and groups, but seldom to the total exclusion of individual interests. The extent to which organizational goals and objectives are coincident with those of the individuals and groups at any given time determines the cohesiveness of the organization at that time. If the organization is very cohesive and the individuals and groups of which it consists share much the same mind, the need for strategic information concerning the environment within the organization is likely to be small. If cohesiveness is low, however, and there is conflict between factions within the organization, the need for such internal strategic information will be as great as the need for strategic information when conflict arises in the external environment.

One view of the primary objectives of management holds that management must ensure that internal administration and operations in the organization allow it to achieve a balance with its external environment.[37] Wilensky states that the more such a balance is considered achieved and the relationship between the organization and its environment is seen in terms of discernible, predictable relationships between elements, the greater will be the tendency to collect information about the environment. This statement may seem in contradiction to the description of his first determinant. However, the statement there refers more to the target of investigations rather than the overall amount. Wilensky's contention is rather that organizations in balance with their environment seem to move towards collection of large amounts of technical, economic, legal, and scientific information. An organization that is not in balance, on the other hand, tends to be more concerned with the characteristics of other participants and the nature of possible natural events and phenomena.

The size and structure of an organization both influence the way in which the effects of the other three determinants just considered manifest themselves. For example, larger organizations generally collect more strategic information than smaller ones. This may be because larger organizations normally have greater resources. The effort devoted to gathering and interpreting strategic information may, therefore, represent a smaller proportion of the total resources. At the same time, there is usually much more informal communication among members of a smaller organization. The need for formal systems for collecting and treating strategic information may, therefore, be less. In addition, smaller organizations are often more closely knit and have less internal dissension and conflict. For this reason, also, the formal allocation of resources to strategic information activities is often given less priority in a smaller organization.

Examples of Inadequate Use of Strategic Information

There has been increasing interest in recent years in analyzing, in retrospect, situations in which available strategic information has been either ignored entirely or not used to its full potential. Most of the situations that have been analyzed refer to military and political events, possibly because there is generally more information available about such events. For example, detailed studies have been conducted in one form or another of the attack on Pearl Harbor,[38] the German

[37] Smith, P. B., *Groups within Organizations,* Harper and Row, 1973, p. 50.

[38] Wohlstetter, Roberta, *Pearl Harbor: Warning and Decision,* Stanford University Press, 1962.

attack on Russia in 1941,[39] the airborne descent on Arnhem in 1944,[40] the defense of Dien Bien Phu,[41] and the start of the Yom Kippur war in 1973.[42] A basic outline of each of these events is familiar to most readers who remember the news stories of the time or who have read of them in historical or popular articles.

Situations of this nature in which private corporations have been involved have often been found to be very similar to the more public political and military events. They are, of course, less significant on a national or world scale. They may, however, be just as beneficial or catastrophic to a corporation as military events can be for a nation. Records of such events in the private sector are more difficult to find than those of their public counterparts. Corporations appear less willing to publish records of their mistakes for understandable reasons. Corporations may also be more able to keep embarrassing details confidential, although accounts of situations involving misuse of strategic information in private corporations are published occasionally.[43, 44] In the corporate field, as elsewhere, disasters and failures seem to attract more attention and investigation than successes and, therefore, provide us with some of our best insights into corporate workings. Perhaps this is an unavoidable result of our desire to learn from past mistakes. The concentration here upon information failures as causes of disasters is not, therefore, intended to in any way suggest that strategic information is not used successfully in a wide range of situations.

There is one common thread that runs through most, if not all, of the descriptions of situations in which there has been "a failure in the area of strategic information." This thread is that at least a portion of the strategic information needed to avert disaster has been available or obtainable within the organization affected. For example, full details of the nature and timing of the Japanese attack were available to U.S. intelligence sources. The British were fully informed of the concentration of German Panzer Divisions around Arnhem. Stalin had several warnings of the exact nature and timing of the German attack.

39 Whaley, Barton, *Codeword Barbarossa,* MIT Press, 1973.

40 Ryan, Cornelius, *A Bridge Too Far,* Simon and Schuster, 1974.

41 Fall, Bernard B., *Hell in a Very Small Place,* J. B. Lippincott Co., 1966.

42 Ben-Zvi, A., "Hindsight and Foresight: A Conceptual Framework for the Analysis of Surprise Attacks," *World Politics,* vol. 28, no. 3, Apr. 1976, pp. 381–395.

43 Argenti, J., "Corporate Planning and Corporate Collapse," *Long Range Planning,* vol. 9, no. 6, December 1976, pp. 12–18.

44 Smith, R. A., *Corporations in Crisis,* Doubleday and Co., Anchor Books edition, 1966.

In each of these cases, and in many other similar situations, available strategic information went unheeded.

A similar conclusion has been drawn in an analysis of three recent civilian disasters in the United Kingdom. The first of these three disasters occurred in 1966 when a portion of a huge coal mine tailings pile at Aberfan in Wales slid down a mountainside and engulfed a school. The second disaster occurred in 1968 at Hixon when a very long road transporter was hit by an express train at an automatically-controlled rail crossing. The third incident involved a fire in a holiday leisure complex at Douglas, Isle of Man in 1973. In each of the three cases, the disaster-causing situation developed over a considerable period of time, during which a great deal of strategic information concerning the situation was collected and analyzed. The general conclusion of the analysis of these three disasters is that "disaster-provoking events tend to accumulate because they have been overlooked or misinterpreted. . . ."[46] During the period of accumulation, considerable amounts of information were available in each case that could have been used to detect the impending disaster situation and initiate steps aimed at averting it.

Causes of Strategic Information Failures

Apparent reasons for the neglect of vital strategic information in practical circumstances fall into three categories: (a) failure to identify information that is significant; (b) failure to interpret correctly the meaning and significance of information that has been acquired; and (c) failure to communicate significant information to those with the power to act in time to take necessary actions.

One of the most common causes of the failure to identify information of vital significance is that such information is normally encountered in disordered fragments intermingled with large amounts of other information referring to a wide variety of subjects. There is normally no annotation attached to the vital data that draws attention to its significance. If the importance of such information is detected at the time of its receipt, it is usually only as a result of the interpretative action of a particularly sophisticated and alert observer.

45 Ryan, Cornelius, *A Bridge Too Far, op. cit.*, pp. 144 ff.

46 Turner, Barry A., "The Organizational and Inter-Organizational Development of Disasters," *Administrative Science Quarterly*, vol. 21, Sept. 1976, pp. 378–397.

It is, of course, much easier to detect and distinguish vital signals in a body of strategic information in retrospect. Knowledge of later happenings causes information signalling significant future events to stand out when it is examined with the advantage of hindsight. At the time of their receipt, however, the vital signals are usually competing for attention with many other signals that seem to be of equal importance. These competing signals constitute a form of noise surrounding the vital information and distracting attention away from it.[47] Quantities of noise, particularly signals concerning other potentially significant problems, tend to act as decoys that draw attention away from the information that later turns out to have been vital.[48]

Attention is sometimes diverted away from significant information by the intentional creation of noise and decoys by a competitor. The elaborate pattern of deception and false reports created by the Allied Command prior to the Normandy invasion in 1944 provides an excellent example of this phenomenon. Its counterpart in the business world lies in practices such as the issuing of many diverse unrelated publicity releases prior to the introduction of a major innovation or the conclusion of a merger.

A second and equally common failure in the use of strategic information is misinterpretation or misperception of its content. Those involved in decision situations act in accordance with their subjective perceptions of the meaning of the information available. As noted earlier in this chapter, individuals, particularly those under stress, tend to interpret information according to preconceived ideas. They may attempt to fit new information to existing theories and convictions. They may ignore, reinterpret, or reconstruct any information that does not conform to these theories and convictions.[49] Nonconforming information is often required "to meet higher standards of evidence and to pass stricter tests to gain acceptance than new information that supports existing expectations."[50]

Examples of preconceptions affecting interpretation of information and influencing plans for action abound in military affairs: "The Germans cannot take the Belgian forts" in World War I; "Singapore will

[47] Wohlstetter, Roberta, *Pearl Harbor, op. cit,* p. 387.

[48] Turner, Barry A., "Development of Disasters," *op. cit,* p. 388.

[49] Holsti, O. R., "Cognitive Dynamics," *op. cit,* p. 30.

[50] George, A. L. and R. Smoke, *Deterrence in American Foreign Policy,* Columbia University Press, 1974, p. 574.

not be attacked by land" in World War II; and "The Viet Minh cannot deploy artillery on the high points" at Dien Bien Phu; to cite a few. There are many counterparts of these beliefs in business and industrial experience. It is a chilling thought that many of the conceptions that we hold unshakable today may be proved wrong tomorrow.

Sometimes a competitor will cultivate convenient misinterpretation of information and misconceptions in others by a pattern of deliberate deception. Several authors have suggested that Stalin was deliberately led to believe that any attack on the USSR in 1941 would be preceded by a formal ultimatum.[51, 52] Speeches to troops giving false information that would eventually be reported to the enemy by spies were apparently used in ancient times as a means of deception and reinforcement of the enemy's existing perceptions.[53] A skillful businessman can produce the same effect in a competitor during the course of a luncheon without actually even offering false information.

Another common reason why available strategic information is not used is failure in communications. For example, even when the danger to Pearl Harbor was clearly recognized, considerable delays occurred in communicating this information to important decision makers. The result was that the alert arrived at the scene hours after the attack.[54] Failure in communications can occur even when the intended recipient is immediately at hand, if he or she is unwilling to devote the necessary attention to the information transmitted. Aguilar found that vital information known within an organization is often not used because recipients "would not listen" to entreaties by subordinates to consider what they thought to be vital information.[55] In many cases, this rejection of information may have been due to the fact that the information was not presented in a form that was acceptable or attractive to the recipient. The importance of proper preparation and packaging of the output from a strategic information system should, therefore, not be underestimated. Even if the information presented to the recipient is vital to his activities he may "screen it out because it does not fit his preconceptions, because it has come through a suspicious or poorly regarded channel, because it is embedded in piles of inaccurate or

[51] Jervis, R., *The Logic of Images in International Relations,* Princeton University Press, 1970, p. 26.

[52] Whaley, Barton, *Codeword Barbarossa, op. cit,* pp. 240–244.

[53] Starr, Chester, *Political Intelligence, op. cit.,* p. 14.

[54] Wohlstetter, Roberta, *Pearl Harbor, op. cit,* p. 310.

[55] Aguilar, F. J., *Scanning Business Environment, op. cit,* p. 116.

useless messages, or simply because too many messages are transmitted to him."[56]

Failures of communication sometimes occur between members of an organization and those who are not regarded as being part of that organization. In two of the cases discussed by Turner, "individuals outside the principal organizations concerned had foreseen the danger that led to the disaster and had complained, only to meet with a high-handed or dismissive response."[57] These informants and the information that they had to offer were ignored because "it was automatically assumed that the organizations knew better than outsiders" about the situations with which they were dealing.

A further example of lack of communication of strategic information sometimes occurs when a number of groups work together on the resolution of a complex problem. It may be that each of the groups has a base of information somewhat different from that of the others. Each, therefore, has a different appreciation of the problem at hand. Lack of communication prevents a reconciliation of these differences. Each group then constructs its own set of theories explaining the observed phenomena and events and reaches its own conclusion about what needs to be done. It may be possible for a number of groups to work together under these conditions, as long as the cooperation required is not very great. However, if a truly concerted effort is needed, coordination of the work of the individual groups is likely to be difficult, if not impossible, due to the lack of agreement between them concerning the information basic to the situation.

Many failures to use strategic information effectively appear to be inherent in the structure of large, complex organizations and in the hierarchy that may surround information gathering and processing in these organizations.[58] Complex organizations require a hierarchical structure in order to control and motivate staff members. As information passes from point to point in this structure it may become distorted as staff members unconsciously report inferences rather than raw data to others. At the same time, there exists the possibility of deliberate distortion and blocking of information by persons who have their own motives for such acts. The degree of specialization required of personnel in large organizations often results in rivalries between different

[56] Wilensky, Harold L., *Organizational Intelligence, op. cit,* p. 41.

[57] Turner, Barry A., "Development of Disasters," *op. cit,* p. 388.

[58] Wilensky, Harold L., *Organizational Intelligence, op. cit,* p. 179.

subunits and sectors. Such friction provides conditions under which information distortion and blocking often flourish.

Activities involving strategic information are sometimes surrounded by a screen of secrecy far more elaborate than is needed to protect the interests of the organization concerned. This screen of secrecy often allows those engaged in gathering and interpreting strategic information to operate in a manner that is different from the rest of the organization.[59] In some cases, the personnel involved lose sight of the overall objectives and interests of the organization and operate in a world bounded by the limits of the security network that they have constructed. Conditions such as these often lead to distortions in the output of the strategic information activity. Similar distortion may occur due to the type of personnel attracted to working under conditions of heavy secrecy and security. Such excessive security conditions also tend to encourage less discussion and less consideration of deviant views than is desirable in the interpretation of strategic information. Under these conditions, executives may bypass the parts of the organization that have been specially established to deal with strategic information and seek to acquire their information firsthand from personal networks of their own. Whereas this may be a successful alternative in some cases, it leads in others to a situation in which the executive concerned remains unfamiliar with any vital information that originates outside his personal sphere of operations.

The above conditions leading to the distortion of strategic information are usually more prevalent in organizations that have been established for some time without having been revitalized by effective reorganization. Newly established organizations are less likely to experience such conditions. Newer organizations usually have more open channels of communications among individuals and components as well as a more flexible management structure.

Foresight

If there is one gift that, if available, would be most devoutly desired by all those who must make decisions, it is the gift of foresight. Foresight is derived from an understanding of existing conditions. Foresight implies a depth of understanding of existing conditions that is such as to "give us some grasp of the novelty which is about to produce

[59] Kent, Sherman, *Strategic Intelligence, op. cit,* p. 168.

a measurable influence on the immediate future." [60] When the Ford Motor Company designed the Edsel, a basic premise for the design was that a high proportion of the North American public preferred large cars. However, the company did not foresee that between the times of design and marketing, public preferences were to swing toward smaller cars. Not realizing that the small-car "novelty" was to become a long-term trend, the company went ahead with production of the Edsel, with results that were nearly disastrous for Ford.

In most organizational settings, "existing conditions" are defined in terms of a set of commonly accepted beliefs about the organization itself, other organizations, and the environment in which the organization operates. In normal circumstances, these conditions are sufficiently understood within the organization to enable it to survive in its environment. The activities of the organization are governed by adherence to a set of normative prescriptions that are based on its beliefs. If any of these norms are violated, the consequences of the violation are taken as evidence suggesting the need for a modification of the beliefs or of the norms. The continued readjustment of these factors allows the organization to achieve its objectives, at least in some part. This readjustment process is analogous to the steering of the ship by the captain, and is a basic function of management and operational control.

Failure of foresight occurs when a discrepancy develops between the way the world is thought to operate and the way it really does. Minor occurrences of such failure do not normally result in significant difficulties for an organization. There is enough time in most such circumstances to make the necessary adjustments. Major difficulties can arise, however, when there is an accumulation of a number of events and phenomena that are at odds with the model of the world corresponding to the organization's norms and beliefs. If such events and phenomena are allowed to accumulate unnoticed, a disaster may be in the making. The time during which the events and phenomena develop has been called the "incubation period" of the disaster. It is in this period that the failure of foresight occurs.[61] It is during this period that alert individuals operating within the interpretation and evaluation segment of the strategic information system can inform management of the dangers ahead.

There is no infallible prescriptive formula that will enable informa-

[60] Donham, W. B., *Business Adrift,* McGraw-Hill, 1931, p. xix.

[61] Turner, Barry A., "Development of Disasters," *op. cit,* pp. 381–2.

tion analysts to foresee impending dangers with certainty. However, a simple accumulative procedure of inductive inference (recently called "strong inference") provides a useful methodology for those engaged in this type of work.[62] Strong inference consists of the formal, explicit, and regular application of the following steps: (a) devising a range of alternative hypotheses related to the problem; (b) devising a series of crucial experiments with alternative possible outcomes, each of which will, as nearly as possible, exclude one or more of the hypotheses; (c) carrying out the experiments in such a manner that the results are unequivocal; and (d) recycling the procedure, making additional or sequential hypotheses to refine the process of analysis. These four steps constitute the minimum sequence necessary for the logical consideration of any situation. The emphasis in application is placed upon generating a number of possible models or explanations of a given situation, rather than on concentrating on only one. The regular and explicit consideration of alternative hypotheses and the resulting elimination of hypotheses after the conduct of experiments provides a systematic method of reaching firm inductive conclusions one after another in the shortest possible time. Such a system is the closest approach to generating foresight that is available to those engaged in the consideration of strategic situations.

Summary

Strategic information is information that relates mainly to the choice of objectives and the selection of future courses of action for an organization. It consists primarily of information concerning the environment in which the organization is operating. Some strategic information may exist within the organization itself. Interesting analogies exist between the use of information in military and political affairs and corresponding activities in the strategic management of organizations. These analogies allow experience in the more widely-discussed military and political fields to be applied to the study of strategic information in organizations.

In ancient times, political leaders were very interested in the political intentions of their neighbors. In the same way, managers in

[62] Platt, John R., "Strong Inference," *Science,* vol. 146, no. 3642, 16 October, 1964, pp. 347–353.

modern organizations are interested in "competitive" information about both the other organizations in their environment and the characteristics of the environment itself. Environmental characteristics can be listed under the headings of social, technological, and natural elements. Strategic information utilized by an organization takes three forms: (a) the basic descriptive form—providing a general overview of a subject drawn from past history; (b) the current reportorial form—providing information needed to up-date the existing overview, and (c) the speculative-evaluative form—containing perceptions about the inferences and possible impacts of current strategic information.

Strategic information is used by organizations to detect future situations that may provide either dangers or opportunities. The first step in this process is to make estimates of existing conditions in terms of the accepted beliefs within the organization itself, concerning both other organizations and the nature of the environment in which the organization is operating. As more strategic information becomes available, it is used to modify managerial beliefs about existing conditions, to make estimates of future conditions, and to adjust the activities of the organization as appears to be necessary. This process is analogous to the steering of a ship. In order that it be carried out effectively, the strategic information must be clear, concise, as unequivocal as possible, timely, consistent, reliable, and wide-ranging. The consequences of a lack of appropriate strategic information may be either disaster or the inability to take advantage of available opportunities.

Search for strategic information in practical situations is usually motivated by the recognition of a problem and suppressed when a means of resolving that problem presents itself. Initially the search centers upon the known and observed symptoms of the problem and currently proposed means of resolving it. More complex search behavior is adopted only if a simpler process does not provide a satisfactory result. The nature of the search process in any particular set of circumstances is influenced by the hopes, expectations, and personal characteristics of the individual or individuals involved.

In studies of actual strategic information gathering in working organizations, it has been found that managers rely overwhelmingly on personal, rather than impersonal sources. Senior managers tend to have a high preference for personal sources that are not in regular business communication with their organization. Managers in large organizations rely more heavily on sources internal to their organization than do managers in smaller organizations. Publications are a major source only for managers who are relatively inexperienced in their job. Slightly less than half of all external information received is solicited and only half of that is obtained as a result of an organizational activity.

The processes of searching for information and evaluating its relevance are intimately intertwined. Both are affected by the perceptions of the individual involved. These perceptions are likely to be biased, especially when they involve issues about which the individual has strong feelings. They are also affected by the needs and expectations of the individual and other characteristics such as his or her aversion to risk. The process of perception is therefore highly subjective. It may be influenced by preconceived concepts. It may be limited by one or more of a number of types of conceptual blocks. An individual's perceptions may be radically impaired if he or she is subject to stress. The behavior of a group of individuals in information gathering and evaluation may be far different from that of each of the members of the group acting individually.

The effort allocated by organizations to activities concerned with strategic information depends in practice on (a) the degree to which competitive forces are felt to be in the environment; (b) the internal condition of the organization; (c) the degree to which the internal operations of the organization are felt to be appropriate to conditions experienced at the time; and (d) the size and structure of the organization.

Many examples of inadequate use of strategic information exist in the military and political fields. Records of such events in the private sector are harder to find. One thread that runs through all such situations is that applicable strategic information is usually available within the organization concerned. There are a number of apparent reasons for neglect of this information. Vital signals may, for example, appear only as disjointed fragments or be overshadowed by what can be seen, in retrospect, to have been signals of little or no significance. This inconsequential component tends to distract attention away from the vital content of the strategic information. In some cases, attention may be diverted away from vital information by the deliberate insertion of noise or decoys by a competitor.

Important strategic information may be misinterpreted or misperceived by those involved, particularly if it does not fit existing theories and convictions. Misinterpretation and misperception is sometimes deliberately cultivated by a competitor. In other cases, vital strategic information may not be used because it could not be communicated at the crucial moment. Sometimes superiors "do not listen" to such information. In other cases, the communicator may be ignored because he or she is viewed as an outsider by the organization. It may be that failure to use strategic information is inherent in large and complex organizations. Such organizations require a hierarchical structure that may be hostile to the development of a competence in strategic information. They may also erect a screen of secrecy around strategic information activities that becomes a barrier between the information activity and its users. In these circumstances, managers may bypass the organizational activity devoted to strategic information and rely primarily on personal contacts for their information.

The most desirable attribute of those concerned with strategic information is foresight. Failures in foresight usually occur when events and phenomena that are not consistent with an organization's view of the current situation are allowed to accumulate unnoticed. This accumulation often occurs relatively slowly, so that alert members of an organization engaged in the strategic information activity can sometimes inform management of the dangers ahead.

Discussion Topics

1/ Do you feel that actions in the military and political spheres are sufficiently similar to the competitive operations of an organization to allow experience in one area to be transferred to the other? Do you see any possible disadvantages and dangers from the use of this analogy? If so, what precautions should be taken to avoid them?

2/ Strategic information is classified under the headings, basic descriptive, current reportorial, and speculative-evaluative. What are the counterparts of these categories in the internal information system?

3/ What forms might an "early warning system" take in an organization? What would be its main activities and functions?

4/ Search for information is usually conducted in a manner determined by the characteristics of the individuals involved. Is there any way of conducting a search more "objectively"? Would it be desirable to install an objective search procedure in an organization? What would be its advantages and disadvantages?

5/ Why do you think managers seem to rely more on personal contacts than on organizational activities for their strategic information? How can this factor be taken into account in the design of the strategic information components of the information system?

6/ Individual perceptions are influenced by pre-conceived notions concerning the factors involved. With this factor in mind, how can the elements of innovation and creativity be introduced into the interpretation of strategic information?

7/ Why do organizations experiencing competitive forces in their environment tend to increase strategic information activities?

8/ Is it true that organizations that feel they are in balance with their environment tend to concentrate more on collecting technological data? Can you think of instances where this has occurred? Has this tendency led to disadvantages for the organizations concerned in these instances?

9/ What is the nature of the strategic information available within an organization? How can this information be gathered? Does any of this information exist in the internal information system?

10/ Why do disasters attract more attention than successes? Why do certain kinds of disaster (such as a miner being killed in a mine disaster) sometimes attract more attention than others in which many more people lose their lives?

11/ What steps would you take to reduce the effects of the noise usually mixed with vital strategic information? Is an analysis of events in the recent past in the area of interest likely to be helpful in this task?

12/ In many adverse situations, it seems that one lone individual foresaw the potential disaster, but his warnings were ignored. Why do you think this happens? What steps could be taken to take advantage of the warnings issued by such individuals?

13/ Difficulties in transmission of strategic information are inherent in the structures that are created in organizations. What are these difficulties and how can they be overcome?

14/ To what extent is secrecy required in the strategic information activities of an organization? What adverse effects can an emphasis on secrecy have on a strategic information system? How can these effects be minimized?

15/ Foresight is said to be derived from an understanding of existing conditions. In what ways can this understanding be developed in an organization to encourage accurate foresight?

16/ It has been said that those who ignore the past are often condemned to relive it. Do you agree? If so, what aspects of the past do you consider to be particularly important to study?

17/ Failure of foresight apparently occurs over an appreciable period of time. What steps would you take to ensure that the novel events and phenomena that must be detected to prevent a failure of foresight are, in fact, recognized?

18/ In your opinion, what points brought out in this chapter have the most bearing on the design and implementation of a strategic information system?

CASE WORK

The following case work is designed to show how strategic information is applicable in a wide range of decision situations. It consists primarily of descriptions of situations with an invitation in each case to list the types of strategic information that might be needed by those responsible for resolution of the problem. As a further elaboration of the exercise, the reader might describe the use to which the information could be put in each case.

Exercises of this nature are more meaningful when they refer to situations with which the reader is familiar. For this reason, a sample case exercise is given first that deals with the hijacking incident that led to the rescue of hostages by Israeli forces at Entebbe in June/July 1976.

The Entebbe Hostage Incident

The Entebbe hostage incident began on June 27, 1976 when an Air France airliner originating in Tel Aviv was hijacked en route from Athens to Paris. The plane was diverted to Libya and was flown from there to Entebbe, Uganda. The passengers and crew were held as hostages in the airport terminal, with the apparent cooperation of the Ugandan authorities. The hijackers subsequently released all passengers other than those who were Jewish and the French crew. In exchange for the safety of the hostages, the hijackers demanded the release of 53 persons convicted of terrorist acts and held in Israeli and other jails. A deadline was set for compliance with the terms of the ultimatum, but it passed without incident and the time limit was extended. A second deadline was due to expire on Sunday, July 4th, one week after the original hijacking on Sunday, June 27th. Just before the last deadline was to expire, Israeli armed forces landed at Entebbe, rescued the hostages, and returned with them to Israel.

The operation was all the more remarkable in that it required a refuelling stop. The whole incident has been recorded in a number of popular accounts written from various standpoints.[63] Many reveal the political opinions of their authors. More analytical, historical accounts will no doubt appear in due course.

The exercise suggested here is to consider the needs of the Israeli cabinet for strategic information throughout the incident. It is proposed that this analysis be divided along the lines of the three stages of their deliberations: (1) when the initial news of the hijacking was received; (2) when the hijacked aircraft had landed at Entebbe and negotiations with the hijackers were being contemplated; and (3) when a military operation was being planned. This division greatly simplifies what must have been a very complex decision problem. It also ignores the needs of other participants (for example, the hijackers, the hostages, the Ugandan government) who must also have had strategic information requirements. However, this simplified framework will suffice for the purpose of illustration as is our objective here.

The initial information requirements when news of the hijacking was first received can be described under the headings of (a) participants and (b) elements of the environment as discussed in this chapter.[64] At this early stage, the only apparent participants were the hijackers, the Israeli government (because of the number of Jewish passengers and the fear that the hijacking was aimed against Israel), Air France, and, indirectly, the French government. Of these, the hijackers were relatively very powerful in the initial stages while the other participants were relatively weak. Potential participants were any other governments that might be friendly to the hijackers and the organizations, such as the Popular Front for the Liberation of Palestine, with which they might be linked.

One of the most pressing needs of the Israeli cabinet at this time must have been to establish the characteristics of other participants and the nature of the relationships between them. This would probably have been expressed in terms of questions such as (a) which organization do the hijackers represent and what are the goals of that organization? (b) which governments will cooperate in maintaining international law and agreements and which will not? (c) which governments and organizations have a past history of involvement

[63] Stevenson, W., *90 Minutes at Entebbe,* Bantam Books, 1976.

[64] See also Radford, K. J., *Complex Decision Problems, op. cit,* Chapter 2.

in such incidents and how have they behaved in the past under such circumstances? (d) what are the likely beliefs and value systems of the participants and what information is likely to be available to them at this time? (e) what commitments have been made by the participants and which of them are they likely to honor? and (f) what are the likely preferences of the various participants for various possible outcomes of the situation?

A second immediate set of requirements must have concerned the technological elements of the environment of the problem. Questions such as the following must have arisen: (a) what constraints are imposed on each of the participants by physical factors such as geography, climate, and man-made objects such as airfields? (b) what technological factors enter into consideration, for example, what are the range and capabilities of the airplane involved and where do facilities exist for handling, resupplying, and refuelling such an aircraft? (c) what factors concerned with human capabilities, behavior, and endurance must be considered at this stage?

A third and less easily defined set of information requirements must have concerned natural elements of the environment that could have an effect on the outcome of the problem situation. Primary among these in the initial stages was probably the state of the weather at points within the range of the airplane. Other considerations might have been the existence of individual leaders who might have had considerable influence on the situation or the possible involvement of potentially influential governments in other problems (such as an election, civil unrest, or economic difficulties) that might divert their attention from the hijacking problem.

The second stage of the problem began when the plane landed at Entebbe airport, Uganda. The Ugandan government (frequently represented in person by the President, Idi Amin) became a participant. The possibility arose that the major powers would enter as active participants. World opinion was aroused and became an element of the environment, posing constraints on courses of action available to the participants. It was confirmed that the Popular Front for the Liberation of Palestine had links with the hijackers, thus bringing that organization into the problem as an active participant. Each of these developments must have imposed additional requirements for strategic information on those supporting the activities of the Israeli cabinet in this respect. Items of interest at this time must also have included details of (a) any factions existing within each of the participants and any possibility that these factions might come into conflict under the stress of the situation; for example, would the apparent cooperation between the Ugandan government and the hijackers remain unbroken under the pressure of events? (b) possible coalitions among the present or potential participants that might affect the relative power of the actual participants in the situation; (c) changes in the characteristics of the participants (particularly in their relative power and their values) as time progressed, as well as any changes in the social, technological, and natural elements of the environment.

In the third stage of the problem, a military operation was planned against the hijackers and the Ugandan forces cooperating with them. The use of force would change the relative power of the participants significantly. It might, however, cause potential participants to take a more active part in the existing situation or in a future situation linked to it, for example, in a future war in the Middle East. World opinion might become a major participant, particularly if the operation failed. Refuelling of the Israeli planes was a necessity. This was arranged to be done in Kenya and this country, a neighbor of Uganda, was thus brought into the situation as an active participant. All these developments no doubt required considerable strategic information activity in order that the characteristics of each new participant and element of the environment could be assessed, while changes were made in existing estimates as dictated by actual and potential events.

The possible interaction of the hijacking problem with other current and linked situations was also, no doubt, a major consideration requiring support from strategic information. New physical, technological, and human factors entered into consideration with the possibility of a military operation. A major factor in this planning must have been that the Israeli government, which had earlier assisted in the construction of Entebbe airport, had retained detailed plans of the runways and the facilities located there.

The situation facing the Israeli cabinet just prior to its decision to authorize the military operation can probably be summarized in table 5.1.

The decision problem facing the Israeli cabinet was whether the use of military force would bring about a situation that was considered preferable to the existing situation, taking into account the risks of failure that were involved. In the actual event, the operation was authorized, it was successful, and the effect on linked situations was negligible.

The foregoing was, of course a very brief summary of a very complex and tragic problem. It does, however, provide an example of the need for strategic information in such a situation. It is interesting as an exercise to consider the parallel case of the hijacking of a

TABLE 5.1 *Summary of the Entebbe Airport Situation Just Prior to the Authorization of the Military Operation* (as it may have been viewed by the Israeli cabinet)

Participants	*Available Courses of Action*	*Present Situation*
Israel	Negotiate with hijackers	Give appearance of
	Take military action	No
	Mobilize world opinion	Yes
Hijackers	Cooperate with Ugandan government	Yes
	Threaten hostages	Yes
	Use violence on hostages	No
	Fly elsewhere	No
Ugandan government	Cooperate with hijackers	Yes
	Use force against hijackers	No
U.S. government	Support Israel	Yes
French government (Air France)	Mobilize world opinion	Yes
	Cooperate with Israel	Yes

Lufthansa plane to Mogadishu in October 1977. This example can also provide a guide for consideration of the following problem situations. It is suggested that the reader attempt an analysis of the strategic information requirements likely to arise in the following situations, in each case using imagination to elaborate the brief details of the situation that are given below.

Situation #1: A Municipal Problem

A contractor in a certain municipality has built a number of medium-priced homes in a subdivision over the past few years. In most of these homes, a new type of electrical wiring was used. No problems arose until recently, when one fire and one near-fire occurred. The causes of these incidents have not been established but the Residents Association has expressed suspicion concerning the manner in which the wiring was done.

At a recent meeting of the Association, a motion was passed calling for action by the municipality or the contractor to have the suspect wiring replaced free of cost to the residents. The contractor states that the work was passed at the time at which it was carried out and that he has met all required standards. The municipality does not feel able to bear the cost of replacing the wiring. The Association is becoming militant and has presented petitions to City Hall. The local alderman and members of the provincial (state) legislature are involved. A civic election is four months away and the standings in the provincial (state) legislature are in very close balance.

It is suggested that the reader records answers to the following questions:

1/ Who are the current and potential participants in this problem, what are their characteristics, and which do you think has the greatest and which the least power to influence the outcome?

2/ What are the most important social, technological, and natural elements of the environment in this problem and what strategic information would you collect in order to assist one of the participants in decision making with respect to it?

3/ What are the possible future outcomes and which outcomes are the most preferred by the various participants?

4/ What new requirements for strategic information might arise as time progresses in the resolution of the problem?

Situation #2: An Industrial Relations Problem

The Omega Transportation Company provides a continent-wide service of rapid pick-up and delivery of goods between major cities. It operates a fleet of trucks based in a number of cities. Headquarters are centrally located on the continent. The largest fleets of trucks are on the east and west coasts. Truck operators are unionized and there is a long history of industrial disputes between the union and the company. Most of these disputes have centered around working conditions, although wages have sometimes been an important point of contention.

At the present time, the union contract with the company is about to be renegotiated. The union has presented its demands and management has stated what it is prepared to concede. The two positions are far apart and a strike is imminent. Customers of Omega will be inconvenienced by the effects of the strike. These customers could probably wait out a short interruption of service without suffering major damage. In the event of a long strike, however, they would probably switch their requirements to a competing method of transferring the necessary goods. Omega is worried that it might not recover a major proportion of its business after a long strike was eventually settled. However, the company has detected that there are a number of competing factions in the union. It seems possible that the union leadership does not represent all these factions and that certain groups could be persuaded to return to work soon after a strike was called, in defiance of the union leadership.

It is suggested that the reader list the types of strategic information that would be useful (a) to management and (b) to the union leadership in the situation outlined. As a continuation of the exercise, suppose that truckers at certain of the depots return to work and that the company encourages this action. Suppose also that the company locks out the remaining striking workers and that civil disobedience and violence in the areas affected are distinct possibilities. How would these developments affect the requirements for strategic information?

Situation #3: An International Problem

A company engaged in mining and smelting is extracting resources from an overseas country in exchange for a levy paid per ton extracted. The government of the country involved has just indicated that it wishes to triple the payment it receives for the resources. At the same time, it is prepared to sign a 10-year contract with only a modest price escalation over this period.

There is another source of the needed minerals in another country. The cost of extraction of the material from this new source would be considerably higher, but the payments demanded by the country involved are much less than triple the existing price. On the other hand, the country controlling the new source will not sign a long term contract and will not guarantee prices after the first year.

There is some indication of unrest in the country that is presently supplying the material. A change of government could occur on very short notice. The board of directors of the company and its management are deeply divided on how to proceed. List, as before, the strategic information that the president of the company might require at all stages and covering all aspects of this problem. Elaborate the problem situation as you see fit in preparing your review.

6

Design and Implementation of the Strategic Information System

The strategic information system is the second of two major components of the overall organizational information system. Its purpose is to provide information in support of decision processes that arise in strategic planning and, to some extent, in management control. Much of the information in the strategic system originates in the external environment of the organization. However, some strategic information exists in the internal environment of the organization and can be collected within its own boundaries.

The nature of the strategic information system is different from that of the internal information system in a number of respects:

1/ The content of a data set in the internal system is well-defined and complete. Each data set is constructed in accordance with specifications that govern (a) the definition of the parameter to which the data refers; (b) the units of measurement used; and (c) the format and coding of the data. Strategic information, on the other hand, seldom presents itself in a form that is well defined. For example, it may not be sorted by context and annotated as to meaning. Items that prove later to be of significance are usually encountered first in a mass of similar material relating to a variety of subjects. Furthermore, once a significant item is separated from other material surrounding it, it is often found to be fragmentary and incomplete. Detection of an important item of strategic information is usually followed by an intensive search for further material with which it can be connected. Relatively greater effort is, therefore, placed on the functions of acquisition and identification of information in the strategic information system than is the case with its internal counterpart.

2/ Information in the internal information system is, in large part, quantitative. This quantitative information and the nonquantitative descriptive material that accompanies it are both well-defined and unequivocal. They refer to familiar aspects of the activities of the organization and their meaning can be readily appreciated. On the other hand, much of the information in the strategic system is descriptive and nonquantitative in nature. It consists of documents in which descriptions of people, organizations, events, and phenomena are recorded. These matters may be much less familiar to those to whom the material is presented. Information in the strategic system is also frequently highly subjective. It often consists of opinions and assessments rather than data that can be considered "factual." Much greater emphasis must, therefore, be placed on the interpretation of strategic information than is needed in the case of information in the internal system. In fact, the task of interpretation in the strategic information system is often inseparable from that of acquisition of information.

3/ The quantitative nature of the information in the internal system makes it readily adaptable to processing by automated techniques. The basic data from the completely specified systems is assembled in routine fashion using prespecified procedures to produce summary reports for presentation to management. Much of the work of the strategic information system is, however, concentrated on the search for clues from which assessments of present and potential future environmental conditions can be made. The emphasis is, therefore, not on routine processing of information, but on individual interpretation and assessment of available material. The designer of the strategic information system must take these considerations into account by incorporating into the system efficient methods of referencing, cataloging, storing, and retrieving information.

It is a natural tendency of managers in modern organizations to collect strategic information through personal contacts and by using their own individual networks of communication. Managers usually regard information that they collect in this manner as confidential. They often retain this information for exclusive use by themselves and their immediate colleagues. The design and implementation of a strategic information system need not oppose these natural tendencies. The facilities provided by the system do not restrict the individual initiatives of managers in the search for strategic information. A successful system can be designed that supports and augments the efforts of managers in both the acquisition and the interpretation of strategic information. This can be done without encroaching upon the confidentiality requirements of individuals. The introduction of a strategic information system often has the effect of broadening and expanding the individual efforts of managers. The result is frequently a greater shared use of information and an accompanying natural increase in the coordination of strategic information activities.

By the same token, managerial involvement in all aspects of the design, implementation, and operation of the strategic information system is of very great importance. Information of this nature cannot be collected and assessed in a vacuum.[1] Information gathering and assessment is an integral part of the decision-making process. It is interesting to note that this need for strategic information was a point not lost on leaders in ancient times. The standing procedure of the Athenian assembly called for introduction of heralds and ambassadors (important sources of strategic information in those times) as the second item of business.[2]

Many organizations have strategic information systems of one kind or another in operation at the present time. The majority of these systems are not fully developed. In many cases, they have been created in connection with a particular committee, task force, function, or activity, rather than to serve the whole organization. The most commonly available strategic information system, although it is not often thought of in such terms, is the reference library. Many organizations have an extensive library dedicated to reference works. When the size

[1] Seale, P. and M. McConville, *Philby: The Long Road to Moscow,* Hamish Hamilton, 1973, pp. 142–143.

[2] Starr, Chester G., *Political Intelligence in Ancient Greece,* Lugduni Batavorum, E. J. Brill, 1974, p. 33.

and scope of these facilities are considered, it is difficult to understand why they are not more widely used. Perhaps it is because a generally-oriented facility is frequently not able to meet the specialized needs of each of its potential users. There are also certain specific difficulties that most users of libraries have experienced at one time or another, which are described in the following paragraphs. This discussion is not meant to imply that all users meet all the difficulties mentioned in all libraries all the time, as such is clearly not the case. Recognition of these negative factors with regard to libraries can, however, provide useful guidance to the designer of a strategic information system.

The user of a reference library often finds that no volume clearly applicable to his particular line of enquiry is available at the location to which he has gone. If a pertinent volume is available at another location, the procedures and delay involved in retrieving that volume often discourage its procurement, particularly if the time available for pursuing the subject is limited. When a volume of interest is available at a particular location, it is sometimes loaned out to another user and is similarly unavailable for immediate reference.

Facilities and methods for pursuing a line of research that is initially poorly defined often discourage search following a preliminary enquiry. The cataloging system and the positioning of books on shelves are generally adopted in the interest of efficient operation of the library. The library's system may, however, be a source of puzzlement to the casual user. In some libraries, procedures almost appear to have been designed to protect the books against the user. Junior staff persons occasionally seem bent on discouraging enquiry. Specialization within the library often has the same discouraging effect. "That's on microfilm and the person who deals with that is on her lunch break" is a statement that has caused many an enquirer to drop the search. The mere fact that the library is in a building geographically removed from a person's office often prevents an enquiry from being made at the library at all.

The above listing will no doubt bring librarians immediately to the defense of their facilities—with some justification. Reference libraries are a source of unlimited information to those who have the time and perseverance to make best use of them. However, busy managers are frequently not in a position to spend the time necessary for the required search for information. It is necessary, therefore, in designing a strategic information system, to include facilities that will provide users with ready and convenient access to information. Such facilities may be expensive and are undoubtedly more costly than many generally-available reference libraries can afford. Nevertheless, ready access to information is the prime factor in ensuring the success and utilization of a strategic information system. The cost is justified by the use to which the information it contains can be utilized in the important and expensive decision processes at the higher levels of the organization.

The above discussion and the material concerning strategic information in Chapter 5 lead to the following initial considerations in the design and implementation of a strategic information system:

- The major functions in a strategic information system are acquisition, interpretation, storage and retrieval, and presentation of the information;
- The functions of acquisition and interpretation are closely interrelated;
- Efficient methods of referencing, cataloging, storage, and retrieval are essential to the success of the system;
- The system must provide convenient and ready access to the information it contains;
- Managerial involvement in the design, implementation, and operation of the system is an important key to its success.

The discussion now concentrates on each of the major functions of acquisition, interpretation, storage and retrieval, and presentation in turn.

Acquisition of Strategic Information

Individuals and organizations are continually bombarded with information. Some of this information arises within the organization and relates to familiar aspects of its operation and management. The fact that an organization has boundaries that are relatively well-defined places some limits on the volume and variety of the information that can arise within it. By contrast, the environment in which the organization is operating is usually quite varied and extensive. The number of sources, the volume of information, and the variety of subjects to which the information refers are, therefore, considerably greater in the external environment. Information originating in the immediately surrounding area of the environment may be more familiar to those with responsibility for important organizational decisions. However, there is no guarantee that strategic information of great importance to the organization will not arise in the further reaches of the environment that may have been less fully explored to date.

It is a natural requirement in organizations that information be gathered on all subjects and in all areas that may have a bearing on current and future decision making and planning. However, this may be impossible in practice due to (a) the very great volume and variety of information that is available; and (b) the constraints on available time and resources that usually apply in modern organizational decision making. The task of information gathering is, therefore, similar to the piecing together of a complex puzzle where the parts that are available may refer to that puzzle or to one or more other puzzles with the same general characteristics. The task involves not only looking for the pieces of the particular puzzle of immediate concern, but also deciding whether a piece that is picked up actually belongs to that puzzle or to one of the others. The difficulty of this task is compounded by the lack of order and completeness with which the information becomes available and by the ever-increasing rate of change in the turbulent (Type 4) environments in which most modern organizations operate.[3]

The required activities of the acquisition function in the strategic information system are, therefore: (a) to gather as much information as possible (within the constraints of time and resources) concerning subjects that are relevant to organizational decision making; (b) to recognize subjects that are relevant, so that the chances of neglecting information that is important to the organization are minimized; and (c) to gather the information required with a minimum of distortion. In order to meet these requirements the acquisition function normally operates in a number of modes. These modes, the relationships between them, and the basis for switching from one mode to another are now described in detail.

Modes of Acquisition

Information gathering in organizations covers a broad spectrum of activities. As one scans this spectrum, the various modes of acquisi-

[3] Aguilar, F. J., *Scanning the Business Environment,* MacMillan, 1967, p. 10.

tion merge imperceptibly into one another. It could be said, therefore, that it is not possible to distinguish any set of acquisition modes that are more important than others. On the other hand, it is possible, for purposes of analysis, to describe three such modes that are spaced across the spectrum. It is then possible to consider the conditions under which the acquisition procedures used in an organizational setting may vary between modes. The three modes of acquisition chosen as reference points on the spectrum are described as (a) general scanning, (b) directed scanning, and (c) active search. The following descriptions of these modes are based on those contained in a similar analysis by Aguilar.[4]

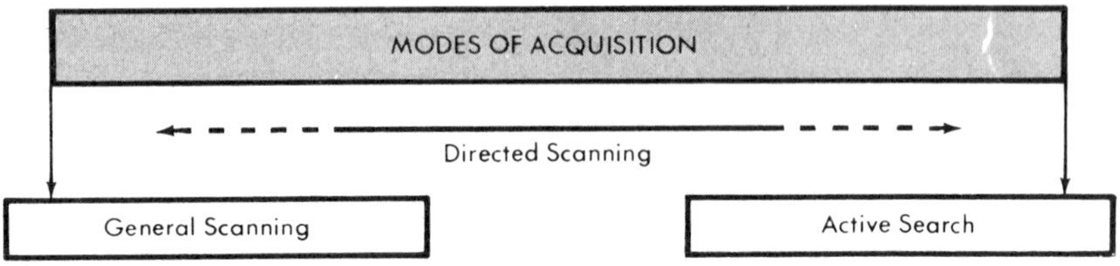

Figure 6.1. Spectrum of Acquisition Modes for Strategic Information

General scanning of the environment is the mode of acquisition in which information is gathered with no specific purpose in mind. It is the equivalent of the activity of the scanning radar in a ship. General scanning covers a wide variety of subjects and a large number of sources. Because the scope of acquisition is wide, the amount of information that is gathered from any one source or on any one subject is generally small. The relevance of the acquired information to any particular problem is tentative in this mode. The material gathered is contributed to the basic descriptive form of strategic information and is useful in compiling descriptions of current developments, phenomena, and conditions. It may also contribute to the current reportorial form of strategic information and be used in updating existing descriptions of this nature.

The second acquisition mode is identified as *directed scanning.* This mode is the equivalent of the use of a zoom lens in photography. The purpose of directed scanning is to concentrate effort on an area of the environment in which it appears that some process of change is under way. The need for directed scanning is often indicated by a

[4] Aguilar, F. J., *op. cit., Scanning the Business Environment,* pp. 19–22.

signal or cue that is detected by chance in the general scanning mode. On the other hand, a series of "criterion checks" can be designed as part of the acquisition function that provide a semiautomatic trigger for the switch to an even more concentrated scanning of a particular area. The need for directed scanning can arise also from requests by individuals working outside the strategic information system. Such requests frequently occur when an individual in an organization has detected the existence of a problem and requires general information regarding the problem area in question to assist him in its resolution. The directed scanning mode covers a wide range of degrees of concentration of the information gathering activity. Note that movement into directed scanning does not preclude continuation of the general scanning mode. Such movement is a matter of altering the assignment of resources between the modes. Design of the acquisition function includes the specification of rules by which the appropriate task assignments can be made in a wide variety of circumstances.

The third mode of acquisition of strategic information is *active search*. This mode consists of a deliberate effort to seek out information related to a specific issue using a preestablished plan, procedure, or methodology. As in the case of directed scanning, there is a wide range of degrees of active search. All are typified, however, by the active involvement of specific methods of information gathering as compared to the more passive activities of general and directed scanning.

Methods of Active Search

Methods of active search for strategic information can be considered under four headings: (a) illicit activities that may actually be illegal as well as unethical in most modern societies; (b) activities that are not actually illegal, but that may be unethical and are best termed "surreptitious"; (c) open search and investigation of sources of information in a nonclandestine and systematic manner; and (d) open search for information from the records of one's own organization.

Illicit and illegal methods of gathering strategic information include: (a) trespassing on the property of other participants; (b) direct theft of records, diagrams, and other information; (c) systematic eavesdropping by electronic or other means; (d) bribing individuals associated with other participants to provide information held confidential by them; and (e) using blackmail and extortion for the purposes of obtaining information.[5] The practice of planting an agent on the payroll of a competitor, while possibly not illegal, is certainly unethical. These methods of gathering information are reportedly used primarily by spies and undercover agents, many of whom claim to operate under conditions and legal restrictions different from those that apply to ordinary citizens. It is clear, however, that such methods have no place in the repertoire of active search techniques that can be used by law-abiding organizations.

Surreptitious or clandestine methods of active search are those probing activities that are not regarded as actually illegal in most societies, but that border on the unethical. These methods include (a) direct questioning of competitors' employees; (b) information-gathering interviews with a competitor's employees arranged under false pretenses, for example, to discuss nonexistent job opportunities; (c) hiring personnel solely for the purpose of obtaining competitive information; (d) direct observation of other participants in the environment under secret and clandestine conditions. The acceptability of such methods depends upon the degree to which they are used. Most executives are accustomed to probing the opinions and reactions of others at business meetings and social gatherings. This method of gathering information is acceptable because there is usually an unspoken agreement between those taking part in the exchange to impose a limit on the extent and scope of the conversation. If this limit is reached, signals to that effect are exchanged and the ethical executive changes the subject. Individuals who attempt to press beyond the ethical limits are soon detected and often obtain less information than the more skillful conversationalist who stays within acceptable bounds. In the same way, commonly-accepted standards of ethical behavior impose limits on the extent and nature of direct observation that can be carried out by clandestine methods, in that a known offender may be cut off from other information or excluded from business opportunities.

Open methods of active search are concerned with investigation of information regarding other participants and conditions in the environment utilizing freely-available documents, records, and reports. These sources include market surveys, trade announcements, com-

[5] Wade, Worth, "Proprietary Information: How It Leaks Out," *Chemical Engineering*, May 23, 1966, p. 160.

petitors' published brochures and reports, brokers' research surveys, government reports, and other published documents. Open methods of active search include also direct and open observation of the behavior of other participants, of the relationships between them, and of the other elements of the environment. Some of this observation can be carried out by members of the organization while they are engaged in their normal work. In this regard, those members of the organization who venture into the environment are the modern-day counterparts of the ambassadors and travellers of earlier times.

By far the greatest proportion of strategic information gathered by organizations in active search is obtained from publicly-available sources and material by open methods. Simple observation of the activities of others and of trends in the environment carried on by an informed individual is usually the most fruitful method of gathering the information needed to support strategic decision making. Recourse to the use of clandestine methods within boundaries set by ethical considerations is sometimes necessary and advantageous. However, as Wilensky observes, recipients often evaluate secret information too highly. The accent on secrecy often "impairs critical judgement in the production and interpretation of intelligence and dulls the sense of relevance." [6] Furthermore, individuals engaged in clandestine activities are often not the most reliable of sources. The nature of their trade sometimes seems to impel them to present apparently significant material whether or not such material exists. The temptation to exaggerate, augment, or even invent information may be all the greater in such individuals since modern society exacts relatively mild penalties for these activities. The deterrents to such activities were greater in ancient times when the common penalty for trickery of this nature was instant death.

A great deal of strategic information can often be gathered from knowledgeable persons who are willing to cooperate in the use of questionnaires. Use of questionnaires is in many ways an inexpensive substitute for personal interviews. The method provides a means of gathering the information held by individuals. However, it lacks the elements of interaction and mutual drawing out of information that are present when a group of knowledgeable persons is brought together in one location to discuss a subject.

A method that is designed to retain some of the advantages of group

[6] Wilensky, H. L., *Organizational Intelligence,* Basic Books, 1967, p. 66.

interaction, while remaining relatively inexpensive, was originally put forward by T. J. Gordon and O. Helmer and called *Delphi*.[7, 8] The Delphi procedure utilizes a sequence of questionnaires submitted in a number of rounds. The first questionnaire is usually introductory and unspecific in nature. For example, it might pose questions about the identity of other participants in the environment and the relationships between them. It is important that the questions posed in the first round not be too structured or restrictive. Such a lack of structure often allows important factors that are outside the knowledge of the director of the enquiry to come to light.

The replies to the first questionnaire are returned to the director, usually, but not necessarily, anonymously. He or she consolidates them into a single set, which is then used as the basis of the questionnaire in round two. The second questionnaire seeks to gather more details on those items from the first round that are judged to be important to the problem at hand. For example, questions might be included that are designed to obtain opinions about the likely plans, objectives, and available courses of action of participants mentioned in the first-round replies. Estimates of the effects of natural and quasi-natural events might be sought, as well as forecast probabilities of occurrence for those events in a given time period.

It is important to note that, in addition to posing questions, the second and succeeding questionnaires provide respondents with information about the views and opinions of the others involved, even though they do not meet face-to-face. The questions in each succeeding round are designed to amplify and investigate the opinions of the respondents and also to verify that the summary of replies in the previous round does, in fact, represent the views of the group. The procedure continues over a number of rounds (usually between three and five) with increasingly specific questions until sufficiently detailed information has been gathered. It is not necessary to limit the enquiry to only one group of similarly qualified or positioned individuals. Questionnaires can be sent to a number of groups with different fields of knowledge or at different levels in an organization or community and the responses either combined or kept separate after each round.

7 Gordon, T. J., and O. Helmer, "Report on a Long-range Forecasting Study," *Rand Corporation Report*, 1964, p. 2982.

8 Delbecq, A. L., A. H. Ven, and D. H. Gustafson, *Group Techniques for Program Planning*, Scott Foresman and Co., 1975, pp. 88–107.

Delphi has two characteristics that distinguish it from other methods of information gathering:

- *Anonymity*—which allows the individuals providing the information to remain unknown to one another and not meet in a group discussion. This factor provides the opportunity for those taking part in the study to change their opinions without loss of face.
- *Iteration with feedback*—information is gathered in a sequence of rounds and the results of previous rounds are fed back to the individuals involved at the start of each new round of questioning.

Delphi has clear advantages over other methods of gathering data from groups when (a) opinions are needed from a larger number of individuals than can be accommodated in a face-to-face meeting; (b) differences of opinion are so great that face-to-face encounters result in unproductive arguments; and (c) when the individuals involved are separated by large distances or when face-to-face meetings might involve large expenditures of time.

Two sources that are often overlooked in active search are the stores of information available within the organization and information in the possession of the organization's individual members. The content of the internal information system has already been mentioned as a source of strategic information. The current activities of the various parts of the organization may also be rich in information of strategic value that does not find its way into the internal system. A prime illustration of this circumstance concerns the decision process shown in Figure 3-5. Details of the strategic analysis carried out with respect to current and past decision situations may contain information that would be valuable in other contexts. For example, previously recorded descriptions of the behavior of a particular participant, individual, or organization in past situations might be of great value to those engaged in a current or future situation in which that participant is involved.

As noted in Chapter 5, individual managers normally seek strategic information from their own personal sources. Such information may not be widely available within the organization and individuals may be unwilling to divulge it to anyone but their immediate colleagues. However, if regular contact can be established between those working in the strategic information system and managers who consistently collect such confidential information, benefits may accrue to all parties. The individual manager's store of information and possibly his or her perception of a decision situation may be enhanced. At the same time, he or she may be able to supply pieces of information that have not yet been acquired by the strategic system and that gain significance in the light of the other information that it contains. Particular emphasis should be placed on the briefing of individuals who are about to travel within the external environment and debriefing them on their return. The nature of strategic information gathering and interpretation is such that the pooling of material by cooperating individuals and organizations most often results in considerable benefits to all concerned.

Management of the Acquisition Function

Each of the three modes of acquisition of strategic information has advantages and disadvantages. General scanning is the most economic method of covering a wide range of subjects and sources. The information that it produces, however, is not specific to a given problem and not concentrated on any one line of enquiry. Furthermore, important developments in a particular area may remain undetected while the scanning process is directed elsewhere. Some of these disadvantages are overcome by directed scanning. However, directed scanning is relatively more costly and, when time and resources are limited, the number of subjects that can be treated in this manner is limited. The diversion of resources away from general scanning may also result in areas later found to have been important being left uninvestigated for a long period of time.

Active search, when properly conducted, is undoubtedly the most effective method of gathering strategic information in specific areas. It is, however, by far the most costly method of gathering information. Investment of a high proportion of available resources in active search may well cause serious deficiencies in the more wide-ranging scanning activities. The manager of the acquisition function, therefore, has a continuing task of ensuring that his or her allocation of resources between the various modes of gathering strategic information is appropriate to the needs of the organization.

In order to visualize how the most appropriate allocation can be accomplished, imagine that the organization concerned is in a tranquil, steady state, much like a ship sailing on a calm and open sea. In this state, all resources are devoted to general scanning, because no specific problems have presented themselves. It is important, however, that the manager of the acquisition function receive early warning of conditions that do not correspond exactly with those expected as these may be the forerunners of even greater change. This early warning can be obtained by continuous monitoring of indicators or standards. Some of these indicators are quantitative in nature in the form of the "criterion checks" proposed by Thomas P. Ference.[9]

Criterion checks are used in the comparison of data received in current scanning with that contained in an historic store of data referring to the same parameter. If the comparison shows a deviation from the established figure, the change may signal the existence of a problem for the organization. The natural reaction is to employ available resources in directed scanning in an effort to gain more information concerning the potential problem area. If this more concentrated scanning effort reveals further indications of divergence between observed and desired conditions, more resources may need to be devoted to directed scanning or to active search. The resources required for these activities may need to be diverted from general scanning. This diversion of effort may lead to either a reduction in the number of areas covered by general scanning or to the examination of areas of interest less often.

Procedures can also be devised to determine whether activities that occur regularly and repetitively in the environment both external and internal to the organization are, in fact, continuing to occur in their normal pattern. If a regular activity or event does not happen on its normal schedule, this may indicate the initiation or existence of a problem situation. The conditions surrounding the nonoccurrence can then be investigated by directed scanning or by active search as is judged appropriate at the time.

There is evidence that criterion checks are the dominant method of detecting problem situations in technologically-based organizations.[10] In other types of organization, the character of the criteria used in problem detection may vary widely from the essentially quantitative criterion checks. The qualitative criteria used in less technological organizations depend upon the nature of their external environment,

[9] Ference, Thomas P., "Organizational Communications Systems and the Decision Process," *Management Science,* vol. 17, no. 2, October 1970, p. B89.

[10] Pounds, William F., "The Process of Problem Finding," *Industrial Management Review* (now *Sloan Management Review*), vol. 11, no. 1, Fall 1969, p. 1–9.

their pattern of management, and the nature of their operations. The different criteria employed may result in different search techniques once a problem has been detected.[11]

The need for changes in the allocation of efforts among acquisition modes may arise from incidents other than the detection of change by the general scanning activity. For example, recognition of a problem situation by individual managers or by those involved in planning and policy making at the higher levels of the organization may dictate a need for strategic information in a certain area. The impulse for change in the acquisition mode may, therefore, come directly from those involved in strategic decisions. Feasible courses of action in a rapidly changing environment can be formulated only as strategic information becomes available. As the available information becomes more precise as a result of concentration of the acquisition procedures in the area of interest, courses of action to respond to the problem situation can be correspondingly better defined.[12] This is a further reason for a close working relationship between the strategic information system and the continuing decision process as depicted in Figures 3-5 and 3-6.

The manager of the acquisition function must devise a system for allocating his resources in such a way that he responds to both deviations detected in general scanning and to the requirements of individuals and groups directly involved in the decision process. The system that he needs might well be called "mixed scanning" if this name had not been appropriated by A. Etzioni for a similar, but somewhat more complex process.[13] Etzioni recommends mixed scanning as a means of both detecting the existence of decision problems and separating the strategic decisions from the less fundamental ones that he says can be treated incrementally. The acquisition function manager's system of mixed scanning has similar characteristics but a slightly different purpose. It combines various modes of acquisition in a mix determined by the conditions experienced. In less turbulent conditions, a more encompassing but less detailed mode of acquisition is predominant. As more problem situations are encountered, the emphasis is changed towards less encompassing modes that provide greater details within the problem areas.

11 Thompson, J. D., *Organizations in Action,* McGraw-Hill, 1967, p. 85.

12 Ansoff, H. Igor, "Managing Strategic Surprise by Response to Weak Signals," *California Management Review,* vol. 18, no. 2, Winter 1975, p. 23.

13 Etzioni, A., *The Active Society,* The Free Press, 1968, pp. 282–288.

The system devised to regulate the choice of acquisition modes also contains a set of criteria that act as a guide to the selection of a mix of modes under operational conditions. These criteria are related to the scope and urgency of the problem situation and to the potential effect of the issue at stake on the future of the organization. In individual cases, the actual mix between modes is often determined also by the availability of information and by the amount and nature of the resources available for use in information gathering in each of the modes.

The Interpretation Function

The purpose of the interpretation function in a strategic information system is to assess the significance of information that has been acquired. This significance may be apparent from the magnitude of the changes and trends that are detected by comparison of new information with that which has been gathered previously. A particular piece of information may, on the other hand, acquire significance from the recognition that it completes a pattern that had not hitherto been noticeable. One of the most important characteristics of the successful interpreter of strategic information is the ability to integrate a vital piece of new information into a background that has been previously available.

Interpretation of strategic information is inseparable from the process of acquisition. The results of interpretation of information acquired in the general and directed scanning modes of acquisition are the primary triggers for the change to a more intensive form of search. Pursuit of more revealing information or of an elusive clue to linkages between parts of previously held material is usually an iterative process. In the course of this process, the emphasis moves to and fro between acquisition and interpretation as the exploration continues. Close cooperation between the individuals engaged in the two functions is essential to a successful search. On the other hand, the persons who seek out strategic information should not, in general, be those who assess its importance or who decide what action should be taken in the light of its implications.[14] Searching for vital information sometimes becomes a consuming obsession for those engaged in this work. It is often necessary to seek a second opinion from one not so

[14] Seale, P., and M. McConville, *op. cit*, p. 161.

involved in order that a balanced judgement on the importance of the information acquired can be obtained.

In much the same way, interpretation of strategic information cannot be done out of context or in a partial vacuum. Successful interpretation requires that the "targets" about which more detailed characteristics are sought be defined by those who need the information. Managers involved in decision processes are sometimes the best interpreters of newly-acquired information. For this reason, the basic information that has been collected in the acquisition function should always be available to those involved in the related decision processes. On the other hand, the manager who insists on using only raw material to the exclusion of reports in the speculative-evaluative form is likely to come to consider the treatment of strategic information a distinct and subordinate function. This will lead him or her to distinguish sharply between the acquisition of strategic information and its interpretation and furthermore to tend to exclude those involved in the strategic information functions from policy and decision making deliberations.[15]

The best results and economy of effort are usually obtained by close and continuing cooperation between managers and their colleagues in the strategic information functions. Two negative tendencies that have been observed in studies of some situations in which strategic information has had, or could have had, important implications are (a) those involved in acquiring and interpreting strategic information sometimes tend to report what they think the responsible managers want to hear; and (b) the responsible managers see and hear what they want, no matter what information is reported to them.[16] A close cooperation between decision makers and information personnel appears to be the best way to minimize these tendencies.

The interpretation placed on strategic information is subject to the personal characteristics of the individual making the evaluation. Each interpreter brings to the task his or her own subjective value systems, perceptions, experiences, and judgement. Individual interpretations can, therefore, be expected to be biased to some degree by these personal characteristics. However, if the evaluations of two or more individuals of roughly the same experience in the subject area are

[15] Wilensky, H. L., *op. cit, Organizational Intelligence,* p. 62.

[16] Ransom, H. H., "Strategic Intelligence and Foreign Policy," *World Politics,* 1975, p. 146.

similar, there is reason to afford the jointly-held interpretation more weight than that of a single individual.

Interpretation of information depends to some extent on the situation in which the evaluation is made. For example, in some circumstances it has been observed that less information was needed to conclude that a favorable event would occur than to conclude that an unfavorable event would occur.[17] The desirability of the event to the individual concerned may, therefore, affect the amount of information that is required to reach a conclusion. In the same way, it has been suggested that more information is required to change a previous conclusion than to establish that conclusion in the first place.[18] Information that is inconsistent with that collected earlier is likewise often rejected. However, the more reliable a source has been in the past or the more power the source appears to have, the less likely it is that the information will be rejected, even if it is inconsistent with material gathered earlier.[19]

Experiments have shown that human beings tend to exhibit conservatism in changing their opinions on receipt of new information. Individuals displaying this characteristic modify their beliefs to a lesser extent than appears to be justified by the content of the new information received.[20] Possibly more disturbing is the observation that individuals in some circumstances tend to undervalue a clear indication of a future hazardous situation. This tendency is often greater when there is ambiguity and disagreement among several parties about the status and the significance of the evidence pointing to the possible danger. Undervaluing of available evidence has been observed to occur particularly when a relatively complacent individual or group was also the most powerful of those involved.[21]

Interpretation may be affected if significant information is unnoticed because of erroneous attitudes or assumptions. This may occur when individuals or organizations adopt rigid stereotypes of the

[17] Morlock, Henry, "The Effect of Outcome Desirability on Information Required for Decisions," *Behavioral Science*, vol. 12, 1967, pp. 296–300.

[18] Pruitt, Dean G., "Informational Requirements in Making Decisions," *American Journal of Psychology*, vol. 74, 1961, pp. 433–439.

[19] Ference, Thomas P., *op. cit.*, "Organizational Communications Systems," p. B93.

[20] Ebert, R. J., and T. R. Mitchell, *Organizational Decision Processes*, Crane Russak

[21] Turner, Barry A., "The Organizational and Interorganizational Development of Disasters," *Administrative Science Quarterly*, vol. 21, September 1976, p. 391.
and Company, 1975, pp. 8–88.

problems and person with which they are dealing. For example, in a study of the final days of the outbreak of several wars, it has been found that all participants suffered from distortion of their images of themselves and their adversaries. They tended to see themselves as honorable, virtuous, and pure and the other participants as diabolical and scheming. In addition, perceptions of power were particularly distorted. In the early stages of a confrontation, participants tended to exaggerate their own power and to underestimate that of their adversaries. At a later point, however, these perceptions often gave way to acute fears of inferiority. In many cases, what appears now to have been pertinent and well-founded information readily available to the participants was ignored while previously formed perceptions appeared to have been practically impervious to change by newly acquired knowledge.[22]

The effects on the interpretation function due to the above types of behavior on the part of one individual can usually be kept to a minimum by a policy requiring all strategic information produced in the speculative-evaluative form to be checked by a number of persons. Consideration of major interpretive statements by a group of qualified individuals considerably lessens the chance that the final evaluation will be biased by misperceptions and stereotyping. However, group consideration of material is not without its difficulties. Situations may arise in which individual members of the group are subjected to subtle pressures that prevent them from bringing contrary opinions to bear once the others in the group appear to be reaching a consensus.[23] This phenomenon, which has been called by the Orwellian term "group think," is often unconsciously reinforced by leaders in the group.

A series of prescriptions have been advanced by Irving L. Janis to minimize the possibility of occurrence of the group-think phenomenon.[24] These prescriptions have particular application to the interpretation of strategic intelligence by a group of individuals. They may be summarized as follows:

- The leader of the evaluating group in the course of discussion should give high priority to the airing of any objections and doubts concerning matters that appear to be in agreement.

[22] Stoessinger, John G., *Why Nations Go to War,* St. Martins Press, 1974, pp. 27–30 and 223–30.

[23] Janis, Irving L., *Victims of Group Think,* Houghton Mifflin Company, 1972.

[24] Ibid., pp. 209–19.

- The leader should be impartial at the outset and not advocate specific interpretations that he or she would like to see adopted.
- If possible, more than one group should work on an important evaluation, with each group having a different leader. As an alternative, a single group should break up into subgroups under different chairpeople from time to time and then re-form and exchange information.
- Members of the group should discuss its proceedings on occasion with trusted associates and report their views and reactions to the group as a whole.
- One or more outside persons with expert knowledge should be invited to meetings of the group on a staggered basis and their views on proceedings to date solicited.
- At least one member should be assigned to act in the role of devil's advocate in each meeting of the group.
- Once a consensus is reached, it should be reconsidered and confirmed or rejected at a later meeting held after time has been allowed for members to collect their doubts and reservations.

Prescriptions with similar intentions have been advocated for use by individuals by Edward deBono in his description of a process known as "lateral thinking."[25] In this description, he compares lateral thinking with the more conventional form which he calls "vertical thinking." In vertical thinking the search for alternatives is continued until a promising one is found, after which that explanation is adopted until there is reason to change. By contrast, lateral thinking is said to have the aim of generating alternatives in a manner that is deliberately nonsequential and unconventional. It seeks to concentrate on dominant ideas and crucial factors, to view situations in different ways and continually restructure information in such a way that new alternatives appear. In this mode of thinking, there is a conscious attempt to break with the familiar, to challenge existing concepts, and to seek different ways of looking at situations.

Lateral thinking is recommended as a complement to the more conventional logical and sequential "vertical" thinking, rather than as

[25] deBono, Edward, *Lateral Thinking,* Ward, Lock Educational Ltd., London, England, 1970.

a replacement for it. The two modes of thought can be used together, one covering areas that might otherwise be neglected by the other. Lateral thinking is often more appropriate during the early stages of consideration of new information, when interpretations can be easily changed and restructured. In advocating lateral thinking, deBono advocates the use of a number of techniques devised to avoid narrow interpretation of evidence. These include (a) rotating areas of attention; (b) designing sessions to provide cross-stimulation of group members; (c) dividing situations into "fractions" and then restructuring the parts; (d) reversing existing situations, ideas, and trends for purposes of analysis; and (e) challenging existing categorizations and labels. The desired effect of these techniques is much the same as that sought by many others proposed as means for maintaining the creativity of those involved in the interpretation of strategic information.

The interpretation function is one in which intuition and creativity play an important part. Interpretation requires an emphasis on communication of impressions concerning matters that are not completely understood. In carrying out this communication, the interpreter must avoid behavior that may distort the message. For example, it has been shown in experiments that persons passing information often exhibit a desire to simplify the message.[26] This may occur because the responsibility of communicating complex information is regarded as troublesome and taxing. People also dislike being required to pass along a message that is, in some respects, incoherent, illogical, or incomplete, probably because it is embarrassing to admit an inadequate understanding of the subject matter. Then again, many people are quite averse to conveying a message that is unpleasant for the recipient, particularly if the recipient is a superior.

While avoiding the tendency toward information distortion, the interpreter must be acutely aware that simple words often have a number of different meanings. The emphasis in preparation of strategic information in the speculative-evaluative form must be on clarity and lucidity of expression. It is also important to distinguish clearly between the actual acquired or observed information and the inferences that are drawn from it by the interpreter. Unless these guidelines are scrupulously observed, significant details may be added,

[26] Haney, W. V., "Serial Communication of Information in Organizations," in S. Mailick and E. H. Van Ness, eds., *Concepts and Issues in Administrative Behavior,* Prentice-Hall, 1962, pp. 150–165.

altered, or omitted in the preparation of the speculative-evaluative form of strategic information. The result may be that the most vital and significant strategic information will go undetected.

The Storage and Retrieval Function

The purpose of the storage and retrieval function in the strategic information system is to provide facilities for the retention of information and its later retrieval.

Information retrieval systems that have proven successful to date have been mostly those systems dealing with well-structured and well-defined data. Strategic information, on the other hand, is likely to be in the form of documents and reports containing very little precisely defined quantitative data. Moreover, the exact meaning, significance, and context of an item of strategic information may not be apparent at the time of its acquisition.

Its ill-defined and often unquantifiable nature together with the wide range and variety of available strategic information, make the storage and retrieval function for this type of material much less efficient than is the case for quantitative information. The relatively low performance level possible in search and recall of documented information is familiar to anyone who has carried out a literature search in a library. Recent experiments have shown that 60 percent recall of documents in an information retrieval system is about the best that can be expected at the present time.[27] In addition, a large volume of documents irrelevant to the current search often accompany the 60 percent of available information that is recalled, adding considerably to the work of retrieval.

The facilities needed for storage and retrieval of strategic information consist of the following components: (a) a series of storage locations (ranging from document racks to microfilm files)[28] in which documents and information are stored and from which they can be easily retrieved; (b) a system of communication with the storage media that allows users to update and reassess the contents; and (c) a system for organization of the stored information that contributes

[27] Ibid., Chapter 1.

[28] Doyle, Lauren B., *Information Retrieval and Processing,* Melville Publishing Company, 1975, Chapter 2.

to effective and efficient retrieval. Each of these components is of great importance to the effectiveness of the storage and retrieval function. Without proper organization of the information stored, however, even the most sophisticated storage facilities and means of communication with them are rendered much less effective.

Organization of the Storage and Retrieval Function

The first task to be undertaken in the organization of the storage and retrieval function of a strategic information system involves deciding which of the wide range of available information to retain and which to discard.[29] Clearly, it is most desirable to retain that portion of the available information that is judged to be most important to the future deliberations of the organization. However, it may not always be clear how this judgement should be made. The views of managers and users of the information are of great value in reaching conclusions in this regard.

After item selection, the second task involves deciding which characteristics or aspects of each item should be stored. The basic choice is between storing the entire document or merely storing a part or an abstract of it.

The third and most complex task consists of determining the relationships between the items stored as a basis for cross-referencing them. The work of classifying the items stored usually results in the assignment of key-words or descriptors to each item. These are most useful in the progressive search of stored information, making a major contribution to the usefulness of the store to the user.

The key to an effective and efficient storage and retrieval system is in accurate, consistent, and precise descriptions of the material that it contains.[30] The type of organization, classification, and indexing system most desirable for a given body of information clearly depends on how well the information is described and structured. If the information is ill-structured, the indexing system should be in the form of a general *directory*. A directory should encourage exploration of the body of information rather than the narrowing down of the area of search. As the information content of the store becomes better struc-

[29] Hare, Van Court, Jr., "Communication and Information Systems," in Joseph W. McGuire, ed., *Contemporary Management: Issues and Viewpoints,* Prentice-Hall, 1974, pp. 207–213.

[30] Wessel, A. E., *Computer Aided Information Retrieval,* Wiley, 1976, p. 9.

tured, a *subject index* or a *catalogue* can be produced. A further step in the classification of the information is the construction of a *thesaurus,* which contains all known linkages and cross references between the items in the store. As the body of strategic information in an organization becomes more sophisticated, so too does the manner in which it can be organized and indexed. A more sophisticated method of indexing information leads to more complex and fruitful search procedures so that, with cooperation, the activities of the user and the organizer of the strategic store build upon each other's efforts.

The primary function of a *directory* is to orient its users within the body of available information.[31] It should stimulate the user to obtain further knowledge and understanding. It should provide facilities so that an individual can locate him- or herself within the entire area of coverage, while, at the same time enabling the user to concentrate on subareas of greater interest. A directory system should be responsive to its users and facilitate interaction, so that attempts at exploration by the user will be immediately rewarded and reinforced by the system. Moreover, the directory should be dynamic, making revisions to keep pace with changes in fields that may be rapidly developing.

The ideal system is a family of directories, the members of which grow in sophistication as the body of information becomes increasingly structured and understood. Earlier versions of such a family of directories are often more suitable for the beginning user of the information store and the later ones for the more experienced users who work continuously with it. Such an ideal family of directories, however, is not achievable in many practical cases.

As the content of the directory develops, the tendency is toward the creation of a classified *subject index* and eventually a *thesaurus.* In the early stages of this development, the concentration is on developing techniques for grouping subjects and documents that result in classifications that are loosely defined, weakly connected, and widely extended.[32] This ambiguity allows for a maximum of exploration and a minimum possibility that connections that are not immediately obvious will be missed. As the size and familiarity of the information body grows, however, the grouping of subjects and docu-

[31] Kochen, Manfred, *Principles of Information Retrieval,* Melville Publishing Company, 1974, pp. 114–116.

[32] Sparck Jones, K., *Automatic Keyword Classification for Information Retrieval,* Archon Books, 1971, p. 11.

ments will tend to become tighter and more selective while the classifications will contain more strongly connected sets. The result, after much development, is a thesaurus, which can be defined as an ordered collection of subject headings indicating the known interrelationships between them.

A thesaurus is usually organized by assigning one or more of a series of descriptors to each of the documents contained in the store. A descriptor is a key word or phrase indicating a significant aspect of a document or record that also relates to important areas of concern to the users of the stored information. Considerations of conciseness of the thesaurus require that the number of descriptors assigned to each record be kept as small as possible, so that the number of interrelationships does not become unmanageably large. On the other hand, the larger the number of descriptors used, the greater is the chance of detecting connections between records in the store. In practice, the number of descriptors assigned to a piece of stored information is decided based upon a compromise between these two conflicting requirements of conciseness and completeness.[33, 34] In most cases, the number chosen lies between one and seven, with an average falling between three and four.

Development of a thesaurus is a task that requires close cooperation between the compilers and the users of the information. Users can supply intuitive and practical knowledge of the relationships between stored documents and records. They can also provide valuable insights into the pertinence of various items of information to the present and future work of the organization. If the users and the compilers keep in close contact, the resulting thesaurus will be a comprehensive listing of relevant topics in the body of information in which the topics are interrelated and coupled to the interests of the organization such that efficient search and retrieval will be greatly facilitated.

Many organizations concerned with storage and retrieval of information have constructed a thesaurus of the type required in the strategic information system. One of the best known of these is the New York Times Thesaurus of Descriptors.[35] This thesaurus is a structured vocabulary of descriptors that is designed to guide information special-

[33] Kochen, Manfred, *op. cit, Principles,* pp. 22–27.

[34] Sparck Jones, K., *op. cit, Automatic Keyword.*

[35] *New York Times Thesaurus of Descriptors,* 2nd Edition, New York Times Co., 1969.

ists in processing and organizing materials from newspapers and other works dealing with current events and public affairs. It consists of terms (descriptors) in a single alphabetical sequence that are used to denote the subjects that may be found in the body of collected information. For each descriptor, some or all of the following information is given in the order indicated:

1/ *Qualifying terms* that make entries more specific, such as, *America:* (continent);
2/ *Scope notes* that describe the scope and range of the entry;
3/ *"See" and "see also"* references that provide reference and cross-reference between topics;
4/ *"Refer from" references* that refer topics in hierarchical form to broader, narrower and related terms;
5/ *Subheadings* that expand and index material on each topic.

A model page from The New York Times Thesaurus is shown in Figure 6-2 to illustrate the use of the above terms to define descriptors and correlate them with one another.

A thesaurus is a catalogue that specializes in relationships between topics. There is one further type of directory that is often valuable in the search for strategic information. This additional catalogue lists the persons, called *agents,* who are concerned with a selected topic or document at any given time under headings referring to the topics themselves.[36] The most important classes of agent are authors (or sources), the interpreters, and users. A directory that matches producers of the information with users of the information can serve as a useful source of contact on particular topics. These contacts can then be used to amplify and augment the information and to suggest further lines of enquiry and search.

The Presentation Function

The presentation function in the strategic information system is concerned with making the information that is pertinent to their current work available to managers and others responsible for decisions. The wide variety and scope of the information in a typical strategic

[36] Kochen, Manfred, *op. cit, Principles,* pp. 124–125.

(reproduced by permission of the New York Times)

Descriptor "See" Reference

ADEN Protectorate
  see South Arabia, Federation of
ADOPTIONS
  Refer from Children and Youth (BT)
ADVERTISING
  See also
    Mass Communications (for inclusion) (BT)
    Premiums, Coupons and Trading
      Stamps (RT)

"See Also" References

    Public Relations and Publicity (RT)
    Trademarks and Trade Names (RT)
    company names
    subjects advertised

  Refer from

"Refer from" References

    Marketing and Merchandising (BT)
    Public Relations and Publicity (RT)
    Publications (BT)
    Retail Stores and Trade (BT)

Subheadings

  Subheadings
    foreign countries
    United States
  Awards
  Direct Mail
    Refer from
      Direct Mail Advertising
      Mail Order Companies(BT)
      Mailing Lists (BT)
      Postal Service (BT)
  Magazine
    Refer from
      Magazines (BT)
  Misleading and Deceptive Advertising
  Newspaper
    Refer from
      News and Newspapers (BT)
      Outdoor
        Refer from
          Billboards (NT)
          Outdoor Advertising
          Roads (for billboards) (BT)
      Television and Radio
        Refer from
          Television and Radio (BT)

Qualifying Terms

AMERICA (Continent)
AMERICA (Jesuit Publication)
AMERIKA (Soviet Publication)
BIRTH Control and Planned Parenthood

Scope Notes

  Note: Material here deals largely with medical, legal, moral and social aspects as they concern individual family
  See also
    Abortion (NT)

Qualified Cross References

    Population and Vital Statistics (for link between birth control and population explosion) (BT)
    geographic headings (specific) (for link between birth control and population explosion) (NT)
  Refer from
    Births (BT)
    Children and Youth (BT)
    Contraception
    Families and Family Life (BT)
    Parenthood, Planned
    Planned Parenthood
    Population and Vital Statistics (BT)
    Pregnancy, Obstetrics and Maternal Welfare (RT)
    Reproduction (Biological) (RT)
BLACK Muslims
  Refer from Muslim Sects (BT)
"BLACK Power"
  See Negroes (BT)
BLACKLISTING

Hierarchical Notations:
(BT) broader term
(NT) narrower term
(RT) related term.

Figure 6.2. Model page from the New York Times Thesaurus of Descriptors

information system precludes presentation of its entire content to all its users. A way must be found of bringing the details of the information available to the attention of the users in a manner designed to attract their interest. The chosen method must also provide users with the least possible diversion of effort from their other tasks and responsibilities.

The most important general aids to presentation of the content of a store of strategic information are a series of comprehensive directories and catalogues and a competently compiled thesaurus. The aim in this most general method of presentation of the data is to display the contents in a form that is of immediate assistance to users in their search for information. This objective can be met over a period of time only if the directories, catalogues, and thesaurus are continually kept up-to-date.

The next step for the user after consulting the directory, catalogue, or thesaurus is to retrieve the selected documents or records for personal assessment. The search procedure then consists of series of repetitions of the three-part process of interpretation of the contents of the retrieved documents, consultation of the various forms of directory, and retrieval of further documents and records. At each stage of this process, continuation of a line of enquiry to a successful conclusion usually depends upon the ability of the user to obtain quick and easy access to the information required.

Establishment and maintenance of easy access to information is a first and continuing objective of the presentation function of the strategic information system. This objective can be achieved by designing the necessary search and retrieval procedures so that they serve the purposes of the users rather than those of the system itself. This may be difficult if there are many users of the system with varied and diverse interests and working habits. However, much in the way of user-responsiveness can be achieved by ensuring (a) that an unresponsive and seemingly impersonal bureaucracy does not grow up, inhibiting access by the user to the information he or she is seeking and (b) that the physical location of the information is convenient to the offices of the user. If the latter condition cannot be achieved, much the same result can be obtained if a swift and reliable delivery service (electronic or otherwise) can be installed linking the location of the documents and records with the user's offices.

Another method for the presentation of strategic information involves the establishment of an information display room located centrally in the organization.[37, 38, 39] Display rooms of this sort are common in military command centers. Their purpose is to bring required strategic information, as well as relevant information from the internal system, to the notice of the decision makers in as comprehensive and interesting a way as possible in a short period of time. This is achieved by the use of display techniques that integrate information from a number of fields and allow concentration on specific issues and situations. The use of modern video display technology allows rapid and flexible movement through a number of subjects. It also facilitates continuous updating of the information displayed.

There may be some opposition within an organization to the presentation in a display room of information that is admittedly subject to interpretation and doubt. Many individuals are reluctant to see subjective information of this nature given permanent display, possibly because they think that permanent display would confer special status to what they regard as only one of a number of possible interpretations of the situation. However, the same individuals do not normally object to a briefing containing strategic information being delivered at a meeting. This suggests that the emphasis in a display center should be on generating interaction between the users and the store of strategic information. This interaction can be encouraged by holding regular briefing sessions for senior managers and also by holding individual discussions of the material with each of the managers involved.

If the display room is equipped with the means of rapid access to the store of basic information upon which the presentations are based, the process of interaction can be all the more meaningful. The intuition and reactions of the individual managers can be rapidly incorporated into the interpretation of the strategic information acquired by the organization and the displays amended accordingly. In the course of this interaction, information in the possession of individuals and not yet integrated into the strategic information system may become available. The reluctance of some members of the organization to impart such information can often be overcome by the installation

[37] Branch, Melville, *The Corporate Planning Process,* American Management Association, 1962, p. 128 ff.

[38] Smalter, D. J., and R. L. Ruggles, Jr., "Six Business Lessons from the Pentagon," *Harvard Business Review,* March-April 1966, p. 174.

[39] Friend, J. K., and W. N. Jessop, *Local Government and Strategic Choice,* Tavistock Publications, London and Coventry, 1969, pp. 279–281.

of a strict security system governing entry into the display room and restricting access to a very few persons with a recognized need-to-know.

Strategic information not requiring strict security can be circulated to a wider set of individuals by the establishment of a regular information bulletin.[40] Articles in such a bulletin can consist of strategic information in the basic descriptive form covering issues and events that are not specifically problem-related. A system of updates can be incorporated, providing information in the current reportorial form on items that indicate a trend or discontinuity in the environment of the organization. An invitation to qualified members of the organization to discuss items in the bulletin at greater depth often encourages interaction with users of strategic information. It may also uncover stores of information that has not previously been available to the central system.

Implementation of the Strategic Information System

The initial stages of the implementation of the strategic information system consist of the establishment of staffs and facilities to carry out the basic functions of acquisition, interpretation, storage and retrieval, and presentation. Decisions regarding the number of persons and the amount of resources to be allocated to each of these functions can be made somewhat arbitrarily in the beginning. It is typical in modern organizations, however, that the resources allocated to the internal information system are far greater than those assigned to the strategic system. This is natural because by far the greatest part of the internal system consists of the completely-specified systems. These systems can rightly be regarded as an integral part of the administration and operations of the organization. Perhaps a realistic initial target for the strategic system should be the acquisition of resources equivalent to those used to establish and operate the common data base, the management reporting system, and the information retrieval system of its internal counterpart.

Once an initial allocation of resources has been made and the functions of the strategic system have been established in an operating

40 Weiner, Edith, "Future Scanning for Trade Groups and Companies," *Harvard Business Review*, Sept.-Oct. 1976, pp. 14, 174, 176.

condition, the major task in the development of the system involves integrating the various and widespread strategic information activities already existing in the organization.[41] The great amount of differentiation and specialization that is a basic feature of modern organizations results in dispersal and fractionalization of these information-gathering activities. The fact that strategic information is generally regarded as strictly confidential usually impedes the process of integration. The reluctance of those involved to disclose and divulge information with a large amount of subjective content is also a barrier to quick and complete integration.

Historically, the same dispersal of activities, feelings of confidentiality and uncertainty about the exact meaning of data encountered by strategic systems existed, to some extent, in the early days of internal information systems. There is no reason to suspect, therefore, that the task of establishing an integrated strategic information system will be substantially more difficult than the earlier task of forming the various internal data processing activities of an organization into an integrated system.

A major factor in the process of integration is the establishment of confidence in the overall purposes and activities of the strategic information system. The growth of confidence can be aided greatly by the continuous and visible support of the system and its basic concepts by the senior managers of the organization. Demonstrated and convincing use of the system by senior members of the organization is far superior to reliance upon written memoranda and pronouncements.

A second and equally important factor fostering integration of the system is the encouragement of interaction between users and the information system staff as discussed in the previous section of this chapter. Vigorous interaction of this sort provides benefits to all parties involved and is one of the most potent factors in ensuring the acceptance of the strategic system.

Other methods of ensuring the integration and growth of the system are also recommended, namely (a) stressing the importance of both strategic information and internal information in organizational pronouncements and policy statements; (b) assigning an executive assistant to each senior manager whose duties specifically include relations with the strategic information system; (c) assignment of middle- and upper-level managers to positions within the strategic information

[41] Aguilar, F. J., *op. cit., Scanning the Business Environment,* pp. 184–194.

system for either short or long periods; and (d) emphasizing the role of the display center in the decision making activities of the organization. Using these and other methods, the strategic information system will develop at a rate determined by the degree of acceptance by the members of the organization. If this acceptance is not given for one reason or another, the system is likely to languish and the effort expended in its development and operation will be largely wasted.

The Security of the Strategic Information System

Security of both the internal and strategic components of the information system is important to an organization. However, the reasons for maintaining the confidentiality of the contents of the two systems are somewhat different. A leak of information from the internal system would provide the recipient with information on the state and characteristics of the organization. This information would probably permit an assessment to be made of the *potential* of the organization to undertake certain courses of action. A leak from the strategic system, on the other hand, might provide information on the *intention* of the organization to take a course of action. A leak in the strategic system might, therefore, be more damaging than a similar disclosure from the internal system, especially if the information were made available to a competitor at a crucial point in a decision situation.

A leak from the strategic system might also provide a competitor with an assessment of the state of knowledge in an organization in regard to a particular problem. A high state of knowledge might reveal intentions, whereas a low information level would indicate unawareness of the existence of a problem. The fact that knowledge in some category is being sought is, in some respects, an indication of the interests of an organization. It is also an invitation to a competitor to surreptitiously supply misinformation related to the interests of the organization in a form advantageous to his or her own interests.[42]

Some of the information in the strategic system refers to the characteristics and intentions of other individuals and organizations who are participants in current decision situations. The information in this

[42] Goffman, Erving, *Strategic Information,* University of Pennsylvania Press, 1969, p. 63.

category may only be of use as long as the participant concerned does not realize that it is known outside his or her own organization.[43] The element of surprise in launching a new product or initiative is lost if the details and timing of the action are known to others. On the other hand, undetected acquisition of such information may be a source of power to the recipient in countering the new initiative. It is not surprising, therefore, that the subject of industrial and commercial espionage has been examined in the literature. However, most of the studies that have been published seem to be only applications of the more popular treatments of international intelligence operations to the industrial environment.[44]

The requirements for protection against espionage can be stated simply—as guarding any information that others might be seeking. Although the nature of the protection required can be stated simply in this form, methods of ensuring the necessary security are seldom easy to implement. Moreover, it cannot always be assumed that even the most intricate and costly methods of protection will guarantee complete security of the information in question.

As in the case of the internal information system, the first steps towards security of information and against espionage consist of a series of physical measures, such as combination locks and their electronic equivalents. These measures can be supported by procedures and protocols designed to ensure that only authorized persons have access to information that has been classified as confidential. However, the fact that individuals must have access to this classified information in the course of their day-to-day work is probably the greatest weakness in the whole security system. It has proved to be relatively easy in both the international and industrial environments for persons intent on stealing information to represent themselves to the organization as bona fide employees. With careful preparation, such persons have often been able to gain access to confidential information in a short period of time. Even the long-time trusted employee must be regarded as a potential espionage agent. The very fact that an individual is a trusted recipient of information may make him or her a high priority target for subversion by a competitor.

[43] Seale, P., and M. McConville, *op. cit*, Philby, p. 197.

[44] For example see T. J. Walsh, and R. J. Healy, *Protecting your Business against Espionage*, American Management Association, 1973; and P. I. Slee Smith, *Industrial Intelligence and Espionage*, Business Books Ltd., London, 1970.

Security of both internal and strategic information requires constant vigilance. The potential spy hopes to discover routine procedures of protection and to design his activities so as to utilize weaknesses in measures that have remained unchanged for some time. The most potent measure against espionage is a program of randomly implemented and generally unannounced changes in protection procedures. Those who have not been informed of a particular change and who are detected probing under the old rules are then automatically suspect. In addition, the continual change in procedures will prevent a potential spy from building up a knowledge of routine. Unfortunately, such measures do not affect the activities of the trusted employee who has become subverted. These individuals are the most dangerous espionage agents. However, the strain under which such persons operate is very great. Only the most sanguine insider spies are able to carry on such a deception for long. Other lesser individuals are detected within a short period of time, but often not before they have passed on vital information to a competitor.

Summary

The strategic component of the overall information system differs from its internal counterpart in a number of characteristics. Information in the internal system is usually well-defined and complete, while that in the strategic system is often fragmentary and ill-structured. Strategic information is mostly nonquantitative. It refers, in large part, to matters in the external environment of the organization that are less familiar to managers than the subjects of internal data. Most strategic information is highly subjective. The emphasis in the strategic information system is, therefore, on acquisition and identification of information, on interpretation of its meaning, and on individual search and enquiry starting from a base of information already acquired.

Managers tend to collect strategic information through personal contacts and individual communication networks. The confidential nature of such information may cause some resistance to the establishment of a more formal system. However, many organizations have established strategic information systems. Procedures in reference libraries provide many clues as to the manner in which a strategic information system can be designed.

The major functions of a strategic information system are acquisition, interpretation, storage and retrieval, and presentation of information. The duty of the acquisition function is to gather as much relevant information as possible within the constraints imposed by available resources. This task is performed by employing a range of acquisition modes ranging from general scanning through directed scanning to active search. Management of the acquisition function includes the task of allocating effort among these modes in a way that is appropriate to the needs of the organization at any particular time.

Methods of active search can be considered under the headings illicit, surreptitious, and open. Illicit methods include theft, bribery, and other activities that are actually illegal. These methods cannot be included in the activities of a law-abiding organization. Surreptitious methods of acquisition, on the other hand, may be unethical but are not actually illegal. Most organizations engage in activities of this sort to a greater or lesser extent. Open methods of information acquisition are, however, the most common and acceptable methods employed by modern organizations. Open methods have also been proven to be the most fruitful in most circumstances.

The Delphi method for the collection of information from persons and groups that may be widely dispersed provides a very advantageous means of searching for information. There is often a great deal of information of strategic value that is overlooked within the organization itself. Methods of acquisition should include some way, such as Delphi, to gather information from this readily-available source.

Proper allocation of resources among the various acquisition modes can be facilitated by procedures based on criterion checks. These checks consist of the comparison of recently acquired information with data previously stored. If a deviation from past conditions is detected, there may be a reason for a more concentrated scanning effort in the area of the deviation. Recognition of problems by managers or others outside the immediate operation of the strategic information system may also provide the cause for more concentrated scanning or active search.

The purpose of the interpretation function is to assess the significance of the information that is acquired. This process is inseparable from the process of acquisition. Interpretation of information is often the primary reason for a change of acquisition mode. Successful interpretation requires that the targets about which more information is required be defined by managers engaged in the organizational decision processes. Interpretation is a highly subjective process. Individuals bring their own personal characteristics into the evaluation of information. The resulting effects are often highly desirable. Any undesirable effects can be kept to a minimum by a policy requiring that all important strategic information in the speculative-evaluative form be checked by a number of individuals. Proper leadership of such a group of individuals can ensure that all possible interpretations are considered.

Information that has been acquired and interpreted must often be stored for later retrieval. Facilities for the storage and retrieval function consist of (a) storage media; (b) a system of communication with the stored information; and (c) a system of organization, cataloging, and indexing of the information. Of these components, the third is of overriding importance. The type of organization, cataloging, and indexing system employed depends upon how well the information concerned is described and structured.

When the information is ill-structured, a directory is required to orient the users of the store and to assist in the exploration of its contents. As the information store becomes better known, a subject index can be constructed. Later still, a thesaurus can be produced that delineates the linkages and cross references between the items of information. A thesaurus is usually constructed by assigning descriptors to each of the items stored. This task is best accomplished with the close cooperation of the users of the store.

A directory, index, or thesaurus is a vital aid in the presentation of the information in the strategic system to its users. The success of the strategic information system depends upon the user obtaining quick and easy access to the information that it contains. It is important that an unresponsive and seemingly impersonal bureaucracy does not grow up between the user and the information that he or she is seeking. It is important also that the physical location of the information be as close as possible to the user or that a speedy and reliable delivery system be available. Some organizations have set up display rooms to facilitate presentation of information. Information bulletins are also used to disseminate some of the less sensitive items.

Implementation of the strategic information system does not depend as much on the creation of new complex systems as does implementation of the internal component of the information system. It is more a matter of integrating activities that already exist to some extent within the organization. There may be some resistance to this process of integration. Support of senior management is essential to lessen this resistance.

Security of the information in the strategic system is vital because the items contained may indicate the intentions of the organization, as opposed to the indication of the potential of the organization that might be gleaned from the content of the internal system. The contents of the strategic system also may reveal the state of knowledge of the organization, an important factor when the element of surprise is considered. Security of the strategic system is provided by a series of physical and procedural methods in the same way as is done for the internal system. The greatest weakness of any security system stems from the fact that individuals must have access to the information protected. Possession of this information may make individuals targets of attempts at subversion.

Espionage seeks out routine as a means of ensuring that probing activities are not detected. The best protection against espionage is continued and randomly-implemented changes in procedures. These measures do not, however, impede the activities of a trusted employee who has become subverted. These most dangerous of espionage agents, on the other hand, seldom remain undetected for long.

Discussion Topics

1/ The strategic information system and its internal counterpart deal with different types of data and information. What basic differences in the design and construction of the two components of the information system result from this fact?

2/ How does the fact that managers tend to collect strategic information on an individual and confidential basis affect the design and operation of the strategic information system?

3/ What relevance does experience gained in the use of a reference library have to the design of a strategic information system?

4/ What surreptitious or clandestine methods of active search might you authorize for your own organization? Under what conditions would you regard such methods as justified?

5/ A great amount of strategic information exists within the organization itself. What categories of information might be included in this internal store? Where in an organization might this information be found?

6/ Are there major advantages to the anonymity and iteration that are characteristic of the Delphi questionnaire method of gathering information? Are there any disadvantages to the method?

7/ List some examples of the criterion checks that you might specify in managing the acquisition function in your own organization. How can such checks be used to assess changes in the environment that cannot be expressed totally in quantitative form?

8/ What training or educational background do you think best prepares individuals for the interpretation function? Would the answer to this question help you in devising a training course for such individuals and, if so, how?

9/ Why shouldn't the individual responsible for gathering strategic information be solely responsible for its interpretation?

10/ Janis has put forward some prescriptions for the leadership of a group engaged in interpretation of strategic information. Can you think of some examples of situations where these prescriptions have not been followed? What were the results?

11/ What procedures would you install in the interpretation function to ensure that narrow and biased assessments are not likely to emerge?

12/ What do you consider to be the major factors that impede the search for information in libraries? How do you think that these factors can be eliminated in formulating procedures for retrieval of information from the strategic information system?

13/ Do you feel that users should be closely involved in the construction of a thesaurus? How can the opinions of a small subset of users be prevented from dominating the selection of key words?

14/ Is a display room likely to be useful in the presentation of strategic information on a continuing basis? What would you consider to be the most important characteristics of such a facility?

15/ What would be the purpose of a regularly published bulletin for the dissemination of strategic information? Would the confidentiality of the information present a barrier to this method of presentation of strategic information? How would a bulletin of this type compare with a management report from the internal system?

16/ What are the primary causes of resistance to the integration of the already-existing strategic information activities into a formal system? How can this resistance be minimized in practical circumstances?

17/ Is strategic information more confidential than information in the internal system of an organization? If so, why?

18/ Is strategic information more important than internal information? If the two sorts of information are of roughly equal importance, why do you think so much more money and effort have been expended on the internal system? What do you think can be done to correct the imbalance?

19/ How would you set out to detect the activities of a subverted employee passing information to a competitor?

20/ What methods of random change of procedures would you institute to protect the information systems in your organization?

CASE WORK

1/ Tom MacDonald was president of MacDonalds Lumber Ltd. until a few months ago. He had founded the firm in 1947 when he established a local lumber yard in a small town. His first year's gross receipts were less than half a million dollars. However, the firm had prospered. By the time that Tom died of a heart attack six months ago, there were seven branch operations in neighboring towns and the annual gross of the company exceeded 34 million dollars.

As president and founder, Tom MacDonald played a dominant role in setting the company's objectives and goals. The managers of his branches (including his son Jim who operated the largest branch about 100 miles away) concentrated on keeping their operations efficient under Tom's general directives. If they had any ideas on policy and objectives, there was seldom time at the regular management meetings to mention them. If the ideas did come up, Tom seemed to be so much more knowledgeable on the subject and the discussion soon stopped. However, Tom was now dead. The firm had passed to Jim and he soon realized how ill-equipped he was to handle the task.

It became clear to Jim soon after taking over the presidency that the firm was not in as good a shape as he had always assumed. Expenses and costs had been increasing and net profits decreasing. There was now considerable competition in some previously uncontested areas from large and powerful firms that were aggressively acquiring a large share of the market. Furthermore, Jim realized that his father had been the only member of the firm who had been gathering and interpreting what we would call strategic information. He himself had very little knowledge of the external environment of the firm. He therefore decided to hire a young executive assistant to fill in the gaps in his knowledge. He also decided to ask you to help him specify the nature of the work that this young person should do. Write a descriptive brief not more than 10 pages long that would be of assistance to Jim in this situation.

Meanwhile, Jim met with his branch managers and explained the situation that he found on taking over the firm. They decided that there was an urgent need to diversify operations in view of the competition from the larger firms. Home hardware and automobile parts and service were suggested as possible areas of diversification. Jim now wishes you to take these ideas into account in preparing your description of the areas of concentration of the executive assistant.

One further development affects your task. At a trade convention a long-time friend tells Jim that he has heard that one of the larger competitors is preparing to make him an offer of merger within the next six months. Jim now wishes to know how this possibility should affect what is included in the brief that you are preparing.

2/ You are the planning director of a large region of the country that includes both urban and rural areas. You are well-advanced in the preparation of a plan for development of the region that proposes a balance between agricultural, industrial, recreational, and other uses of land. The plan must be presented to Council in six months' time. The content of the plan is naturally of great interest to developers, citizens groups, and a number of other parties. You have conducted the preparation of the document in great secrecy, although you have arranged public hearings and briefings in all parts of the region.

It is now necessary to make details of the plan available to members of the regional staff. You have decided to set up a display room to which only authorized persons will have access. Describe how you would do this, what information would be on display, and how it would be updated. How would you try to ensure the security of the information on display?

7

The Organizational Information System

Introduction

The designs for the internal and strategic components of the information system that have been discussed in the preceding chapters can now be combined into a single diagram illustrating the basic structure for an overall information system in an organization. This generic diagram is shown in Figure 7-1. Each part of the diagram represents detailed functions that have been discussed in previous sections of the text. The data management component, which facilitates the transmission of data and information throughout the system, has been omitted, however, for the sake of clarity.

The basic design illustrated in Figure 7-1 meets the initial specifications for an organizational information system derived in Chapter 1 in that

- The emphasis of the system is on satisfaction of managerial needs for information;
- The system provides facilities to support routine operational and administrative functions as well as to support the various functions of management at the middle and higher levels of the organization;

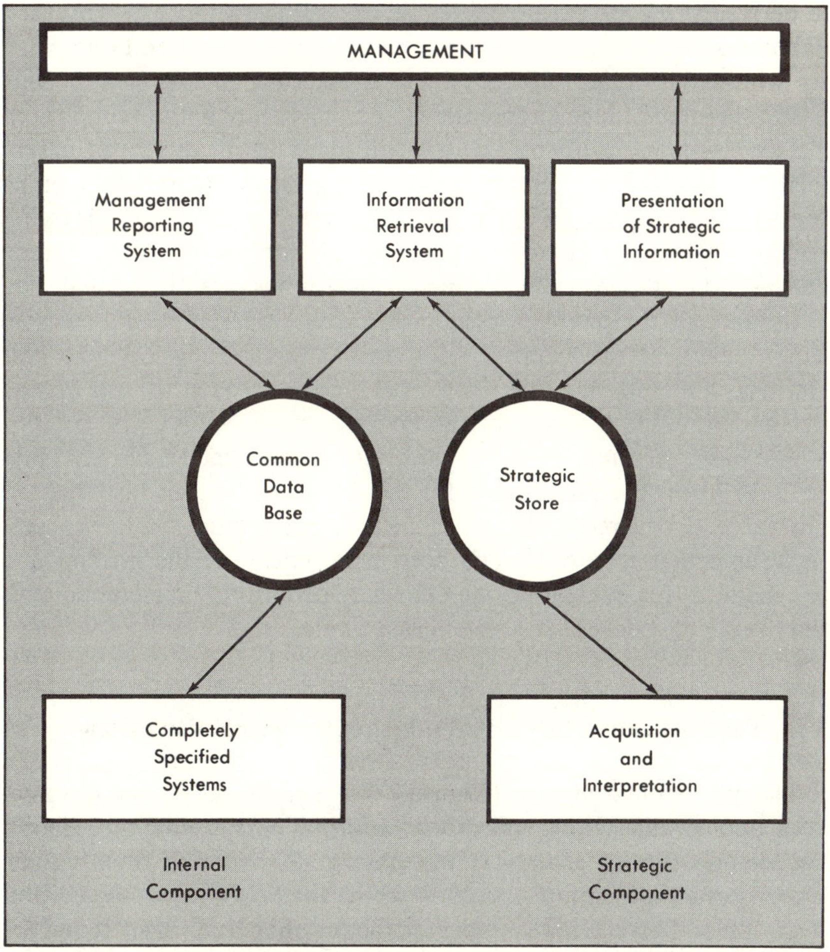

Figure 7.1. The Organizational Information System

- The system outlined in this design matches the pattern and structure of decision making and management within the organization;
- The design allows for flexibility and modular implementation so that any necessary changes in the system can be introduced quickly, economically, and with a minimum of disruption;
- The design allows that the system's output be matched to the capacity of managers to absorb information so that the problems associated with information overload can be avoided.

ed design that is adopted in any particular organization can d from the basic conceptual diagram of Figure 7-1 by such on as is suitable to the circumstances and conditions exist- in the organization and in its external environment. Many existing systems place preponderant emphasis upon the completely-specified systems. This has occurred in many cases due to an urgent need to meet the rapidly expanding requirements of record-keeping and transaction processing. In these and other cases, little effort has been made to establish the essential strategic component of the system. This aspect of the overall information system has often been neglected in the face of the pressing need to meet the apparently more urgent requirements of the internal component. Future development can, however, hopefully lead to a more balanced approach to information system design, implementation, and operation.

The basic diagram for the organizational information system (Figure 7-1) forms the background for the discussions in this last chapter. The subjects covered include (a) factors contributing to the success of the information system; (b) costs and benefits of the system; and (c) methods for evaluating the efficiency of the system's components and the effectiveness of the system as a whole.

Factors Contributing to the Success of the Information System

The conceptual diagram (Figure 7-1) provides only a basic framework upon which an organizational information system can be built. The detailed design that is appropriate to a particular organization depends upon the circumstances in which the organization finds itself at the time. There are a number of factors that have been found by experience to contribute to the success of an information system. Most of these have already been discussed in the preceding text. However, a few of the more crucial factors bear repeating at this point. These factors are discussed below:

1/ It is of primary importance that the information system be designed and implemented to meet the requirements of those who will use it in the discharge of their day-to-day duties. In the past, potential users have often been unable or unwilling to articulate their needs. As a result, specialist designers have sometimes produced systems that have been more oriented to utilizing the latest in technical sophistication or to serving the designers' ideas of managers' requirements than to meeting the existing needs of the organization. The emphasis has also often been on producing a system in a short period of time rather than spending the longer period needed for a study of user requirements and drawing plans accordingly. In many cases, the pressure to meet rapidly expanding routine data processing requirements has provided the major impetus for the introduction of a new information system. With many of these requirements now met, at least temporarily, the emphasis can now move from the completely specified systems to those areas where the needs of managers for information are less well satisfied. The objective of the installation of an information system must be to provide each manager with the type of information that he or she is attuned to and that will be used most effectively in the situation confronting the individual involved.[1]

2/ The work of specifying the detailed requirements of an information system and of implementing the resulting specifications is best undertaken with close cooperation between managers and systems specialists. With such cooperation, the long and detailed experience of managers in the administration and operations of the organization is brought to bear on the system design. In addition, the technical knowledge of the systems specialists is incorporated into the plan for implementation. The result of this cooperation is that both the design and the implementation incorporate a sensitivity to user requirements and a tendency toward proper human factors design. The system that is finally put into operation becomes a natural adjunct to the work of managers rather than a little-understood technical innovation that has been imposed on them.

3/ The best starting point for an information system design project is an examination of the system that already exists in the organization at the time. The first step in such a project is the cataloguing and documentation of the existing system in terms of a conceptual design such as that illustrated in Figure 7-1.

[1] Mason, R. O., and I. I. Mitroff, "A Program of Research on Management Information Systems," *Management Science*, vol. 19, January 1973, p. 478.

The steps necessary to convert the existing system into one that can operate under the new design concept can then be specified in detail. In this way, parts of the existing system that fit into the new design can often be left in place with only minor modifications and a consequent saving in costs. Available resources can then be assigned to areas in which major deficiencies exist. Disruption of those parts of the system that are judged to be satisfactory is minimized by this approach and the time required to implement a system conforming to the new design is correspondingly shortened.

4/ Development of an information system is an evolutionary process rather than one that can be accomplished by the sudden implementation of a comprehensive and radically new set of procedures.[2, 3] The emphasis in implementation of the new design is, therefore, placed on the phased introduction of selected portions of the system that have been designed on a modular basis. This approach facilitates integration of the portions of the existing system that have been judged to be satisfactory and appropriate to the new system. It also provides insurance that the failure of one component that has been newly designed will not disrupt the operation of the whole system. The ability to fall back to the previous version of the system ensures that operations can continue in all circumstances.

5/ Flexibility of design is a most desirable characteristic of a modern information system.[4] In the first place, the development of the system is evolutionary. The objectives of the system and the environment in which it is operating may change in such a way as to require modification of the system during the course of implementation. Second, the objectives and structure of the organization that the information system serves may change. Third, the requirements of managers for

[2] Powers, Richard F., and Gary W. Dickson, "MIS Project Management: Myths, Opinions and Reality," *California Management Review*, vol. 15, no. 3, Spring 1973, pp. 147–156.

[3] Aaron, J. D., "Information Systems in Perspective," *Computing Surveys*, vol. 1, no. 4, December 1969, pp. 233–234.

[4] Emery, James C., "An Overview of Management Information Systems," *Data Base*, vol. 5, nos. 2, 3 and 4, December 1973, p. 4.

information may change with time as the organization matures or as it moves from one mode of operation to another. All these possibilities provide good reasons for flexibility in design. The penalty for inflexibility is the continued vulnerability of the information system to change and the likelihood that any modifications that become necessary will be both time-consuming and expensive.

6/ Successful implementation of a management information system requires adoption of a competent project management scheme based on the chosen design. The type of project management effort required to implement a modern information system is different from that required in the case of standard data processing projects in many respects. Whereas the design and implementation of a completely specified system is similar to the analogous task in data processing, all other parts of the overall system deal with other technologies and other aspects of management. Some of these technologies, such as classification of documents, are not as well specified as most data processing techniques. Nevertheless, project management needs to provide for adequate consideration of these lesser-known but vitally important aspects of the system. As in all project management, emphasis must be placed on time and cost estimates and on documentation and control techniques. Overrunning of projected time and costs figures and lack of documentation have been major irritants in projects of this nature in the past. However, project control in a management information system implementation must be devised so as to facilitate the evolutionary process mentioned previously, rather than to prevent it.[5]

7/ Employment of experienced staff in the design and implementation of a management information system is a major factor ensuring its success. There is sometimes reluctance on the part of senior managers to assign their best individuals to this work for sufficient time to allow them to make a contribution. There is also a temptation, on occasion, to use less experienced systems specialists, because they may be less expensive or because there is a shortage of more fully trained persons.

[5] Powers, Richard F., and Gary W. Dickson, *op. cit,* "MIS Project," pp. 154–156.

In all cases, it is wise to use experienced individuals, even if the cost is higher or the search for such people results in some delay in starting the project. The benefits in terms of competent design and smooth implementation resulting from such an approach amply compensate for any initial disadvantages.

8/ Success of an information system often depends upon the level or the specialization in the organization to which the officer responsible for the activity reports. The completely-specified systems can be disassociated from the other systems in this respect. Each of these completely-specified systems is best integrated into the operation or administrative procedure that it serves. It can then come under the direct supervision and responsibility of the manager responsible for that aspect of the organization's activities, subject only to the requirement that the overall rules and standards of the information system be observed where necessary. The remainder of the information system is much more concerned with the interests of the organization as a whole. The information in these remaining parts of the system is of use to middle and senior managers acting primarily on behalf of the whole organization rather than for parts or specializations within it. Many companies with experience in this area have, therefore, taken the view that those responsible for the design, implementation, and operation of the information system (minus that of the completely specified systems) should report to the most senior levels of the organization.[6] This is a major deviation from earlier practice in which responsibility for the information system was delegated to the most prolific user of data, usually the accounting section. The gradual move in modern organizations is towards having responsibility for the information system being held at the most senior levels. This move appears to be the result of a growing appreciation of the importance of the system in the support of decision processes at these senior levels.

9/ Computer support for the various parts of the information system is an issue that arises early in the design process. In the past, this issue has sometimes dominated all other considera-

[6] See, for example, Hanold, Terrance, "An Executive View of MIS," *Datamation,* November 1972, p. 69.

tions in both the design and the implementation of the system. The presence of a computer has often been the major factor in decisions concerning the scope of the system and the services that it provides. In modern information systems, the role of the computer is to provide support to the functions of acquisition, use, retention, and transmission of information. Decisions with regard to computer support should, if possible, be taken after the operational requirements in each of these functions have been assessed and the activities needed to meet these requirements have been specified. These decisions can be taken independently for each of the elements of the system, as long as the necessary compatibility between the methods of handling data and information in each of the elements is preserved. The major part of the computer processing in the information system takes place in the completely specified systems. The basis for decisions concerning computer support in these systems generally involves the efficiency of the operations or procedures that are supported. In modern organizations the responsibility for these decisions is increasingly delegated to the managers responsible for the systems concerned. Many organizations are now making use of minicomputers or taking service from external installations as alternatives to the acquisition of a large in-house computer to support the information system. A number of minicomputers can be linked together with communications facilities to form an economical and flexible network of support. The fact that a minicomputer can be dedicated to each specific function often allows significant improvements in efficiency over the use of larger multiprogrammed computers.

10/ The most successful information systems are usually those in which existing procedures for acquisition, use, retention, and transmission of information are facilitated, augmented, and improved. New systems that employ complex models or that are otherwise hard to understand or operate often have little impact on the decision making process in an organization.[7]

[7] Dickson, G. W., J. A. Senn, and N. L. Chervany, "Research in Management Information Systems: the Minnesota Experiments," *Management Science*, vol. 23, no. 9, May 1977, pp. 913–923.

Systems that include complex or unfamiliar elements may produce low user confidence and satisfaction, even though, to the systems specialist, they appear to be singularly appropriate to the needs of the organization and quite economical. Resistance to such systems may not be overcome even after substantial effort is expended by the organization on familiarization and training of users.[8]

11/ Considerable attention should be paid in the design of the information system to the provision of output in a form that is most appropriate for managers. In the first place, output that contributes to information overload should be avoided. Individuals in responsible positions require that information be presented in a form that facilitates maximum appreciation and retention of its content in a minimum of time. Cathode ray tube devices and systems providing graphic outputs may be of assistance in this respect. Many managers like to have the ability to interact with the system.[9] Output devices that provide easy interaction with the information store are of particular importance in the strategic component of the information system.

12/ A final important consideration concerns the confidentiality and security of the system. An information system contains material that refers to the most vital aspects of the organization that it serves. Loss or leakage of information from the system may result in irreparable damage to the organization. Unless adequate security measures are taken to safeguard information and unless these measures are seen to be effective, managers and users may lose confidence in the system. This observation refers particularly to the strategic component of the system. Facilities must be available in that component for individuals to conduct searches in confidence and without dissemination of the results even within the organization until the individual is ready to release them.

[8] Argyris, Chris, "Management Information Systems: the Challenge to Rationality and Emotionality," *Management Science,* vol. 17, no. 6, February 1971, pp. 275–292.

[9] Dickson, G. W., J. A. Senn, and N. L. Chervany, *op. cit,* "Research in Information Systems," p. 921.

Costs of the Information System

Information can be considered to be a resource in modern organizations. It has many of the characteristics of material resources.[10] It can be acquired, stored, distributed, and used. It is perishable in that it may become outdated. However, it is not consumable in the sense that it can be used up. Information has value in the same way as do other resources. There are costs associated with its use that must be taken into account in the design of a system to process it.

The costs of the acquisition, use, retention, and transmission of information are most apparent in those parts of the information system in which its handling has become formalized. The formal descriptions of information processing operations in the completely specified systems, for example, allow precise estimates to be made of the cost of these systems in normal everyday use. In less formal processes, where the use of information cannot be completely specified, the cost of acquiring and using the necessary information resources is much more difficult to estimate. In many of the more complex decision processes, for example, a substantial portion of the time of the managers responsible for resolving the problem is taken up with the acquisition and use of information. In such situations, the human system is essentially part of the organizational information processing activity. The cost of the human component could, therefore, be regarded as part of the cost of the overall information system in these cases. However, it may be very difficult to obtain precise estimates of costs of this nature.

It is natural that measurements of the costs of information systems should have been concentrated on those elements for which more precise data are available. In a study reported in 1966, for example, the costs of computer supported completely specified systems in 33 United States companies ranged from 0.13 percent to 1.33 percent of their annual revenue.[11] The average for these companies was 0.54 percent of revenue. Companies that were judged in the study to be of higher effectiveness spent an average of 1.0 percent of revenue on

[10] Johnson, Robert L., and I. H. Derman, "How Intelligent Is Your MIS?" *Business Horizons,* February 1970, pp. 55–62; reprinted in J. W. Borge, and B. P. Coleman, eds., *Concepts for Corporate Strategy,* MacMillan 1972, pp. 37–47.

[11] Taylor, James W., and Neal J. Dean, "Managing to Manage the Computer," *Harvard Business Review,* Sept.-Oct. 1966.

these systems, while those with lower rated effectiveness spent only an average of 0.23 percent of revenue in this area. More recent studies show that these percentages may be rising, possibly to as high as 4 percent of revenue in some cases.[12]

In many present-day organizations, the cost of the completely-specified systems is taken as the total cost of the information system. The other elements of the system, such as the common data base, the management reporting system, and, particularly, the strategic component are much less developed. The costs of the embryonic versions of these elements that do exist are often unwittingly included in other budgets, rather than being attributed directly to the information system. Development of more formal versions of these elements is, therefore, sometimes taken as an additional cost to the organization. This additional cost is often seen as requiring separate justification when, in fact, the activities involved have been continuing for some time under other auspices and in cruder forms.

The greatest proportion of the cost of operating the completely specified systems is that of the computer support required and of the personnel associated with the data processing procedures. In the past, the innovative characteristics of computers have often resulted in service from these installations being regarded as an expense to be borne as an overhead in the organization. This concept has been reinforced in many cases by the creation of a central computer installation in the organization that is supported by its own budget and funding.

The modern tendency is to delegate the responsibility for arranging the computer support of the completely-specified systems to the managers in charge of the operational and administrative activities that they serve. Funds for computer support are then included in the budgets of these activities and the service is obtained in much the same way as other services that are necessary to the activity. This arrangement has an advantage in that the responsible manager can be held accountable for the efficiency of operation of his completely-specified system as part of the budgetary and management process.

The remaining elements of the overall information system are less directly related to particular activities and more connected to the work of the organization as a whole. Funds for the common data base, the

[12] Head, Robert V., *Manager's Guide to Management Information Systems*, Prentice-Hall, 1972, p. 94.

data management system, the management reporting system, the information retrieval system, and the strategic component are, therefore, best provided through the budget of one centrally located office in the organization.

Normal managerial prudence requires that the cost of all elements of the information system be kept as low as possible, consistent with the necessary level of service being maintained. There are a number of methods of ensuring that costs do not rise beyond a level that is considered appropriate. The first of these methods is concerned with the level of service that is offered by the information system compared with that which has been available in the past. Computer-supported systems have the potential of providing service in routine tasks at a considerably reduced cost due to the very high speed and accuracy of computer operations. There is a tendency, however, to increase the level of service markedly just because the computer service is available. For example, reports may be produced daily rather than monthly. The increased level of service may be convenient and pleasant to have. It may, however, not be necessary to effective operation of the organization. The cost of providing the higher level of service may be small for one activity, but the total cost of such extravagances over the entire organization may be much more significant. Constant vigilance is needed to ensure that provision of unnecessary services in the information system does not lead to an escalation of costs.

A second method of ensuring that the cost of operations does not rise unduly is to insist at the design stage that the response of the information system is no quicker than is necessary to meet the reasonable needs of management. Quick response in retrieval of information or in compilation of reports is expensive in terms of computer services. There are some situations in which such rapid response is necessary. These situations are mainly concerned with the demands of customers in applications such as hotel and airline reservation systems. In many management activities, however, the difference between virtually instantaneous response and a short delay of minutes is not significant in terms of the effectiveness of the retrieval of information, while the difference in cost between the two modes of operation may be very great.

A third method of reducing the cost of information systems consists of keeping the amount of on-line communications between geographically separated parts of a system to a minimum. Rates for some communication lines during prime business hours are much higher than those available for overnight use. If long-distance communications within the system can be conducted mainly during off-peak hours, the cost of this part of the system can be made significantly less. Applications that require on-line communications need to be furnished this service, but they should be required to justify their expense on the grounds of need or efficiency.

Benefits of an Information System

The development of an organizational information system requires a significant commitment of resources. Many managers may feel that these resources should be devoted to other activities that they consider more worthwhile. It is necessary, therefore, to develop a clear idea of the benefits that will accrue from the system at an early stage in its design and implementation. Unfortunately, many of the benefits that can be envisaged at the start of a project of this nature are not easily expressed in tangible terms.[13]

In the past, the greatest portion of the effort involved in development of an information system was concerned with the introduction of completely-specified systems. These systems were required to service transactions and routine decisions that exist at the lower and middle levels of the organization. The objective of these systems, in many cases, was cost reduction. In other circumstances, the aim was to replace a labor-intensive operation with one that is capital-intensive.[14] This latter situation occurred in many clerical applications such as accounts receivable and payable, inventory control, and some aspects of personnel administration. In some cases, such as in telephone exchanges, the replacement of people by capital-intensive devices such as computers was forced by the shortage of persons available and willing to do the work.

The benefits of such capital-intensive projects were clearly measurable in terms of the cost reductions achieved or the services maintained per unit of human effort expended. The benefits that were expected were not always achieved, mainly because estimation techniques in a situation involving an emerging and developing technology are not

[13] *Ibid.*, p. 93.

[14] Kriebel, Charles H., "The Evaluation of Management Information Systems," *IAG Journal*, vol. 4, no. 1, 1971, pp. 2–14.

always reliable. Costs and development times were often underestimated and potential cost-reduction benefits were sometimes lost because levels of service were increased significantly. Nevertheless, the benefits that were to be had were tangible and relatively easily measurable in well-understood units such as dollars. The benefits to be obtained from implementation of the completely-specified systems in a modern organization are similarly relatively easy to assess. The benefits that may be realized from other parts of the organizational information system are less tangible and much more difficult to measure in readily-appreciable terms.

The parts of the information system other than the completely-specified systems generally serve managerial decision making in management control and the strategic direction of the organization. The benefits obtained from these decisions contribute to organizational well-being but it is seldom that overall benefits can be attributed to individual decisions and assessed independently. Benefits from the nonspecified information system manifest themselves in terms of a greater awareness and alertness on the part of the members of the organization to both the external and internal environments in which they are working. This can result in

- A clearer appreciation by members of the organization of its objectives, intentions, values, preferences, and available courses of action;
- A clearer understanding by its members of the environment in which the organization is operating, in particular an awareness of the characteristics of other participants and of the social, technological, and natural elements of that environment;
- A greater appreciation by managers of the progress made towards achieving the organizational goals and objectives and of the resources required to achieve further progress in this direction;
- An increased communication and exchange of information between members and parts of the organization, particularly in the realm of strategic information;
- A greater availability of consistent historic data and information for use in planning and other related activities.

One other potential benefit must be added to the above considerations. This benefit is just as intangible as the above factors, but it is often just as clearly seen in hindsight. It is the avoidance of the cost of *not* implementing a competent and comprehensive information system. In some cases, this cost can be estimated in readily-measurable parameters. At the operating level, for example, it may take the form of loss of money, profitability, or time. At higher levels, however, the lack of appropriate information may cause an organization very severe losses and difficulties.[15] In some cases, the loss may involve the actual existence of the organization.[16] Catastrophic events have been seen to follow the lack of information, or the lack of the ability to appreciate available information, at both the community[17] and the international level.[18]

Clearly, it would be most desirable if ways could be found to quantify the intangible benefits of the implementation of an information system. Progress in this area is, however, likely to be slow. Managers responsible for the decision about whether or not to expend significant resources in this area will, therefore, probably be left for some time without a completely quantified and well-defined method of estimating the benefits that are likely to accrue.

Evaluation of the Information System

Evaluation of the information system is an essential follow-up to the design and implementation process. It is also part of the implementation process, in so much as evaluation of the existing information system is a necessary preliminary to the design of a replacement. However, very little progress has been made in devising acceptable methods and criteria for evaluation of an information system. Evaluation remains what it was called in 1971—the most conspicuous and weakest stage in the process of development of an information system.[19]

The basis of evaluation of any system is the set of objectives and goals that are laid down at the start of its development. The first step

[15] Smith, R. A., *Corporations in Crisis,* Doubleday, Anchor Books Edition, 1966.

[16] Johnson, Robert L., and I. H. Derman, *op. cit,* "How Intelligent," p. 46.

[17] Turner, Barry A., "The Organizational and Inter-organizational Development of Disasters," *Administrative Science Quarterly,* vol. 21, September 1976, pp. 378–397.

[18] Stoessinger, J. G., *Why Nations Go to War,* St. Martin's Press, 1974.

[19] Kriebel, Charles H., "The Evaluation of Management Information Systems," *IAG Journal,* vol. 4, no. 1, 1971, pp. 2–14.

in the process of design and implementation of an information system is a review of these goals and objectives and the revision or replacement of existing statements of this nature as is judged appropriate. The revised statements should be in a form that is easily understood by the individuals involved in the design and implementation. Each goal and objective should be stated, as far as possible, in a form that allows criteria and measures to be formulated so that the degree to which it has been achieved can be determined at any given time. Some aspects of the information system, such as those involved with accounting, lend themselves more readily to quantitative criteria and measures of performance.[20] Others, particularly those in the areas of high-level decisions and strategic information, are less susceptible to evaluation in quantitative terms.

As in all other systems, evaluation can be conducted in terms of both efficiency and effectiveness. Efficiency is concerned with the best use of resources to achieve a given result. Effectiveness is a measure of the achievement of the goals and objectives set out at the start of a project. It is possible to be efficient without being effective, as has been demonstrated in many cases in which technically efficient information systems have been rejected by the members of the organizations that they were designed to serve. It is possible to be effective without being highly efficient. The desirable condition is to obtain a high level of both efficiency and effectiveness.

The Efficiency of Elements of the Information System

One system or part of a system is more efficient than another if it attains the same effectiveness in carrying out an operation or set of procedures at a lower total cost. In practice, however, assessments of the efficiency of different approaches to an operation are very difficult to make. It is often the case, for example, that two approaches to the implementation of a system provide different levels of effectiveness at different costs. A meaningful comparison is possible in such cases only if the effectiveness of the two approaches can be measured in terms of the same quantitative parameter. This can usually be achieved only when certain elements of a system are considered, rather than the more complex operation of the system as a whole.

Assessments of efficiency are usually carried out in connection with

[20] Montgomery, David B., "The Outlook for MIS," *Journal of Advertising Research*, vol. 13, no. 3, June 1973, pp. 5–11.

the provision of computer support for elements of an information system.[21, 22] The procedure is to list the costs of the proposed computer equipment and services and to compare them with the costs of the existing operation. The assumption is that the computer-supported operation will be at least as effective as the existing system. Considerable cost savings are often estimated to accrue from the introduction of the computer, not to mention other less tangible benefits. In some cases, however, neither the cost savings nor the other benefits have materialized in the actual implementation. This has often been due to the fact that the original estimates had been derived more in a spirit of enthusiasm than one of realistic evaluation. Despite the difficulties involved, however, it is sometimes possible to reach the conclusion that one approach to the implementation of a part of the system is clearly superior and at the same time significantly less costly than others that have been proposed.

Measurements of efficiency are possible for specific operations in the information system, such as retrieval of documents or records in the strategic component.[23, 24] If it is known, for example, that the strategic store contains 100 references to a certain key word or descriptor, it is a relatively simple matter to determine the percentage of these references that can be retrieved by any given method. There is a danger, however, that such measurements will be confused with an estimate of the effectiveness of the system. Measurements of the effectiveness of a strategic information system must take into account whether the information retrieved was useful to the individual concerned in the resolution of his problem.

The Effectiveness of the Information System

Estimates of the effectiveness of an information system must be related to the basic objective of that system—to support decision making processes in the organization of which it is an integral part. The support provided by the information system is the provision of

[21] Davis, Gordon B., *Management Information Systems: Conceptual Foundations, Structure and Development,* McGraw-Hill, 1974, Chapter 16.

[22] Calingaert, P., "System Performance Evaluation: Survey and Appraisal," *Communications of the ACM,* January 1967.

[23] Kochen, Manfred, *Principles of Information Retrieval,* Melville Publishing Company, 1974, section 7.3.

[24] Vickery, B. C., *Information Systems,* Butterworth and Co., London, 1973, Chapter 11.

information that can be used to ensure that "better" decisions are made. The questions arise, therefore, of the value of information in decision making and of the manner in which this value might be measured. There are three possible approaches to answering these questions.[25]

The first approach is to make measurements of the value of information after the consequences of its use are known. If all other conditions could be held equal while the results of a decision are observed with and without certain information, then the value of that information might be measured. This approach, while attractive at first sight, has many difficulties that combine to make it impractical for other than the most routine of decisions. In the real world, there is seldom, if ever, the chance to repeat a major decision process under identical circumstances. The consequences of one resolution of the problem usually affect the circumstances of the next, so that any comparison between the two outcomes would be inconclusive. In addition, the results and benefits of a decision are often slow to appear and they may be difficult to measure for a number of reasons.

A second approach is to study the results of application of a given decision rule under different conditions of information. This may be possible in the case of decisions that are completely-specified, so that the conditions of the decision process and the pay-off function are well known.[26, 27, 28] However, the approach is not applicable to complex decisions that are new and unique and for which a complete specification cannot be written.

The third approach is to ask users of the system to make subjective assessments of the value of the information that the system provides in the decision processes in which they are engaged. This approach is much less quantitative than the two just discussed. It relies on recording the perceptions of individuals and on designing methods of enquiry that minimize the possibility that use of these perceptions will result in bias and inaccuracy in the results of the assessment. The use

[25] Gallagher, Charles A., "Perceptions of the Value of a Management Information System," *Academy of Management Journal,* vol. 17, no. 1, 1974, pp. 46–55.

[26] Gregory, R. H., and R. L. Van Horn, *Automatic Data Processing Systems: Principles and Procedures,* Wadsworth, 1960.

[27] Feltham, Gerald A., "The Value of Information," *The Accounting Review,* vol. 42, 1968, pp. 684–696.

[28] Stigler, G. J., "The Economics of Information," *Journal of Political Economy,* vol. 69, 1961, pp. 213–225.

of subjective assessments is the primary method of evaluating information systems, given the limitations of the other approaches. It has been advocated both for evaluation of the overall system and for assessment of selected portions of it.[29, 30]

The emphasis in the collection of subjective assessments in the evaluation of the information system is on its value to users in support of their decision making activities. In certain instances, this value may be expressed in quantitative terms, such as the amount of money saved by virtue of possession of a particular piece of information. In most cases, however, the impressions of users that are recorded are more qualitative and provide a more subjective evaluation of the system.

It is often useful to collect opinions concerning the characteristics of the system at the same time as views on its overall effectiveness are solicited. Questions can be posed to obtain the reactions of users to areas that have been sources of complaint and dissatisfaction with information systems in the past. Examples of such questions are

1/ Do you feel that the information system exists to provide service to you in your day-to-day work? How has it helped you in this respect?

2/ Has the information system provided the service that you feel was promised at the start of its design and implementation? In which areas has it (a) failed and (b) excelled in your opinion?

3/ Do you consider that the system has been implemented with due regard to costs and benefits? Are there any areas in which you consider costs are excessive?

4/ Do you feel comfortable using the system? Could more attention have been paid to matching the output of the system to your needs and, if so, in what areas?

5/ Is the system flexible enough in your opinion? If not, where should changes be made?

6/ Do you still keep a personal store of information in a notebook or elsewhere? If so, will you share that information with the system? Do you see any benefits in so doing?

[29] Toan, Arthur B., Jr., *Using Information to Manage,* The Ronald Press Company, New York, 1968, Chapter 9.

[30] Cooper, William S., "On Selecting a Measure of Retrieval Effectiveness," *Journal of the American Society for Information Science,* March–April 1973, pp. 87–88.

7/ Do you think that the information system is still evolving? Can you influence this evolution and, if not, why not?

8/ Does the system provide you with timely, relevant, and accurate information? Are there any areas of deficiency in this respect?

9/ Do you think that the information system makes too much use of complex procedures and models? Can you suggest areas in which less complicated techniques might be used to advantage?

10/ Do you consider that there has been sufficient attention paid to the confidentiality and security of the information in the system? Can you suggest areas for improvement of these aspects of its operation?

There are many other possible questions of the same sort that could be included in an evaluation of the information system by users. Not all managers in an organization would take the time to respond to such a questionnaire and not all that did would record all their views on the questions posed. Nevertheless, an assessment of this nature, conducted periodically in an earnest and sincere fashion is probably the most practical and fruitful method of evaluating an information system available at the present time.

One extension of the method of direct questioning of users involves the construction of a set of parameters by which it is thought that the information system can be evaluated. The procedure consists of weighting these parameters in terms of their perceived importance and having users rate the system in terms of each parameter. Users may also be asked to provide opinions on the appropriate weighting of the parameters. This method of evaluation is useful if the parameters selected can be regarded as reliable evaluators of the system and if the weightings used are reliable indicators of their relative importance. However, if these conditions are not met, the method and its results may be misleading.

There are a number of methods of evaluation that can be employed that do not require the active participation of users. The most useful of these methods is *events logging.*[31] When using this method, events

[31] Carlson, Eric D., "Evaluating the Impact of Information Systems," *Management Informatics,* vol. 3, no. 2, 1974, pp. 57–67.

that might indicate the relative effectiveness of the system are recorded. Events in this category might be heavy use of a particular facility, user complaints, or congratulations. An event log kept over a period of time can be useful in diagnosing causes of deficiencies in the system and can help in establishing connections between phenomena that might otherwise not be realized.

A special type of event log can be designed to record usage of certain parts of the information system. Provision can be made, for example, to note each time that a particular descriptor, key word, or subject appears in requests for retrieval from the strategic store. In the same way, a record can be kept automatically of the frequency with which access to an item in the common data base is requested. The records that are built up provide a basis for understanding present usage of parts of the system. Access to heavily used items can then be made easier and those parts of the system that appear to be underutilized can be brought to the attention of users.

Despite the above methods for assessing the effectiveness of an information system, evaluation is still the most neglected aspect of the design and implementation process. This is unfortunate because evaluation is a necessary part of the introduction of an information system. Without it, management does not have the means to assess whether the effort and resources that have been expended have been put to good use. Without a strong evaluation component in the design and implementation process, desirable future directions in this basically evolutionary process are much less easy to determine.

Summary

The basic designs for the internal and strategic components of an information system that have been developed in the preceding chapters can be combined into a conceptual diagram which provides a general foundation for the design and implementation of an information system in a modern organization. This concept of an organizational information system meets the initial specifications that were developed early in the text. It provides a system that is flexible and responsive to managerial needs for information, while also supporting routine operational and administrative functions.

There are a number of factors that contribute to the success of the design and implementation of an information system. The system should be designed to meet the needs of managers and it should be planned and implemented in close cooperation with them. The design should start from an assessment of the system already existing in the organization and implementation should be planned as an evolutionary process. The design should be flexible and competent project management should be placed in charge of the implementation. The use of a competent and experienced staff produces superior results. When operational, the officer responsible for the system should report at the highest possible level in the organization. Considerations of computer support should not dominate system design and implementation. Due regard should be paid to the confidentiality and security of the system and to the design of output in a form that is most appropriate for managers.

The costs of an information system can be thought of in the same terms as the costs necessary in handling any important resource in the organization. These costs are more easily measured and appreciated in the parts of the system that are the most formalized, notably the completely-specified systems. The costs of these systems can be regarded as part of the operating costs of the routine operations and administrative functions that they support. The other parts of the system, the common data base, the management reporting system, and the strategic component serve managerial activities that are related to the interests of the organization as a whole. The costs of these parts are usually borne from a budget that is held at the executive levels of the organization. Costs of all components can be kept to a minimum by close attention to design. This ensures that the level of services offered is no higher than is necessary and that the most economic way of providing these services is used in all cases.

Benefits to be obtained from the implementation of a planned information system are both tangible and intangible. The most tangible benefits, and those on which attention has been concentrated in the past, are in the form of cost reduction and the replacement of labor by capital-intensive devices. These benefits are realized mainly in the completely-specified systems. The efficiency of these systems can be made the responsibility of the managers in charge of them. The less tangible benefits of other parts of the system are not as easily measurable. They can be seen in a clearer appreciation by managers of the objectives, intentions, and preferences of the organization and in a deeper understanding of the environment in which the organization operates. One major intangible benefit, often appreciated only in hindsight, is the avoidance of the difficulties and costs that can arise if an appropriate supply of information is not available in the organization.

Evaluation of an information system is an important part of the evolutionary process of design and implementation. Evaluation can be carried out in terms of both efficiency and effectiveness. The aim is to obtain a high level of both efficiency and effectiveness, but the primary factor is effectiveness which concerns the extent to which the objectives of the system are met.

Measurements of efficiency are, in practice, applicable only to elements of the system, such as retrieval of information or a completely-specified process. Estimates of effectiveness are closely related to the provision of information that is vital to a decision process. These estimates are usually obtainable only by collecting opinions from users in questionnaires. This method of evaluation can be augmented by collection of information by other means that do not require the active participation of users. Continual and consistent use of all the available, applicable methods of evaluation can contribute significantly to what has been the most neglected aspect of the design and implementation of an information system.

Discussion Topics

1/ Do you feel that the basic conceptual design diagram of Figure 7-1 is helpful as a guide to information system design and implementation? What are its strengths and weaknesses? How do you think it could be improved?

2/ Information can be considered as a resource in a modern organization. How would acceptance of this view affect your approach to information system design. Can information be managed in the same way as any other resource?

3/ How would you go about estimating the costs of the information system existing in an organization at the start of the design of a new system? What elements would contribute to the costs?

4/ List some of the intangible benefits that you think might accrue from the implementation of a planned information system. How would you persuade senior managers of the value of these benefits?

5/ What steps would you take to ensure that your design and implementation of a new information system (a) met the needs of managers and (b) was conducted in close cooperation with them? How would you attempt to lessen any resistance that you encountered?

6/ What are the advantages of starting the design phase only after a thorough examination and documentation of the existing information system? How would you go about such an examination? What criteria would you use to select those parts of the existing system that should be retained?

7/ How can the design and implementation of an information system be made a truly evolutionary process?

8/ What steps would you take to ensure that the design and implementation of the information system is sufficiently flexible to meet possible changes within the organization and in its external environment?

9/ What advantages do you see in the assigning of operating managers and administrators to temporary work within the information system? Do you think such a policy would work in an organization with which you are familiar and, if not, why not?

10/ How can the stigma of unfulfilled promises be avoided in the design and implementation of an information system?

11/ To which level of an organization do you think those who manage the information should report? Is there any particular office that you consider particularly appropriate to oversee this function? Do you think John Dearden's suggestion of an administrative vice-president ("MIS is a Mirage" *Harvard Business Review,* Jan.–Feb. 1972, p. 98) is appropriate?

12/ Is MIS really a mirage? Contrast Dearden's arguments with those of Terrance Hanold ("An Executive View of MIS" *Datamation,* November 1972) and record your conclusions.

13/ Do you think that information system design and implementation is merely a matter of acquiring the right computer? Have computer considerations overshadowed other matters that have been important to a successful system in the past? If so, what can be done to avoid this pitfall in the future?

14/ In your opinion, is dispersal of computer capabilities likely to be a major feature of future information system design? Do you consider this development advantageous? Does it have any potential disadvantages?

15/ What can be done to ensure that the information system does not become overly complex? Are complicated models necessary in parts of the design other than the completely specified systems?

16/ Why is evaluation of the system after implementation so important? Are measurements of efficiency sufficient in the evaluation process? In what terms can the effectiveness of the system be assessed?

17/ Can you suggest some points that you would include in a questionnaire designed to obtain an assessment of the effectiveness of the system during operations? How would you formulate questions to ensure that the assessment was valid and unbiased?

18/ Draw up a list of the type of events and phenomena that you think should be logged by the information systems staff. How can the information obtained in an event log of this type be used to improve system performance?

CASE WORK

The Delta Corporation continues to have its problems. The president has received the report on the recommended goals, objectives, activities, and structure that the team of which you are a member prepared earlier (see the case work at the end of Chapter 2). However, he is still worried about the overall condition of the company. He has just called the team to a meeting with senior managers and made the following observations:

- There has recently been an increasing percentage of orders that are not filled by the promised delivery date.
- It appears that the Vancouver plant is not as efficient as the others. However, it has been difficult to obtain exact figures to substantiate this apparent situation. This seems to be due to the fact that reporting procedures from Vancouver to the head office, while appearing to be in company standard form, do not contain information comparable to that from other plants.
- Morale among employees seems to be dropping. In particular, at the largest plant in Winnipeg, the union has become militant prior to forthcoming contract renewal negotiations.
- Procedures and products at Gamma Inc. are so different from those in the main part of Delta that it is difficult to obtain a firm estimate of the relative contribution of Gamma to company profitability.
- Management reports in the head office are becoming much more complex and they are often late. Much of the time in meetings

between senior managers is taken up in discussing the validity of the information that is presented.

- Head office staff has increased by 45 percent in the last three years.
- The computer supported system introduced two years ago to automate the order and production process in the firm has been more costly than originally estimated and has not yet met initial specifications for work to be done. At the present time, only the Winnipeg plant order and production system is operating on the new system. Other plants are still using the original manual system.
- Managers seem to be increasingly at a loss to explain developments outside the corporation and to recommend changes in strategy to cope with them.

The president ended his summary of the troubles of the corporation by saying that one of the steps that he is recommending to correct the situation is a review of the company's handling of information. The task of undertaking this review and of preparing a plan for the new information handling system was assigned to the team of which you are a member.

Prepare in as much detail as is possible in the time available a summary of the plan that you believe might be produced in the above circumstances. Let your imagination fill in any details that may be missing from the above description of the case. Include in your summary (a) the method that you would employ to review the existing handling of information in the company; (b) a basic design for the proposed new system and a plan for implementation; (c) an outline of the project control that will be needed during the implementation phase; (d) an analysis of the staffing requirements of the project, including how it will be directed; (e) a summary of the major cost areas and; (f) a plan for evaluation of the system once it has been implemented.

Epilogue

I should like to say one thing more about the functions of an Intelligence System, the importance of which, unlike collection and collation, is not generally realized. With perfect collection and collation you may succeed in building up an accurate picture of what the enemy is going to do. But the test of a good Intelligence Service in war is not merely that you were right: it is that you persuaded your operational staff to take the correct countermeasures. To do this, it is necessary first to build up a reputation for accuracy and timeliness so that from experience they find that they can trust your pronouncements. And as I said before, it is not good enough to bark at the slightest approach of danger: you must first learn enough about the danger to be able to tell your operational staff what it is, so that they can take definite action. Otherwise you merely distract them with something that may not materialize. . . .

If you pursue the policy I have described, you will undoubtedly, from time-to-time, make yourself unpopular. You will at all times be accused of hoarding information: at other times you will be called an alarmist and will be told that you have no business to interfere with operational policy. But in the end, you will be justified by events.

—R. V. Jones, "Scientific Intelligence"
Royal United Service Institution Journal,
Vol. 92, 1947, pp. 352–369

Index